D0999713

Design of Very High-Level Computer Languages

Other McGraw-Hill Books of Interest

ISBN	Author	Title
0-07-005397-9	Birnes, Ed.	*Microcomputer Applications Handbook*
0-07-021623-1	Fortier	*Handbook of LAN Technology*
0-07-010889-7	Chorafas	*The Complete Local Area Network Reference Guide*
0-07-002394-8	Arnell	*Handbook of Disaster Recovery Planning*
0-07-005395-2	Birnes	*Online Programming Language Reference Guide*
0-07-005394-4	Birnes	*High-Level Languages and Software Applications*
0-07-067211-3	Vassiliou, Orenstein	*Users Guide to Systems and Languages*
0-07-040235-3	Marca, McGowan	*SADT: Structured Analysis and Design Techniques*
0-07-036964-X	Lecarme, Gart	*Software Portability*
0-07-057299-2	Shumate	*Understanding Concurrency in Ada*
0-07-046536-3	Nielsen, Shumate	*Designing Large Real-Time Systems with Ada*
0-07-042632-5	Modell	*A Professional's Guide to Systems Analysis*
0-07-001051-X	Alford	*Requirements-Driven Software Design*
0-07-016803-2	Dickinson	*Developing Quality Systems*
0-07-065086-1	Towner (Ranade, Ed.)	*Implementing CASE*
0-07-023165-6	General Electric Company Staff	*Software Engineering Handbook*
0-07-010646-0	Wallace et al.	*A Unified Methodology for Developing Systems*
0-07-010645-2	Charette	*An Introduction to Software Engineering Environments*
0-07-067922-3	Wallace	*Practitioner's Guide to Ada*
0-07-044093-X	Musa et al.	*Software Reliability*
0-07-050783-X	Pressman	*Software Engineering: A Practitioner's Approach*
0-07-050790-2	Pressman	*Software Engineering: A Beginner's Guide*
0-07-030550-1	Howden	*Functional Program Testing and Analysis*

Computing That Works

ISBN	Author	Title
0-07-053923-5	Ross	*Data Exchange: PC/MS DOS*
0-07-029748-7	Hood	*Using AutoCAD with AutoLISP*
0-07-008845-4	Buerger	*LATEX for Scientists and Engineers*
0-07-029749-5	Hood	*Easy AutoCAD, 2/E*
0-07-057552-5	Simon	*How to Be a Successful Computer Consultant, 2/E*
0-07-036968-2	Lebert	*CICS for Microcomputers*
0-07-023477-9	Gliedman	*Tips and Techniques for Using Low-Cost and Public Domain Software*
0-07-056565-1	Sheldon	*Introducing PC DOS and MS DOS, 2/E*
0-07-056556-2	Sheldon	*Hard Disk Management in the PC and MS DOS Environment*
0-07-035089-2	Kliewer	*EGA/VGA: A Programmer's Reference Guide*

Design of Very High-Level Computer Languages

A User-Oriented Approach

Melvin Klerer
Professor of Computer Science
Polytechnic University

J. Ranade, Consulting Editor

McGraw-Hill, Inc.
New York St. Louis San Francisco Auckland Bogotá
Caracas Hamburg Lisbon London Madrid
Mexico Milan Montreal New Delhi Paris
San Juan São Paulo Singapore
Sydney Tokyo Toronto

Library of Congress Cataloging-in-Publication Data

Klerer, Melvin.
Design of very high-level computer languages : a user–oriented approach / Melvin Klerer. -- 2nd ed.
p. cm.
Rev ed. of: User–oriented computer languages. 1st ed. 1987
Includes bibliographical references and index.
ISBN 0-07-035098-1
1. Programming languages (Electronic computers) I. Klerer, Melvin. User-oriented computer languages. II. Title.
QA76.7.K58 1991
005.13--dc20 90-22115
CIP

The AUTOMATED PROGRAMMER System is a registered trademark of KGK Automated Systems, Inc.

1 2 3 4 5 6 7 8 9 0 DOC/DOC 9 8 7 6 5 4 3 2 1 0

ISBN 0-07-035098-1

The sponsoring editor for this book was Theron Shreve, the editing supervisor was Jim Halston, and the production supervisor was Suzanne W. Babeuf. It was set in Century Schoolbook by McGraw-Hill's Professional & Reference Division composition unit.

Printed and bound by R. R. Donnelley and Sons.

The first edition of this book appeared under the title *User-Oriented Computer Languages*.

This book is dedicated to Fred Grossman and Robert Klerer, who have joined with the author in putting some of the language design ideas expressed herein into forming "real world" computer software.

Contents

Preface

The primary audience for this book comprises the professionals who want some insight into "friendly" programming language design, particularly for the scientific/engineering/mathematical applications areas. It may also be used as supplementary reading or as a second text in the conventional academic course in programming languages.

The basic purpose of this book is to examine the analysis and design methodologies relevant to user-oriented (user-friendly) computer-language systems and consistent with some fifth- and sixth-generation computer concepts for very high-level languages. This book also analyzes some conventional programming languages to illustrate the aspects that can be regarded as user-friendly and those that are antithetical to that concept.

It is a widely accepted belief that communicating with computers using conventional programming methodology is expensive, inefficient, and unreliable. There is also widespread dissatisfaction that it is currently necessary to employ professional programmers for large or difficult problems and that programming is not easier for users who are not computer scientists. Along with the author, many computer scientists feel that current academic programming methodologies have become too arcane and even sterile.

The view of this book is that languages used to communicate with a computer should enable users who are professionals in their application fields but not necessarily trained in computer science, to solve application problems in ways that are economically efficient, that enhance the reliability of the problem solution, and that are comprehensible (self-documenting) to someone other than the program originator. The basic idea of this approach is to design a specific language, appropriate to a broad application domain, that has the essential characteristic that the description of the computer-acceptable problem solution (that is, the *program*) is expressed at such a high level that it has most of, if not all, the properties of the original problem-solution statement in algorithmic form (the solution specification).

For some application areas, we demonstrate that it is possible to design a language system such that the solution specification is essentially the program. Further, we show (particularly in Chapter 8) that the requirement for algorithmic form need not be detailed or even strictly unambiguous, at the specification level. Thus it is feasible to automate certain aspects of the programming process, which in turn enhances the reliability of complex programs. With such languages, the debugging process becomes one of proofreading the specifications, and the specification itself is the documentation. Where these considerations hold only in part, the methods of conventional program verification need be applied only to those aspects where program and specification differ. Also, those differences can be diminished, in some cases, by reformulating the program or the specification.

The approach of this book is not grounded on an a priori, abstract mathematicized model of the programming process considered as a set of formal procedures. Rather, it starts from the concept of a person communicating with a machine and addresses the pragmatic feasibility of constructing a language interface that will appear to be substantially "natural" for that application domain. *Natural* here means that the difference between the structure/notation of the program and that of the problem-solution specification is diminished. This applies to specification structures/notations which are historically customary and linguistically efficient in the specific application domain. For example, in the scientific/engineering field, textbooks are written in technical English and nonlinear mathematical notation. Thus there is a substantive problem in proceeding from a problem-solution specification expressed in technical English/nonlinear notation to a programmed solution using a conventional programming language.

The feasibility of implementing the techniques discussed here has been demonstrated in journal publications by the author and his colleagues, as well as by others who have published in the fields of two-dimensional programming, two-dimensional text editing, and user-oriented language structures. There are now even some commercially available programming tools that use some of the concepts discussed in this text. Principal among these is the AUTOMATED PROGRAMMER system which is illustrated in Chapter 8. Currently, however, there is no other text that reviews in detail the utility and design considerations associated with these techniques for pragmatic implementation in specific application domains.

Also, conventional computer-language systems have been dominated by keyboard input and linear output. Thus input/output structures have been relegated to minor roles in conventional approaches. The present state of the art, however, allows other types of computer-recognizable input and more flexible output.

Other topics usually found in texts on programming languages are considered in this book from a user-oriented analysis and design point of view, with a critical study of the important elements of conventional languages. Particular attention is given to the FORTRAN-like and ALGOL-like languages, to demonstrate the inadequacy of many of their linguistic structures and notational devices when considered from a user-friendly viewpoint. Such analysis lends credence to the concept that a principal reliability problem stemming from the use of these languages—programming errors—can be linked to the use of specific linguistic structures that have a tendency to generate errors. Specific examples are given of alternative user-oriented structures and notations that we believe are far less error-prone.

The title of this book does not refer to *programming* languages because we want to emphasize that language used to communicate with a computer should be such that the programming burden is minimized as much as possible. Thus we have used the phrase *computer languages* in the title instead of the more conventional *programming languages*. We are concerned with communicating the problem-solution specification to the computer for execution, as far as that is possible. We look for a specification language that minimizes the transformation to an executable program and simultaneously uses linguistic forms and notational representations which minimize user training and error propensity. Such a specification language enhances readability to the point where the program becomes self-documenting, understandable and easily modified by others. That is the goal of what we term *user-oriented computer language design*.

An underlying assumption of this volume is that it is inappropriate to design a universal language applicable to all conceivable applications, since it would be so complex as to be unwieldy in actual usage. That somewhat negative view turns into the positive assertion that specific languages must be designed and tailored for specialized applications areas. Only in this way can user-oriented design be successful.

This text attempts to develop design themes for structuring a language for a specific application domain so that, given precise computational specifications, programs can be easily understood by others and programming protocols characterized by conceptually simple abstract structures.

Chapter 1 examines the nature of the computer-language problem. The communication of instructions from person to machine is viewed as a linguistic process. Such an approach to "computer languages" differs from the one conventionally used in the design of "programming languages." Programming, in its pure form, is a translation process. An important purpose of this volume is to inquire how appropriate user-oriented language design can reduce the economic cost of the programming process.

Chapter 1 goes on to discuss the relationship between machine architecture and language to give an integrated view of hardware/software. It also examines the historical dependency of conventional language design on available hardware. In particular, certain linguistic attributes of FORTRAN-like languages are shown to result from historical machine architecture and specific input/output devices available at the time FORTRAN was designed. A design problem is presented for a situation where there is a very large programmer population but only a very small set of input devices.

Additional characteristics of nonmachine computer language are examined. The essence of the programming problem is defined. The concept of "powerful" is given a quantitative definition. The issue of economic efficiency as dependent on the phenomenon of (large) individual programming variability is mentioned. The concepts of *problem-oriented, user-oriented, generality, simplicity, user definition, naturalness, artificiality, self-documentation, error proneness, procedure-oriented*, and other aspects of languages are examined.

Chapter 2 discusses methods of language definition. This chapter is also an introduction to some elements of conventional language theory. The lexical attributes of a language are discussed from a general point of view. Details are given for various kinds of lexical-type distinctions applicable to computer languages.

Syntax, semantics, and pragmatic aspects of language design are treated. An introduction to some methods of syntactical representation is given. Examples of the representation of syntax for a limited programming language are shown, and elementary parsing considerations are discussed. An introduction to the Chomsky classification of languages is given. A distinction is made between language theory and the mathematically interesting notational structures used for the representation of language.

Chapter 3 analyzes the assignment statement. The concept of the assignment statement is generalized, and its importance for scientific/mathematical/engineering applications programming is discussed. Various lexical considerations in the representation of the assignment operator are treated. The issue of the complexity of assignment representations is clarified in terms of the distinction between problem-solution specification and program representation. The interplay between language design and the complexity of language structure is discussed, as well as certain psychological constraints that affect the programmer.

Examples of a generalized form of assignment are given and their relation to mathematical formulas elucidated. Examples of equivalent program structures, relating to the generalized form of assignment, are also displayed. Various forms for multiple assignment and other aspects of assignment are given. The concept of symbolic equations is briefly considered. We summarize the conclusions of this chapter by showing that the conventional assignment statement can be replaced by a more general structure that is sentencelike and multiline, that admits qualifying phrases for iteration, and that permits boolean control.

Chapter 4 considers basic control structures. The control structures of conventional languages are discussed in the context of conventional machine architecture. Topics examined are

- Sequential execution, explicit and implicit
- Statement terminators
- Nesting, *if...then...else* considerations
- Parenthesization (linear and two-dimensional)
- Precedence of nested loops
- The unconditioned branch; null operation interpretation; side effects; subroutine calls; alternatives to the GOTO; the viability of the GOTO
- Conditional structures, the computed GOTO; relationship to the IF statement; the CASE statement; the COND statement; the GUARDED statement; IF structures of various complexity, with examples, associated ambiguity considerations for various languages, use in assignment statements, parenthesization considerations, as an object for GOTO
- Decision tables, with an example; relationship to *if...then...else* structures
- Loop qualifiers; importance of loops in the computational environment; loop control variables; DO structures; WHILE structures; FOR/FROM structures; other structures; the role of FOR/FROM phrases as qualifiers; comparison to conventional languages; execution efficiency; use of indentation and esoteric forms; relationship to good programming style

Chapter 5 deals with input and output. This chapter analyzes the inadequacies of conventional approaches to input/output and shows how more powerful language forms for I/O can be designed using conventional hardware input/output devices. Specific topics are

- The difference between data processing and pure computation
- The pragmatic importance of I/O design and its historical neglect
- The inadequacy of FORTRAN-like input/output structures

- Free format
- Problems of conventional format structures
- PICTURE format
- I/O in PL/1
- I/O in ALGOL-like languages
- A user-oriented approach to input/output; examples of input and output structures; specification of output type; heading; user-oriented formats using alphanumeric literal strings and value placeholders for the linear case, with examples and figures; a user-oriented format for two-dimensional pictures, alphanumerics, and embedded value placeholders; the IMAGE format statement, with figures to illustrate

Chapter 6 examines declarations, types, and scope considerations. We discuss the effects of declarations, type, and scope with respect to minimizing programming effort. Topics covered are

- Historical considerations
- Storage declarations in various languages; feasibility of automatic assignment of storage and elimination of storage declarations
- Type declarations in various languages; the advantages and disadvantages of strong typing; relationship to machine architecture; declarations and spelling errors; examples of pathological results of typing; the difference between numerical type and numerical representation; declaration considerations for multiple precision; relationship of conventional machine architecture to the concept of type
- Binding, with examples in PASCAL, FORTRAN, PL/1, ALGOL, Ada, APL; dynamic binding and its effect on program correctness analysis, program comprehensibility, and implementation efficiency; binding by definition; MACRO binding
- SCOPE as used in various languages; blocks; subprograms; default rules; pointers and scope; nested scopes, complexity of scope rules and side effects; simplification of scope rules; use of global variables

Chapter 7 considers procedures and parameters. It also discusses iteration and recursion. Topics in this chapter include:

- Multiuse subprograms, macrocalls, procedures, functions, implicit definition, implementation considerations, terminating symbols

- Various options for syntactical representation of function definitions
- Formal parameters, actual parameters
- Passing parameters
- Functions without arguments
- Input/output parameters
- Key word terminators
- Attributes of parameters
- Side effects
- Calling syntax
- Symbols with more than one interpretation
- GOSUB routines
- CALL section name
- Other types of functions and value structures, user-oriented implications
- Detailed consideration of passing of parameters; call by value, call by reference, call by name, with examples of side effects; example of a useful applications of call by name
- Other considerations, distinction between system names and user-defined functions, generic functions and subroutines, concurrent processes
- Iteration versus recursion, examples of iteration, equivalent examples of recursion, multiple integration by recursion, the user status of recursion

Chapter 8 illustrates language design principles by doing a case study of a specific scientific/engineering/mathematical applications language system. Simple examples of programs written in that language are given and compared to computationally equivalent programs written in conventional languages. The advantages and disadvantages of these differing approaches are then analyzed, and more complex program representations, programmed in this "designed" language, are illustrated. In addition, specific aspects are considered for this language, including

- The goal of minimizing the difference between the problem solver's specification and an equivalent executable program
- Achieving that goal by having the representations of the program-

ming language mimic technical English and use notational forms and syntax rooted in conventional (two-dimensional) mathematical representations

- The flexibility of specific syntax, thus providing alternative forms and control structures
- The use of synonymous key words
- Avoiding notation that is psychologically unacceptable to users in the applications domain
- Basing ambiguity resolution on contextual analyses, a cognitive model of the user, and feedback of the system's interpretation of the user's program
- Minimal programming rules and a program that is self-documenting
- Powerful and error-avoiding format structures

The reasons for allowing syntactic flexibility are based on the notion that such an attribute reduces cognitive complexity and thus is error-avoiding. The representation of the underlying grammatical rules can be articulated in a simplified form. That approach also permits a brief reference manual and minimal programming training in the specific language. The concept of "hidden rules" is also analyzed, and the anthropomorphic problem associated with "natural" language is discussed. The overall design is related to the concept of automated programming.

Chapter 9 discusses additional user-oriented concepts. Topics treated are

- Design of human-machine interface
- Natural-language input and natural-language front ends
- Programming style, program verification, and software engineering
- Direct manipulation techniques
- Language design and artificial-intelligence techniques
- Fifth- and sixth-generation concepts

Acknowledgements

The author expresses his appreciation to his colleagues at Polytechnic University for their support and to his students there for their willingness to listen to and examine new ideas. The author owes a particular debt to his long-time research colleagues Fred Grossman and

Robert Klerer who have contributed to some of the notions expressed herein. However, any faults that this work may reveal are strictly the responsibility of the author.

Melvin Klerer

Design of Very High-Level Computer Languages

Chapter

1

The Nature of the Computer-Language Problem

Introduction

We are in the midst of an accelerating computer revolution. Prior to the mid-1950s, this technology was regarded somewhat ambivalently and merely as a curiosity. Since then, computers have become indispensable in carrying out scientific and engineering tasks. Their superhuman speeds allow us to address problems that we could not even hope to solve otherwise. Computers are also essential to the administrative operation of both government and business. More recently, computers have been used to deal with problems in ways that some experts would label as "intelligent." Increasingly, computers have become the crux of the automated factory, a phenomenon that will undoubtedly cause fundamental changes in the economic and social structure of society, indeed in our daily lives. Computers also have great potential as an educational device, or "knowledge transmitters." In these and many other ways, digital computers have become vital to the basic mechanisms of society, and their importance keeps increasing at an ever more rapid rate.

Thus it is important to consider how we "tell" computers what we want them to do. All present-day computers (considered as pieces of hardware) are designed to carry out specific instructions. The communication of those instructions from human beings to the machines is a linguistic process. Although not as general as the linguistic process that occurs when human beings communicate to one another, it is nonetheless a linguistic process. This text is concerned with the particulars that apply to this process of human-machine communication.

Nearly all books that consider the general linguistic problem involved in causing a computer to do what is desired use *programming languages* as the key phrase in their titles. This book, on the other hand, stresses the subject area of *computer languages*. An explanation is necessary, since the difference in phraseology is not insignificant.

Stripped to their essentials, currently available computer hardware units can be regarded as manufactured devices with at least the following five properties:

1. A memory, whose elements are addresses, usually expressed as a positive integer number, can receive, output, and store a sequence of w "bits" of information into each memory element. The integer w is the word size of memory. The computer hardware bit has only two states, 0 and 1. The word size for different computer models may vary. In principle, it is possible to make memory elements whose parts can assume more than two states. But for reasons of engineering reliability and manufacturing economy, the two-state bit is standard.

2. The capability of receiving bits of information into the computer is the input process. At some subsequent time, the output process emits bits of information that are the result of a particular input and the state of the computer at the time of that input. The pattern of bits stored in the memory and other storage units of the computer constitutes part of that particular state.

3. A component, which we shall call an *instruction decoder,* can be directed to specific locations (addresses) in memory and can retrieve strings of bits stored therein. The decoder may (1) interpret these strings as specific instructions to do arithmetic operations on the information stored in certain other memory locations; (2) test this information for various conditions (for example, = 0, not = 0, positive, not positive) and take the next instruction from alternative memory locations, depending on the result of the test; or (3) transfer information from memory to certain special registers of the machine, transfer information between registers, or store the results of those operations at locations. Normally the decoder will retrieve instructions from sequential locations in memory until it encounters a GOTO instruction. A GOTO instruction causes the decoder to take the next instruction from an address different from the next sequential address. There is also a special GOTO instruction that will cause its own address in memory to be recorded for future use.

4. Operations such as arithmetic operations and testing are usually done in special registers.

5. The representations in memory of data (input or transformations of input) and of instructions are, in general, indistinguishable. (In princi-

ple, the categories could be "marked" with special bits or placed in special sections of memory.) Normally what is interpreted as an instruction depends on the address sequencing of the decoder component.

The conventional design of computers[1] is such that they can decode only a very specific set of instructions. Those instructions, their meaning (the actions they cause), and the set of rules that determine how they may be properly sequenced can be considered to be the *machine language* for a particular computer. The vocabulary of machine (computer) language is usually a string of binary bits, that is, a string of 0s and 1s. To get the computer (machine) to do what is intended, we must, on the most elementary level, give it a sequence of instructions coded as strings of 0s and 1s, along with data whose values are also represented as binary numbers (strings of 0s and 1s). Since people do not ordinarily specify problems in such terms, this gives rise to the *programming* process.

Ideally, the input to the programming process should be a well-formulated, unambiguous problem-solution specification expressed in a language that is not a machine (computer) language. Normally, this will be a "natural" language such as technical English, which has evolved historically, or some sort of mathematical notation that may predate the use of computers and that precisely describes the problem, and its solution. Some (but not all) of the characteristics of those noncomputer languages are

- A vocabulary of item names or processes that is either larger or more complex than the specific machine instruction set
- A set of language rules that are more complex than the rules of the computer language
- A nonlinear representation, such as a mathematical expression, for example,

$$y = \frac{a^n}{b}, A_i, \sqrt{a + b}, \sum_{i=1}^{n}, \text{etc.}$$

In other words, the problem-solution specification, even if it is in a complete and precise algorithmic form, is usually expressed in a language that is rich compared to the sparse language used by the computer. Programming, therefore, is the process of transforming such a

[1]For the sake of completeness, we must note that there is currently a great deal of research directed toward the design of novel computer architectures that do not conform to the above description. These new designs, however, will not seriously affect our discussion of computer languages.

problem-solution specification into a sequence of statements acceptable to the machine either directly or indirectly. That transformation is direct if the statements are machine language. It is indirect if the statements are in some higher-level language that is automatically transformed into machine language. *In its pure form, programming is a translation process.* It translates the complete and precise problem-solution specification expressed in some rich language into a computationally equivalent form expressed ultimately in machine (computer) language. The programming process is not comparable, however, to the process involved in translating English into French, for example. Because the structure of elementary machine language differs so greatly from the usual specification language, the translation problem is qualitatively different from the translation of, say, English into French.

When the programming process is applied to a nontrivial problem, the result, that is, the program (even in current higher-level languages), can be said to have certain attributes:

- The program may not be understandable to the original programmer after a certain length of time.
- The program may not be understandable to others.
- Long and complex programs are not reliable in the sense that it cannot be guaranteed that they will always give the correct results for different data.
- Complex programs always seem to have errors, or bugs, associated with them. It seems that no matter how long an arbitrarily complex program has been used and tested out, one cannot guarantee flatly that there are no bugs in it. This is an extremely serious problem with software today, and the large amount of work to find a theoretical solution to the general problem of program correctness has not yet been successful.
- Hardware has become relatively cheap compared to its historical costs. Software, however, has become relatively expensive. Under current conditions, for a complex problem application, it is not unusual for the software costs (that is, the costs involved in writing the program) to far exceed the costs of purchasing and running the computer hardware. *It is the central purpose of this book to discuss how to reduce the economic cost of the programming process.* In other words, how can we minimize the amount of transformation from the original problem-solution specification (assuming that it is well formulated, precise, and relatively unambiguous) into a computer language that the machine can assimilate? Historically, that has not

been the criterion used in designing many higher-level languages. Their design structure has been motivated more by efficiency of execution as a function of a specific machine architecture, theoretical completeness, amenability to proof of correctness, programming succinctness, mathematical aesthetics, or just obtuse ad hoc whims lacking any rational justification.

The Relationship between Machine Architecture and Language

Machine language, as noted previously, is directly implemented in the hardware in the sense that a program represented in machine language is directly executed as presented. A so-called higher-level programming language, however, requires either a special program to effect execution or translation in n steps into a machine-language representation, which is then executed.

Even the smallest general-purpose computer has the capability of computing anything that is computable by any other more complex or larger digital computers. (The qualification is that some memory device of the machine is sufficiently large to handle the input, the intermediate results, and the output of the computation.) The major differences between a small machine and a large machine are that the large machine essentially does the computation at a much faster rate and that it may be easier to program the problem-solution specification for the larger machine. Computers can be constructed where their machine language is much more complex than that evidenced by a set of machine instructions consisting of strings of binary bits. For example, it is possible to make computers that will accept a program written in a language such as FORTRAN or ALGOL directly without the need to write a special program to interpret the input or to translate the input into a lower-level machine language.

For all practical purposes, the binary states of the most primitive machine components are invisible to the user. Therefore we can say that the distinction between the hardware and the software that drives the machine is essentially an artificial distinction. That is, *the hardware plus the program software really constitute the machine as it exists at a particular moment.* If we regard the computer as a "black box," then we cannot distinguish what portion of our program is due to the hardware architecture and what portion is due to the software we have written for that particular machine. Therefore, for any realm of applications, the proportion of hardware and software designed is essentially an engineering decision based on reasons of economy, efficiency, reliability, and aesthetics. The distinction between hardware and software is essentially arbitrary. *A machine loaded with a new piece of software functionally becomes a new machine.* One can therefore consider that any particular programming language (or as we would prefer to call it, computer language) can be *either* "machine" or "higher-level," depending on the engineering decisions concerning the complexity of the general-purpose computer hardware available. In general, the viewpoint of this book will be guided by the assumption that we will always be dealing with standard commercial computers. We pose the problem keeping in mind the properties and features of a designable computer (programming) language that will ensure efficient solution to the problem. We will, however, also inquire into designing new input or output devices that will facilitate or minimize the particular programming process associated with a specific computer language.

If our aim in designing a language is to ensure the efficient solution of problems appropriate to the domain of that language, we see that the extent of the programming necessary to transform the problem-solution specification into "sentences" in the language is a *function of language design.* Therefore we regard the phrase *computer language* as more precise than the conventional *programming language,* since in certain problem domains (see Chap. 8) a computer language can be designed that is totally identical to the problem-solution specification. In this limiting case, there would be no programming process whatsoever. The problem-solution specification itself would be the program.

Language as a Function of Hardware

Practical languages cannot be entirely independent of computer hardware, particularly the hardware used for input. In fact, historically speaking, the properties of many current programming languages have been derived directly from the internal architecture of computers, particularly the input and output devices. These considerations are particularly evident in the case of FORTRAN, which came on the computing scene during the mid-1950s. At the time, FORTRAN was a major advance in the development of programming languages. It influenced, with some exceptions, most of the currently available programming languages. FORTRAN is still the most widely used language for scientific and engineering computation, even though many other languages have since appeared on the scene and claim superiority.

In looking at FORTRAN as a language, we can ask why it has certain characteristics. FORTRAN originally was an acronym for *formula translator.* The intent of FORTRAN was essentially to allow easy programming of mathematical formulas. For example, the mathematical equation $y = ab$ or $y = a \times b$ or $y = a \cdot b$ would be represented in FORTRAN as Y = A * B. FORTRAN requires an equation written in precomputer mathematical notation (1) to have an explicit multiplication symbol (implicit multiplication is not allowed) and (2) to have the precomputer explicit multiplication symbol (× or ·) replaced by * .

Similarly, the mathematical equation

$$y = \frac{a}{b}$$

translated into FORTRAN is Y = A/B. In this case, FORTRAN takes the ordinary numerator-over-denominator notation of mathematics, which is a two-dimensional form (in the sense that it requires two cartesian coordinates to specify the location of each particular symbol), and translates it into a *linear* form. The linear form uses a unique symbol, the slash (/), for division instead of the equally appropriate mathematical symbol ÷, which was conventional in precomputer mathematics.

We should note that in the programming-language representation of the "sentence" Y = A + B, the equals symbol does not really mean that Y is equal to the sum of A + B. Rather, this command (called an *assignment statement*) is meant to instruct a computer to add the value associated with the name *A* to the value associated with the name *B*, then to take that result and associate it with the name *Y*.

Why does FORTRAN ignore the convenient convention of implied multiplication and use an asterisk symbol instead of the more common × or · symbol? Why does it abandon the much more convenient numerator-over-denominator form in trying to express division? Why are only capital English letters permitted? And why does it not clarify the mathematical process involved in assignment by using, for example, a left-pointing arrow instead of an equals sign, which might be confused with the operator for relational equivalence in a "phrase" such as...IF (A = B) THEN...?

The reasons for those rigid linguistic constructions stem from the input devices available to the FORTRAN designers. At the time that FORTRAN was invented by a group associated with IBM, the only widely used input device available for IBM computers was the 026 keypunch (cardpunch). The keyboard of the 026 keypunch was designed essentially for punching data into 80-column by 12-row cards for commercial applications. It punched one or more holes in a left-to-right manner, one coded symbol per column. It was impossible, therefore, to punch codes for the form $\frac{a}{b}$. If a formula was to be input into the computer via cards coded by the 026 keypunch, it had to be translated into a linear form somewhat like A/B. A slash symbol was used simply because the ÷ symbol was not a character on the 026 keypunch. Similarly, the asterisk was used for explicit multiplication because the × and · symbols also were not available on the keypunch. The = symbol was used because no left-pointing arrow was on the keypunch. As a historic note, it should also be added that the strict policy of most computer manufacturers of that time was not to permit modifications of input devices. The keypunch did not have a lowercase character set, let alone commonly used Greek or mathematical symbols. Thus FORTRAN programs were expressed in uppercase characters only, and the rigid syntax was line-oriented, corresponding to the columns of the original punched card. Line numbers, a character code to indicate continuation of a statement, a code to indicate a comment line, and statements were restricted to specific positions in the line corresponding to specific numbered columns of the card.

Essentially, because the designers were stuck with the very limited 026 keypunch, the *only* generally available input device for IBM computers, this critically influenced the development of FORTRAN. The structure of the entire FORTRAN statement is thus dominated by the 80-column card! The FORTRAN statement consists of only a certain set of characters limited by the character set of the historical IBM keypunch and the coding restrictions of card inputs. The statement number must appear in certain columns of the card image, and the length of a statement is limited for each card image.

There are other aspects of FORTRAN that reflect the internal design of computers in the 1950s. For example, the limitations on the numerical size of FORTRAN constants and the number of characters for FORTRAN variable names have to do with the word size that was extant with the then-current IBM 700 line of computer models, as well as the view that liberalization of those restrictions was either too difficult or too impractical. Implicit multiplication was not allowed by the designers of FORTRAN because they believed that the analysis of implicit multiplication, to distinguish it from the case of a variable name with more than one character, would be too difficult, if not impossible, for the compiling techniques of that time. As we will show later on in the text, all these restrictions can be removed for practical programming (computer) languages and current input devices.

Thought Problem

To illustrate the interdependence between computer-language design and the nature of machine architecture, particularly the input device, consider the following situation.

An institution attempts to teach FORTRAN to 2000 students, all of whom will need access to a central computer, via an input device, during a limited time period. It would be impractical to purchase 2000 input units, or anywhere near that amount, to satisfy the requirement of essentially simultaneous use for those students. The question then arises of how to simplify either FORTRAN or the input process, so that 2000 different users can simultaneously input programs in some practical way.

Devices that read pencil markings on cards or paper sheets rapidly and cheaply are available, as are cards that have partially precut holes that can be punched manually. Therefore one can modify FORTRAN so that each simple FORTRAN statement can be put on one card or extended to a continuation card. For example, the first column of the card might contain the digits appropriate for a statement number. Those digits could be repeated in the second available column so that a pencil mark would indicate the particular statement number, thus limiting statement numbers to a value between 0 and 99. The next two columns of the card could indicate which particular FORTRAN command is to be used in a statement. The other columns of the card could be used to select a particular operator or a variable name. An alphabetic character would require *two* marks in a column. For example, the character C would be entered by marking the A–I (A *to* I) row *and* the CLT (C *or* L *or* T) row *in the same column.* A digit would be entered by marking *one* row only in a column of alphabetic characters. Columns with no marks would be considered to be nonexistent, thus permitting multicharacter names and multidigit values to be entered. Such a system was once implemented at the West Point Military Academy around 1965. Figure 1.1 illustrates a similar mark-sense form for mass input of simple FORTRAN-like programs. Locations blocked out by pencil markings are easily picked up by a mark-sense machine.

Additional Characteristics of Nonmachine Computer Languages

On standard machines, most conventional computer languages have no obvious one-to-one correspondence to machine code. When using such languages, one need not consider what registers or specific hardware instructions are available, although there are some special languages where this is possible. One also need not know the internal representation of the data. This leads, on occasion, to a certain amount of confusion, because in the translation from the usual type of numerical notation (for example, decimal input) to an internal binary representation, there may be a loss of bits both in the transformation to input and in the transformation to output. Thus the computation Y = A * (1/A) may not turn out to be exactly 1. It may come out to be 0.99999 or 1.00001 or worse because of the loss of some bits during the decimal-to-binary conversion or some other more subtle numerical

Student Name: ____________________

STATEMENT		C-Card	GO TO	A − I	+	A − I	+	A − I	+	A − I	+	A − I	+
NUMBER		RETURN	IF(	J − R	−	J − R	−	J − R	−	J − R	−	J − R	−
0	0	PAUSE	REAL	S − Z	*	S − Z	*	S − Z	*	S − Z	*	S − Z	*
1	1	CALL	DO	AJ	**	AJ	**	AJ	**	AJ	**	AJ	**
2	2	FUNCTION	CONTINUE	BKS	=	BKS	=	BKS	=	BKS	=	BKS	=
3	3	FORMAT(	STOP	CLT	(	CLT	(	CLT	(	CLT	(	CLT	(
4	4	SUBROUTINE	ASSIGN	DMU	)	DMU	)	DMU	)	DMU	)	DMU	)
5	5	READ	PRINT	ENV	,	ENV	,	ENV	,	ENV	,	ENV	,
6	6	EQUIVALENCE		FOW	.	FOW	.	FOW	.	FOW	.	FOW	.
7	7	DIMENSION	END	GPX	/	GPX	/	GPX	/	GPX	/	GPX	/
8	8	COMMON	RETURN	HQY	√	HQY	√	HQY	√	HQY	√	HQY	√
9	9	INTEGER	EXIT	IRZ	BLANK	IRZ	BLANK	IRZ	BLANK	IRZ	BLANK	IRZ	BLANK

A − I	+	A − I	+	A − I	+	A − I	+	A − I	+	A − I	+	A − I	+	A − I	row	12
J − R	−	J − R	−	J − R	−	J − R	−	J − R	−	J − R	−	J − R	−	J − R	row	11
S − Z	*	S − Z	*	S − Z	*	S − Z	*	S − Z	*	S − Z	*	S − Z	*	S − Z	row	0
AJ	**	AJ	**	AJ	**	AJ	**	AJ	**	AJ	**	AJ	**	AJ	row	1
BKS	=	BKS	=	BKS	=	BKS	=	BKS	=	BKS	=	BKS	=	BKS	row	2
CLT	(	CLT	(	CLT	(	CLT	(	CLT	(	CLT	(	CLT	(	CLT	row	3
DMU	)	DMU	)	DMU	)	DMU	)	DMU	)	DMU	)	DMU	)	DMU	row	4
ENV	,	ENV	,	ENV	,	ENV	,	ENV	,	ENV	,	ENV	,	ENV	row	5
FOW	.	FOW	.	FOW	.	FOW	.	FOW	.	FOW	.	FOW	.	FOW	row	6
GPX	/	GPX	/	GPX	/	GPX	/	GPX	/	GPX	/	GPX	/	GPX	row	7
HQY	√	HQY	√	HQY	√	HQY	√	HQY	√	HQY	√	HQY	√	HQY	row	8
IRZ	BLANK	IRZ	BLANK	IRZ	BLANK	IRZ	BLANK	IRZ	BLANK	IRZ	BLANK	IRZ	BLANK	IRZ	row	9

Figure 1.1 Illustration of a mark-sense form card for simplified FORTRAN.

failure in the algorithm used for computation. Whether a language should be able to effect specific registers and directly input into the internal representation of the machine is a matter of opinion; we shall discuss some relevant considerations later on in this work. It is generally agreed, however, that a language *should* have a certain amount of machine independence. For example, a program written in FORTRAN should be able to run unmodified on machines that use different machine codes. In actual practice, this is rarely possible for complex programs without some rewriting. Another difficulty is that use of similar languages may produce program segments that, even though they are identical, have different interpretations.

The Essence of the Programming Problem

It would seem that the crux of the matter in communicating with computers is that the essential *linguistic distance* between the effective language of the computer and the language used by a human being to describe the problem to be solved has to be minimized.

Therefore we can state that the amount of programming that is necessary is directly proportional to the distance between the language in which we specify the problem and the language that runs on the computer. In this respect, we must note that by *computer* we mean both the hardware and the software that translates the incoming program into machine instructions in the event that the machine architecture is not directly structured for immediate execution. Minimizing the linguistic distance between the specification language and the computer language not only maximizes the economics of the programming process, it also increases the reliability of the software that is written.

Reliability is directly joined to the capability to verify that a program is correct. It seems obvious, without much formal justification, that the closer a program is to the statement of the problem, the easier it is to demonstrate that the program is correct, that is, the program is equivalent to the problem-solution specification. In other words, an optimum programming language would allow the user to specify the problem solution in terms of structures, abstractions, and notations that are relevant to the problem rather than dependent on a particular machine organization or some artifact introduced by a programming language that has goals other than the maximizing of economic efficiency.

Perhaps these notions can be made clearer by narrowing our considerations to a limited application area, for example, scientific and engineering applications programming, in which FORTRAN has been and still is dominant. In these areas, the specification language is usually technical English and formal symbolic notations, mathematical or logical. Formal symbolic notations have proved to be not only sufficient but indispensable in the specification and precise formulation of mathematical problems. They are also of great value as an aid to efficient reasoning in the solution of such problems. Thus it would seem that in scientific and engineering applications the historically derived mathematical notations are ideal in minimizing the distance between the specification language and the computer language.

The general objection to that point of view, however, is that the notational structure of mathematics cannot be implemented on computers, except in an extremely limited sense, largely because of the very limited capability of conventional input devices. That objection has not been argued explicitly; rather, it is assumed to be obvious that computer languages *must be* linear in form and that the use of computer languages to make a problem-solution specification executable on a computer *must* involve complex programming for complex problems. Equally important as a historical factor has been the lack of inventiveness of language designers who have regarded the computer-language design problem as purely a "software" task distinct from input hardware design. In part, the objection to precomputer mathematical forms arises from the fact that computers can be characterized by a finite set of states and their word units in memory can contain only a finite set of bits. Furthermore, internal operations within the computer may lead to truncation errors and other serious errors of precision, since what is computed is, at best, usually only an approximation to the theoretically correct value. For the most part, however, those are not relevant objections from a practical point of view. Objections to using conventional mathematical forms as a programming language are based on a fundamental misunderstanding of what can be implemented. In our opinion, those objections stem from the historical misunderstanding that arose from the implementation of FORTRAN as a linear language and the failure of subsequent language designers to reexamine the historical constraints. It is not generally understood that modern input devices remove the necessity of linearity of input and that it is possible to use full-blown mathematical notation, which is essentially two-dimensional. Mathematical notation is two-dimensional in the sense that a character has two degrees of freedom. The position of the character must be specified by an x coordinate and a y coordinate in a rectangular cartesian coordinate system. As we shall show in Chap. 8, historically derived mathematical notation not only is implementable, but is decidedly practical to use in a computer language to narrow the linguistic difference between the specification language of the problem and the computer language executed within a digital computer. For application areas outside the scientific, mathematical, and engineering domains, it is also possible to incorporate into computer languages syntactic structures that are much more flexible than those found in current languages.

Powerfulness

Occasionally the term *power of a language* is used to describe the similarity between that language and the machine language of the particular machine on which it is implemented, that is, to describe the extent to which it can directly use all of the facilities of that machine. But more generally, the concept of *powerfulness* implies that a succinct statement in that computer language will cause a great deal of computation. Loosely speaking, a program written in a powerful, high-level computer language should result in a much larger set of machine code.

To give a quantitative measure to the concept of powerfulness, we can define the power of a language over a set of programs as the inverse ratio of alphabetic characters (or words) of the higher-level computer program to the equivalent set of characters or code of the machine-language program. Therefore the *comparative power* of two high-level languages is the inverse ratio of characters or words between equivalent programs.

As a somewhat extreme example, consider, in ordinary mathematical notation, the specification of a problem such as

$$\text{Compute } y = \int_5^{10} \int_3^4 \frac{\tan x^2}{\sqrt{z}}\, dx\, dz.$$

Then compare that to the corresponding program in FORTRAN, ALGOL, or a computer language *that can take the expression as direct input.* According to our definition, the third computing language would be, in principle, the most powerful because it would require no more additional characters than the original specification of the problem. In fact, for the third language, the specification of the problem would be identical to the computer program. Thus in certain application areas the type of computer language used and the particular notation associated with that computer language determine the degree of powerfulness.

Economic Efficiency

If we were to time, over a set of programmers, how long it took them to program correctly the same problem in different languages, the time expended would measure the economic utility of each language. In practice, however, economic utility is difficult to measure, for several reasons. First, there is a learning effect. When a programmer formulates the same problem into different languages, the second time he or she does the problem it will be done much more efficiently than the first time. But more important is the phenomenon of the "hot-shot" programmer.

There is experimental and anecdotal evidence that a hot-shot programmer can produce from 50 to 100 times more correct, debugged code than the average competent programmer. This is an amazing phenomenon that seems to occur in only a few fields. Aside from computer programming, the only other intellectual fields in which this phenomenon tends to occur is in scientific productivity and inventions. In these areas, a few individuals produce scientific discoveries and inventions quite out of proportion to their numbers in a general population, even when in a homogenous group in terms of education, technical experience, and IQ. Because of this and other factors, it is difficult to measure precisely economic efficiency. The most we can attempt to record is gross variations in economic efficiency among languages in different situations. Put more precisely, the variance associated with programming activity is so great that usual statistical measures must be used with great caution to gauge the effectiveness of different languages.

Problem-Oriented Languages

A language is said to be *problem-oriented* if its notation and/or syntax are similar to the actual technical language commonly used in a specific technical field. As we mentioned before, FORTRAN, which originally stood for *formula translator,* is oriented toward mathematical solutions.

User-Oriented Languages

The term *user-oriented* was first coined in the 1960s. It is more common now, as is the equivalent term *user-friendly.* Generally the meaning of either term is that a language (1) is easy to use, (2) is easy to learn, and (3) resembles the user's "natural" mode of communication.

The general idea of the user-oriented approach to designing a language is to take into account, indeed, to give priority to, the psychology and the practices of the user. To do that, the designer must take care that the computer language in some sense resembles the language of the subject matter in which the user has been trained. Also, the list of rules for the computer language—the manuals—should be succinct and easily readable. Ideally, programs should be self-documenting. In many respects, the language should be self-teaching;

that is, the output from use of the language should be designed to increase the user's linguistic competence, without the need for formal instruction.

Generality

Languages characterized by the term *generality* can be used for a wide range of applications. When PL/1 was designed, it was meant to be a universal and general language. The intention was to have it do what any other language would be able to do. As a result, PL/1 is an extremely complex language that, according to many users, is difficult to use because of its great many features. Ada has since been designed to replace PL/1 and the various versions of FORTRAN, PASCAL, and COBOL as a general, universal language in which it is hoped it will be possible to do everything and anything.

Simplicity

A language can be considered simple if it is (1) easy to use, (2) easy to learn, and (3) easy to implement.

In many respects, the language BASIC satisfies all three conditions. Historically, BASIC has shown itself easy to use. In fact, it is so easy to use it became the prevailing language in the early days of timesharing. In fact, from one point of view, BASIC may have been responsible for the widespread use of timesharing in the late 1960s and the 1970s. Because of its very simple linguistic structure, BASIC is also easy to implement. There are innumerable cases where BASIC has been implemented by high-school students with no prior knowledge of compilers or interpreters. The major drawback of simple languages such as BASIC is that they are inadequate for complex applications.

User-Defined Languages

The essential idea of user-defined languages appears, at first glance, to be very attractive. The basic intent of a user-defined language is to allow users to build in those capabilities they want; that is, users have the ability to design their own language structures from a simple framework. Unfortunately, although the idea of a user-defined language has been prevalent for a relatively long time, it is never been shown to be practical. Perhaps the design of computer languages requires an essentially professional background to avoid many of the pitfalls that we shall point out in the remainder of this text.

It is relatively easy to think of certain valuable user-defined facilities that would not alter the actual structure of the language. For example, we might want to define highly complicated mathematical processes by the use of a particular symbol. Say we define ∇^2 as the partial derivatives

$$\frac{\partial}{\partial x^2} + \frac{\partial}{\partial y^2} + \frac{\partial}{\partial z^2}$$

Then, in the particular program, it would be necessary only to write ∇^2, which the computer-language processor would interpret as our definition above, assuming that each partial derivative had been appropriately defined as a recognizable function of the program and the computer language recognized such notational forms.

Naturalness

Some languages are more "natural" than other languages. Intuitively, the idea is that a language resemble the precomputer method of dealing with the problem-solution specification. However, it is not at all clear that natural is better. How can we analyze the attribute of naturalness in weighing its attractiveness in the design of a computer language? One example we might consider would be mathematics.

Examine the following forms:

1. $\frac{A}{B} + C$
2. A/B + C
3. (A/B) + C
4. A/(B + C)

There is no question what form 1 means. It is a totally unambiguous form expressed in the common notation of mathematics familiar to any grade-school child. But what does form 2 mean? Should one divide first and then add, as in form 3, or add first and then divide, as in form 4? In FORTRAN, for example, form 2 would be interpreted as *program* 3; in APL, however, form 2 would be interpreted as *program* 4, which will give different results. FORTRAN uses different precedence rules for operators than APL. Thus we see that the normal mathematical form tends to resolve certain kinds of ambiguities that are introduced by the linear nature of most computer languages used for programming. That is equivalent to stating that the historically derived mathematical notations imply more information than the syntax of conventional computer languages. Another example along that line is given in Chap. 8, together with possible liabilities associated with a computer language that is too "natural."

Natural versus Artificial Computer Languages

All computer languages are artificial in the sense that they have

- A finite, and usually fixed, limited vocabulary, that is, a dictionary essentially of fixed size in terms of allowable operators, words, punctuation, and the type and range of names to be associated with variables and constants
- Inflexible notation
- A definite linguistic structure or syntax
- An essentially unambiguous grammar
- The intent of well-defined semantics

On the other hand, a natural language may have

- *A nonfinite vocabulary.* Natural languages are characterized by an ever-expanding set of words that, while they may be understood by a large number of people, do not appear in any current dictionary of the language.
- *A flexible notation.* In the course of speaking or writing a natural language, one may vary or invent new notations that either are explicitly defined or have meanings that are made clear by the context.
- *A vague, incomplete, or inconsistent syntax.* Many expressions in natural language, while having clear meaning to the listener or reader, are difficult to analyze under any "official" rules of grammar or are clearly incorrect according to such rules (In a *conventional* computer language a sentence or its equivalent that has an incorrect syntactical structure is rejected by the associated compiler at the point in the process when the syntax error is discovered. Translation and concomitant code generation are not attempted for an "incorrect" sentence. Put another way, for a conventional computer language, a syntactically incorrect sentence has no meaning whatsoever, since it cannot be executed by the machine. On the other hand, sentences in a natural language, even if grammatically incorrect, may have precise meaning and thus be "executable.")
- *An ambiguous grammar.* When a given sentence is broken into a

sequence of component parts and the form, function, and syntactical relationship of each part is explicitly identified, that sequence may not be unique. That is, there may exist one or more other sequences that are equally admissible. In some cases, the ambiguity can be resolved, (e.g., by using a different grammar); in other cases, it cannot and the sentence is labeled as inherently ambiguous. If it were otherwise, there would be no need for extensive legal considerations as to the exact meaning of laws and treaties. Since a great deal of time in modern civilization is spent in the clarification of both written and oral communication, we can only conclude that natural languages are characterized by fuzzy grammatical constructs and attributes of meaning.

- *A complex and muddy semantics highly dependent on the speaker/writer, the listener/reader, and the context of the situation.* In the case of computer languages, the semantics of a program is, from a technical viewpoint, simply the machine code generated by the compiler for that language. We note, also, that a meaningless program, for example, a program that does not generate any output, will not be rejected by current compilers.
- *A complex evolutionary history.* In contrast, artificial languages are usually created by one or two individuals or, at most, a committee, and their structure, purpose, and historical circumstances are relatively clear.

As we have indicated before, a computer language that mimics the notation and syntax of a natural language has many desirable attributes. It is easy for the user to learn and use and, if properly constructed, less prone to error. Concomitantly however (as discussed in Chap. 8), an undesirable attribute appears when the language is used by naive people. Essentially, a naive user confronted by a language that mimics a linguistic form with which he or she is familiar may assume that the language-plus-machine has some attribute of intelligence. As a result, the user may impart more intelligence to the machine than is warranted by the capabilities of the language system.

Self-Documentation

Computer languages have various degrees of self-documentation. By this, we mean the attribute associated with a program, including comments, that make it understandable to either programmers other than the originator or individuals who are technically versed in the problem area but who are not professional programmers. In this respect, a computer language that has been modeled to resemble some noncomputer form of linguistic communication is usually more understandable and therefore more self-documenting than a language based on some abstract model unrelated to historically prevalent linguistic forms. Documentation is widely recognized as valuable to any software system. Therefore a computer language that in some substantive sense is self-documenting carries with it a desirable attribute.

Error Proneness

Different languages have different rates of error and different error types. There has been some experimental work to differentiate errors associated with different languages, but the data are not extensive enough so that we can unequivocally label one language as less error-prone than another. It is obvious that a language that has intricate linguistic constructs will be susceptible to syntactic errors in programming. A language that requires a complex notation, for example, the use of highly detailed nested sets of parentheses to delimit certain types of grammatical constructs, will also probably be error-prone. Likewise, a language that has a tremendous range of syntactical categories and complex rules to invoke its many procedures will be very difficult to use correctly, not only for the average user but also the professional programmer.

The field of measuring error as a function of language type needs much more study before we can go further than making plausible arguments and guesses as to the projected errors that one might associate with a particular language design. Nonetheless, it seems clear that a computer language that has been successfully designed to mimic some language structure conventional to a given problem area could anticipate less error. Error analysis in such a language would be reduced to a matter of proofreading.

Procedure-Oriented Languages

The term *procedure-oriented* is used to label most of the current languages that require the user to specify, in sequence, a set of operations. For example, to set an array a_i equal to the values 1, 2,..., 10 and then to print a_i, one might write the simple program

```
    I = 1
(1) A(I) = I
    PRINT A(I)
    I = I + 1
    IF I > 10, CONTINUE, ELSE GO TO LABEL (1).
```

A less procedural language design would accept the form

```
Print a_i = i for i = 1 to 10.
                              <a_i assumes the value printed.>
```

Additionally, in a nonprocedural language, we might program the instruction to compute a definite integral as

$$Y = \int_b^a F(x)\,dx \text{ where } F(x) = x^3 + \frac{\sin x}{x}$$

Application-Oriented Languages

In general, the term *application-oriented* is used to designate languages that have a narrow purpose. For example, the language APT is used to program instructions for cutting machine tools. The language COGO is used in the very specific area of civil engineering. Generally, application-oriented languages tend to be much less procedural than more general languages in the sense that the user need not specify in detail the computational algorithms used to do tasks specific to the application area. For many of these languages, the program is equivalent to a sequence of procedure calls.

Reference, Publication, and Hardware Languages

Historically, in the context of computer languages, the terms *reference, publication,* and *hardware* were introduced by the designers of ALGOL. The *reference* version of a language uses a definitive character set for that language. For conventional computer languages, it is a one-dimensional string of symbols. The *publication* version of a language is a variant of the reference language that makes it more practical for publication. For example, the reference language may contain the string A ↑ 2. For publication purposes, however, it may be more feasible to print A^2. Similarly, the *hardware* language is a variant of the reference language that accommodates the limitations of computer input and output devices. For example, the reference symbol ↑ may not be available on certain input devices; thus the hardware languages would translate the symbol to, say, a series of two asterisks. Hardware languages which use sequences of symbols, e.g., ++ , == , >= , to represent a single "token" are difficult to read and are error-prone. Similarly, operational commands for specific hardware which require the pressing of more than one key simultaneously are error-prone.

Chapter 2

Methods of Language Definition

Any computer language has a basic set of characters, or *keystrokes,* each of which is represented by a unique binary code. A particular language may have a fixed set of characters, or it may have some means of defining additional characters. One way of expanding the language set is to allow a sequence of characters or keystrokes to represent a single new character. For example, the keystroke sequence $= b$ / could be interpreted as the $\neq$ (not equal) symbol where the keystroke b stands for backspace. Similarly, if the computer-language system has associated with it an input device with graphic capability so that symbols can be constructed from more primitive characters, then a *single* symbol can be represented by a *sequence* of strokes and space (cursor) movements to compose the desired graphic character.

The basic linguistic unit of a computer language, however, is the *lexical item.* By this we mean the set of allowed words from which sentences in the language can be constructed. For a particular computer language, a word may be a single character (keystroke) or a combination of characters and *spaces.* The latter may be in a linear sequence: overlaid, as in the construction of the $\neq$ symbol, or in strokes that have a two-dimensional relationship, for example, A^2, where the 2 has the relationship *superscript to A.*

In other words, regard the cluster of characters as concatenated to form a single lexical unit where the lexical unit may be termed a word, a primitive, a token, or an atom of the language. Once this lexical-recognition process takes place, the original sequence of *characters* that constitute the input of the computer language can be replaced by the sequence of *words* in a different representation of that language. In the process of translating a computer language into its machine-coded representation, it is usually desirable to replace the sequence of input codes (representing sequences of characters) with codes representing the recognized words of the language as soon as possible. By doing so, one can pick word codes in such a way that they not only identify a particular word but also, by the numerical value of the code itself, characterize various features of that word. For example, the value of the code representing an arithmetic operator can determine its precedence with respect to another arithmetic operator.

Types of Words

Key words are the special words of a particular language that can be used as commands, operators, labels, prefixes of certain procedures, or punctuation. They include simple operators such as +, −, ∗ , /, ADD, SUBSTRACT, >, <, and GREATER THAN, and the more complex operators such as SORT, Σ, and ∫.

The words IF, GOTO, FOR, and DIMENSION are typical key words in many conventional languages. Key words have the same meaning when used in all programs of a specific computer language. Thus key words, while usually produced by a sequence of keystrokes, could be produced by one special-character keystroke on a terminal where this entire word is treated as one character. A key word may or may not, however, be a *reserved* word in a particular language. A reserved word is one that may not be used as a user-defined name or label. For example, in FORTRAN IV (as well as in FORTRAN 77 and FORTRAN 90), a key word need not be reserved. The phrase IF = 5 means that we want to assign the value 5 to the *name* IF, whereas the phrase IF (A.GE.B) Y = 5 means that if the value associated with the name A is greater than or equal to the value associated with the name B, then we want to assign the numerical value 5 to the name Y. Clearly a language that requires all key words to be reserved will facilitate programs that are linguistically simpler and easier to compile than languages that do not.

Key words may also be *noise words* in the sense that they have no meaning (that is, they generate no executable machine code) and are inserted simply to make the program easier to read. For example, we might say COMPUTE Y = X + Z. Here, the word COMPUTE is a noise word since it adds no meaning to the assignment statement Y = X + Z. It is a characteristic of certain complier implementations that parts of certain key words are, by the idiosyncrasies of a specific implementation, interpreted as noise since they are redundant to the translation process. For example, in some compilers, the input word DIMWIT will be recognized as the word DIMENSION, since the lexical identification is made after scanning only the first three characters.

Blanks also act as special delimiters in the sense that in many languages they separate lexical items or words. However, it is a peculiarity of many historic languages, for example, FORTRAN IV and ALGOL, that blanks are suppressed when the input program is read. One advantage of eliminating blanks upon input is that it allows more compact storage of the input program in memory. Recent hardware developments, however, have made restrictions on memory size relatively unimportant. Thus that particular feature of many languages can be regarded not only as redundant, but as introducing an unnecessary difficulty into the lexical phase of the compilation or translation process. Such difficulty is particularly aggravated in those languages that do not reserve key words.

User-defined words can be categorized as names of variables, functions, procedures, modules, etc., or as constants or literals or comments.

Names of variables, functions, procedures, and modules. Depending on the specific programming language, there may be restrictions as to the number of characters in a name (*identifier*) and the type of characters that can be used in such a name. For example, most conventional languages require that the first character of a name be alphabetic and that the total number of characters in a name not exceed n, where n varies from 6 to 36 characters, none of which may be a special character, that is, not alphanumeric. The restriction that the first character be alphabetic simplifies the lexical analysis phase of compilation. The restriction on the number of characters is not particularly necessary, however, since it can be waived without inducing substantial difficulties in the compilation process. The fact that such restrictions have persevered can be regarded as an historical anachronism. Also, many computer languages require that the identifier be declared as to type and range. The programmer, usually at the beginning of the program, must indicate whether the variable is of integer type, real type, string type, and so on. If the identifier indicates a multi-dimension array variable, then most conventional languages require that the user supply the values of the corresponding dimensions of that array. Similarly, names of labels can be used to indicate particular points in the program where one can "branch to" from other points of the program. Identifiers can also be used as names of particular locations or sets of locations in memory, although, as we shall discuss later, the relationship may not be unique.

Constants. In conventional programming languages, there are many restrictions on constants. For example, depending on the language, constants may be restricted, by declaration or otherwise, to an integer format; a fixed-point format, such as 123.4; or a floating-point format, such as .1234E + 3 (where the signed number following the E must be an integer). Constants may be considered to be numerical to base 10, base 2, base 8, or even to base 16, depending on the particular language. Constants may also be considered to be logical in the sense that they can exist only as two values, true or false. There may be restrictions on the magnitude of constants, restrictions that historically have their origin in the particular machine architecture in which the original language design was implemented. Similarly, the number of dimensions associated with a particular array variable may be restricted, depending again on the architecture of the machine on which the original language was implemented. For some languages, punctuation can be used to distinguish one data type from another. For example, in some languages, the phrase X = 2. would be considered to assign the type REAL to the name X and its value, whereas the phrase X = 2 might mean that X and its value are of either type INTEGER or type REAL, depending on whether or not X had been previously declared. Most programming languages, however, will not distinguish between a name of a variable and a name that can have only one (constant) value, as in π = 3.1415....In some languages such as FORTRAN, if a name begins with a letter such as I, J, K, L, M, N, then it and its values, unless contrarily declared, are considered to be of type INTEGER. Therefore the statement I = 2.987654 would result in the assignment of the value 2 for the name I. This is so because the FORTRAN compiler will automatically truncate to an integer the value assigned to an integer variable. If one is concerned with execution efficiency, that is, the minimization of the running time of a program for a particular machine, then one can make arguments to support the distinction among integers, real numbers, and floating-point representations. But from the point of view of the user and the language designer who wishes to accommodate the user, it is not clear that any real advantage is gained from such categorical division and separate numerical representations into integers, fixed point, and floating point by requiring rigid type declarations of names. For modern processors, even the efficiency gain is minimal if an effective optimizing compiler is used.

Literals. A *literal* is a string or cluster of characters that has no other objective meaning besides itself. An entire literal is simply to be regarded as a *sign* (or picture) because it or its coded representation is treated as a single unit by the program and is not to be interpreted as having any particular functional meaning. Although a literal's usual purpose is as an insert into complex data output, this does not mean that it cannot be modified by the program. In fact, literals can be modified by arithmetic or logical operations, in the sense that graphic signs can be modified by various additions or erasures. Put another way, a literal is not to be interpreted as a name of either a variable or a location nor as a key word in the sense that it is a command to do something.

Comments. *Comments* are introduced into a program to explain those things that are not clear. They do not translate into machine code. The restrictions or signs indicating that a particular string is a comment depend, of course, on the specifics of the language. For example, comments in early FORTRAN were restricted to those cards that had been punched in column 1 with the character C. Thus the inflexible card format used in FORTRAN does not allow the insertion of comments within a single FORTRAN statement. In ALGOL 60, the restrictions on the insertion of comments are less rigid. For example, a comment is any string of characters starting after the characters ; COMMENT or BEGIN COMMENT and terminated by a semicolon. A comment is also any string of characters starting after END and terminated by a semicolon, or END, or ELSE. In most conventional languages, the use of comments involves some sort of restriction on the structure or the placement of the comments themselves. For the type of sentencelike structure defined in Chap. 8, we introduce a relatively unrestricted comment format that requires only that a comment be initiated by a { and terminated by a } placed *anywhere* in the program.

The point we want to emphasize is that language designers have introduced many restrictions either because of historical anachronisms—simply carrying over what was done before—or because they misunderstand the difficulties of certain types of language implementation.

Syntax, Semantics, and Pragmatics

One can analyze a language systematically by constructing an appropriate grammar for that language. If we regard a language as a set of strings of words, then the grammar for that language determines the acceptable or "legal" strings in that language. Grammar itself can be divided into various categories. For example, *morphology,* roughly speaking, is the study of word formations. Another category is *syntax,* or how words are put together to form phrases, clauses, and sentences. Syntax is the *set of rules that state the permissible relationship of words in a sentence of a language.*

Syntactical rules can also be called *rewriting* rules, in that a given syntactical category can be replaced or rewritten as a series of other syntactical categories, a sequence of actual words of the language, or a mixed sequence of syntactical categories and actual words of the language. For example, a syntactical category in most natural languages would be *sentence.* In English, we could use the rewriting rule so that the syntactical category <*sentence*> becomes the sequence of the syntactical categories <*subject phrase*> <*verb phrase*> <*object phrase*>. Similarly we could rewrite the syntactical category <*subject phrase*> as *the man,* where the words *the man* are actual words of the language. The rules of syntax tell us what sequences of words are proper in a specific language and what sequences are improper. For example, in the natural language English, the statement *John hit the ball* is syntactically proper. However, the statement *John the ball hit* is syntactically improper.

The most striking difference between the syntactical rules of a natural language and those of a computer language is that a syntactically improper sentence in a natural language may still have a clear and unambiguous meaning. But in conventional computer languages, a program that has been constructed according to an improper syntax will be rejected by the compiler or translating system. Thus the syntax of computer languages is a rigid set of relational rules between words that admit no flexibility, whereas in a natural language, improper syntax can, in many cases, simply be construed as a nonsubstantive failing in grammar. We should point out that in a computer language an improper syntax is rejected by the compiler not as a theoretical necessity but rather as a dictum of historical practice. In principle, one could conceive of computer languages that, in a certain sense, have a "fuzzy" syntax.

Another crucially important subdivision of grammar is *semantics.* Semantics concerns itself with the meaning of strings of words. For natural language, *semantics is the essence of communication.* The elucidation of meaning from linguistic communication is, in the domain of natural language, a highly complex procedure for which there is yet no definitive understanding. If there were, there would be no need for courts of law to interpret laws, nor would there exist the whole range of human misunderstanding about the meaning of speech or text.

By comparison to the role it plays in natural language, semantics has a minor role for computer languages. For example, in one language the string $A + B$ means that the value associated with the name A is to be added to the value associated with the name B. In another language, the phrase $AB +$ would mean essentially the same thing. In yet another language, the string $A + B$ might mean the union of set A with set B. Thus, for a computer language, semantics can usually be dealt with by a set of simple rules associated with the relatively precise meaning carried by names and those symbols used as operators.

Alternative meanings can usually be resolved by straightforward contextual rules. In a more technical sense, the semantics of a *specific* program is simply the machine code generated by the compiler associated with the language in processing that program. For a machine with a *consistent* architecture (that is, bug-free), there can be only one precise meaning for each item in the machine code of that particular architecture. Therefore there cannot be any question about the meaning of a set of machine codes for a *given set* of input data. It is precisely predictable (at least in principle) how that program will operate on that specific set of data and, assuming the program terminates, what the result will be. The only way that fuzziness or ambiguity in semantics might come into play is if two different compilers for the same language were to generate different sets of machine code for an identical language category. From a nontrivial point of view, it is the role of the language designer to attempt to specify precisely what a given phrase in the computer language will do in the most general sense. If the designer succeeds in precisely defining the action associated with a given linguistic phrase, there can be no possibility of ambiguity or imprecision as to the effect of the *specific* machine code. In that case, differences of output between two compilers can only be different coding structures that are computationally equivalent. Different coding sequences that are not computationally equivalent are the result of an implementation error (not semantic ambiguity).

The term *pragmatics,* as it is currently used in a computer environment, is much less precise in terms of the meaning it conveys. Essentially, pragmatics concerns itself with how the user *intends* to use the program in a given system environment, where the system environment includes a particular machine architecture, the associated storage peripherals, the associated input/output devices with their own idiosyncrasies, and even the quirks and restrictions of a given operating system. From this rather imprecise point of view, the pragmatics of a given computer system might explain why it would be inadvisable to run a program on a machine with a 16-bit word, even if the program has shown itself to produce correct results for a range of data when run on a machine with a 32-bit word. For the same data and the same program (using the same computer language), the results may differ, even radically so, because of the imprecision of numerical results introduced by going from a 32-bit word to a 16-bit word. In principle, an appropriate compiler for the machine with the smaller bit size *could* compensate for the reduction in word size. In practice, however, that is usually not done; thus the situation becomes a *pragmatic* consideration that advises caution in assessing the portability of a program from one machine to another.

Pragmatics can also be said to account for the phenomenon of a program yielding different results when run at different times, even when the same machine, the same compiler, and the same input data are used. The causes of inconsistency are extremely varied and usually indeterminate. The cause could be a transient effect in the hardware itself, that is, an intermittent failure; a voltage peak in the communication line; an imprecise synchronization in the printing mechanism of the output device, causing it to print an incorrect character; and so forth. Such inconsistency may also be a signal that a "virus" is resident within the local or network software environment.

Formal Description of Languages

To describe the various characteristics of a language in a formal or abstract way, we need another language, called a *metalanguage.* Of course, to describe the formal characteristics of the metalanguage, we would need a meta-metalanguage. And it follows that to describe the characteristics of a meta-metalanguage, we would need a meta-meta-metalanguage, and so on. From a practical point of view, it is sufficient just to describe the characteristics of the metalanguage by explicit examples. The most commonly used metalinguistic notation for the syntactical structure of programming languages is known as BNF (Backus-Naur Form). Using BNF, we could write the syntactical definition for a digit as

<digit> ↔ 0|1|2|3|4|5|6|7|8|9

This would be called a *production* or *rewriting rule* for the language, where it is more common to use the *BNF symbol* :: = instead of ↔. We prefer the symbol ↔ because it emphasizes the fact that any occurrence of the left side of the rule can be rewritten as one of the alternatives on the right side of the rule, where each alternative is separated by the symbol |. Conversely, any occurrence of the symbols in any alternative definition on the right side of the rule can be replaced by the symbol on the left side of the rule. If we replace a symbol that appears on the left side of a rewriting rule with one of the sequences of symbols that appear on the right side of the rule, we are rewriting "top-down." If we replace one of the alternative occurrences found on the right side of the rule with the symbol found on the left side of the rule, we are rewriting "bottom-up." If the set of rules completely describes the structure of a "sentence" of the language, then the consistent application of the rewriting rules can be described as *parsing* the sentence in order to assign a particular syntactical category to each component or sequence of components that constitutes the sentence.

In rewriting rules, symbols fall into two classes. Those that have the

< > symbols around them are *items of the metalanguage,* while those symbols that are not enclosed by the < > symbols are items of the computer language, more commonly called the *terminal symbols* of the language. For most computer languages, the rewriting rules can appear with only one *metasymbol* on the left side of the rule and a sequence of alternative symbols on the right side of the rule, each of which may be a *metasymbol* or a *terminal symbol.* The notation is general enough, however, that it may include rules that have on the left side more than one metasymbol and maybe even terminal symbols if the structure of the language so warrants. For example, a computer language that allows synonyms, such as the lexical item PLUS or the symbol + could include the rule

PLUS ↔ + .

A description of a simple syntax for a limited programming language might be

(1) *<sentence>* ↔ *<program>*
(2) *<program>* ↔ *<assignment>* | *<assignment>* ; *<program>*
(3) *<assignment>* ↔ *<variable>* = *<arithmetic expression>*
(4) *<arithmetic expression>* ↔ *<term>* | *<arithmetic expression>*
<add operator> *<term>*
(5) *<term>* ↔ *<factor>* | *<term>* *<multiply operator>* *<factor>*
(6) *<factor>* ↔ *<variable>* | *<integer>* |
(<arithmetic expression>)
(7) *<add operator>* ↔ + | −
(8) *<multiply operator>* ↔ * | /
(9) *<variable>* ↔ **A|B|C|D|E|F|G|H|I|J|K|L|M|N|O|P|Q|R|S|T|U|V|W|X|Y|Z**
(10) *<integer>* ↔ *<digit>* | *<integer>* *<digit>*
(11) *<digit>* ↔ **1|2|3|4|5|6|7|8|9|0**

These rules may also be represented graphically by enclosing each metasymbol and each terminal symbol within a rectangular box. Each box for a metasymbol has three possible pointers: one pointing to its definition, the second to an alternative symbol, and the third to the successor symbol in the definition string. Terminal symbols do not have definition pointers, as they stand for themselves. The graphical representation of the above syntax[1] is shown in Figure 2.1.

Notice that some of the syntactical rules contain, in one of the alternatives on the right side, *the term that is being defined,* that is, the term that is on the left side. If the symbol that appears on the left side of the rule appears again as the first symbol of one of the alter-

---

[1]The style of graphic structures of Fig. 2.1 and the corresponding example syntax are modeled, with some changes, after the notation used by D. J. Cohen and C. C. Gotlieb, "A List Structure Form of Grammars for Syntactic Analysis," *Computing Surveys,* vol. 2, no. 1, March 1970).

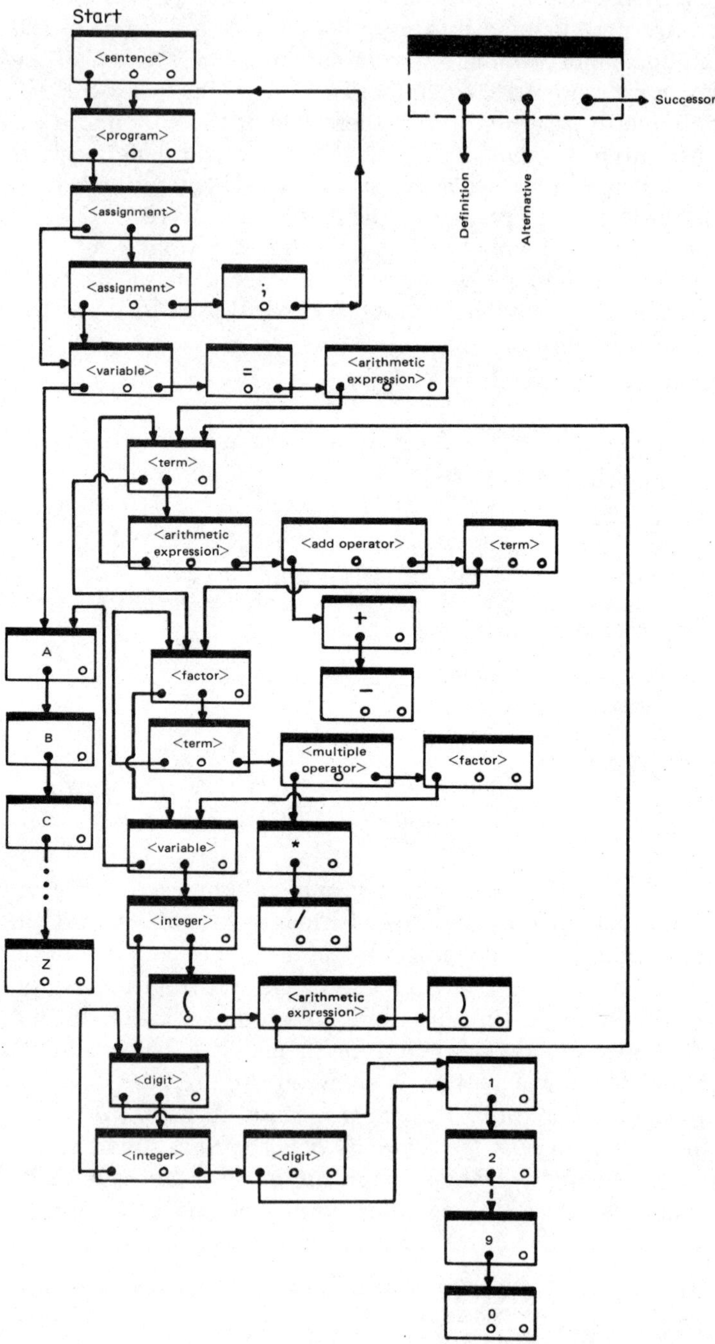

Figure 2.1 Graphical representation of syntax.

native definitions on the right side of the rule, then this rule is called a *left-recursive rule.* Similarly, if the symbol being defined appears as the last symbol of one of the alternative definitions on the right side of the rule, it is a *right-recursive rule.*

The use of rules in recursive forms may cause difficulty when applied in a mechanical way to the analysis of sentences of the language. For example, suppose we are scanning a sequence of terminal symbols of a computer language and we *expect* that an integer will appear. We might want to apply the rule

<integer> ↔ *<digit>* | *<integer>* *<digit>*

to the sequence of symbols 123. We can first scan the symbol 1 and ask if it is an *<integer>* . The first alternative definition of *<integer>* is *<digit>* . The rule that defines *<digit>* does include the number 1 as an alternative on the right side of the rule. Applying the same reasoning to the subsequent symbols 2 and 3, we might then come to the conclusion that *123 is a sequence of three integers.* On the other hand, we might want to use the alternative definition of *<integer>* ↔ *<integer>* *<digit>*. In that event, we would scan the code representing the symbol 1 and ask whether it is an *<integer>*, since the rule states that the first symbol encountered should be an *<integer>*. Then we would apply the definition of *<integer>* that, by the rule we are using, has as a first component *<integer>*, and so on. We are thus in a nonterminating loop, or *circular definition.* The problem may be resolved in many cases by reformulating the rule in a nonrecursive fashion. For example, we could rewrite the rule as <integer> ↔ <digit> < * > <digit>, where the metasymbol < * > is to be interpreted as meaning that the symbol that *follows* it occurs *n* times, where *n* equals 0, 1, 2,.... Of course, there are other notations, or mechanisms, that can be used to transform a rewriting rule from recursive to nonrecursive.

The set of productions or rewriting rules thus specifies the acceptable *phrase structure* for sentences in the language. For example, consider the "sentence"

```
(S1) Y = A * B + C
```

and the "sentence"

```
(S2) X = A - B/C
```

If we consider parentheses to be symbols that imply the grouping of the string of symbols contained within them, then the first form (S1) can be *interpreted* as (S1a)Y = (A * B) + C or as (S1b)Y = A * (B + C). Similarly, the form (S2) can be *interpreted* as (S2a)X = (A − B)/C or as (S2b)X = A − (B/C). If we use the additional *precedence rule* that * and / have greater precedence than + or −, it is clear that forms (S1a) and (S2b) are correct. However, these results can also be implied by the syntactical rules of the language, which not only indicate which form is correct, but also the *phrase structure* of a sequence of symbols by assigning to each symbol an identification corresponding to one of the metalinguistic symbols used to formulate the set of productions. For example, starting with the first production rule and the first symbol, called the *starting symbol,* we can generate the interpretation (S1a) by writing the series of transformations

(1) <*sentence*> → <*program*> → <*assignment*> →
(2) <*variable*> = <*arithmetic expression*> →
(3) Y = <*arithmetic expression*> →
(4) Y = <*arithmetic expression*> <*add operator*> <*term*> →
(5) Y = <*term*> <*add operator*> <*term*> →
(6) Y = <*term*> <*multiply operator*> <*factor*>
<*add operator*> <*term*> →
(7) Y = <*factor*> <*multiply operator*> <*factor*>
<*add operator*> <*term*> →
(8) Y = <*variable*> <*multiply operator*> <*factor*>
<*add operator*> < *term*> →
(9) Y = A <*multiply operator*> <*factor*> <*add*
operator> <*term*> →
(10) Y = A * <*variable*> <*add operator*> <*term*> →
(11) Y = A * B <*add operator*> <*term*> →
(12) Y = A * B + <*factor*> →
(13) Y = A * B + <*variable*> →
(14) Y = A * B + C

From this we see that in the sentence (S1), the *sequence* of symbols A * B is generated by the metalinguistic symbol <*arithmetic expression*> starting at level (4) and therefore *associate* (link) as one expression. The single symbol C can be identified as the metalinguistic symbol <*term*> at level (4). At level (3), the expression A * B and the term C associate to form an <*arithmetic expression*>. A tree diagram of this process is shown in Fig. 2.2.

We can also generate the *interpretation* (S2b) by writing the series of transformations

(1) <*sentence*> → <*program*> → <*assignment*> → <*variable*>
= <*arithmetic expression*> →
(2) X = <*arithmetic expression*> →
(3) X = <*arithmetic expression*> <*add operator*> <*term*> →
(4) X = <*term*> <*add operator*> <*term*> →
(5) X = <*factor*> <*add operator*> <*term*> →
(6) X = <*variable*> <*add operator*> <*term*> →
(7) X = A <*add operator*> <*term*> →
(8) X = A - <*term*> →
(9) X = A - <*term*> <*multiply operator*> <*factor*> →
(10) X = A - <*factor*> <*multiply operator*> <*factor*> →
(11) X = A - <*variable*> <*multiply operator*> <*factor*> →

(12) X = A - B *<multiply operator>* *<factor>* →
(13) X = A - B/ *<variable>* →
(14) X = A - B/C

In the sentence (S2), the symbol A is identified as the metalinguistic symbol *<variable>* at level (7), while the associated (linked) symbol sequence *B/C is identified as the metalinguistic symbol <term> at level (7).* A tree diagram of this process is shown in Fig. 2.3.

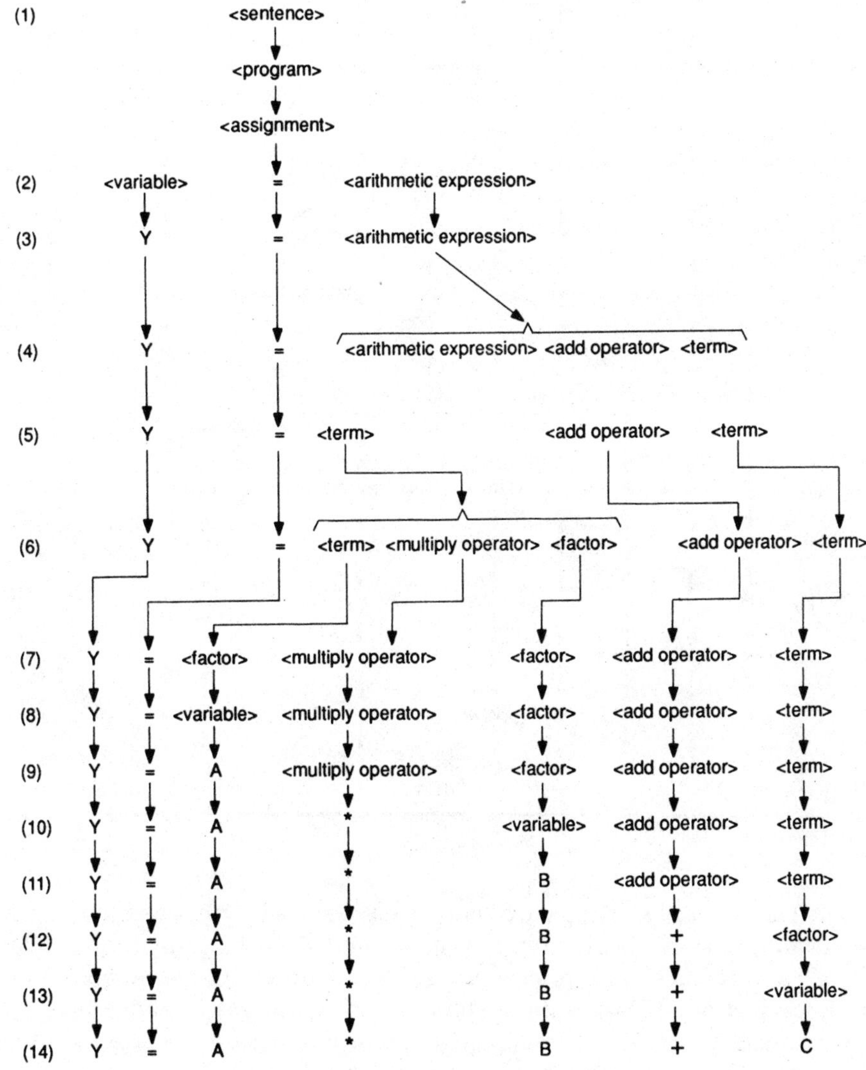
(1) <sentence>
<program>
<assignment>
(2) <variable> = <arithmetic expression>
(3) Y = <arithmetic expression>
(4) Y = <arithmetic expression> <add operator> <term>
(5) Y = <term> <add operator> <term>
(6) Y = <term> <multiply operator> <factor> <add operator> <term>
(7) Y = <factor> <multiply operator> <factor> <add operator> <term>
(8) Y = <variable> <multiply operator> <factor> <add operator> <term>
(9) Y = A <multiply operator> <factor> <add operator> <term>
(10) Y = A * <variable> <add operator> <term>
(11) Y = A * B <add operator> <term>
(12) Y = A * B + <factor>
(13) Y = A * B + <variable>
(14) Y = A * B + C

Figure 2.2 Derivation of Y = A ∗ B + C.

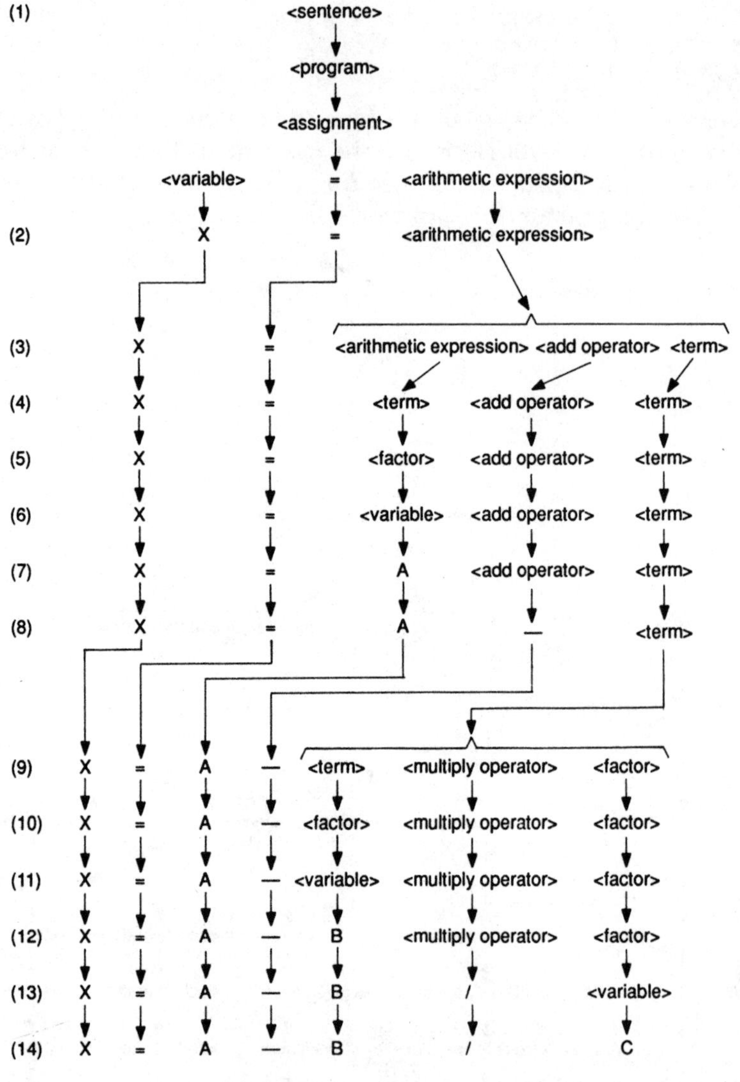

(1) <sentence>
<program>
<assignment>
<variable> = <arithmetic expression>
(2) X = <arithmetic expression>
(3) X = <arithmetic expression> <add operator> <term>
(4) X = <term> <add operator> <term>
(5) X = <factor> <add operator> <term>
(6) X = <variable> <add operator> <term>
(7) X = A <add operator> <term>
(8) X = A — <term>
(9) X = A — <term> <multiply operator> <factor>
(10) X = A — <factor> <multiply operator> <factor>
(11) X = A — <variable> <multiply operator> <factor>
(12) X = A — B <multiply operator> <factor>
(13) X = A — B / <variable>
(14) X = A — B / C

Figure 2.3 Derivation of X = A − B/C.

The set of rewriting rules that we have stated cannot be used to generate the symbols given in *interpretation* (S1b) or *interpretation* (S2a). Therefore these *interpretations* can be regarded as not acceptable or incorrect according to the given rules of syntax for the language. For example, we might attempt to generate *interpretation* (S1b) by a top-down rewriting, similar to that used for (S1a). Thus

(1) *<sentence>* → *<program>* → *<assignment>* →
(2) *<variable>* = *<arithmetic expression>* →
(3) Y = *<arithmetic expression>* →
(4) Y = *<arithmetic expression>* *<add operator>* *<term>* →
(5) Y = ?

At this point, generating item A from *<arithmetic expression>* would interfere with generating the second terminal symbol *, since *<add operator>* ↔ + | −. We could back up to level (4) and write:

(4) Y = *<term>* [using rule (4), first alternative], then rewrite as →
(5) Y = *<term>* *<multiply operator>* *<factor>* → [by rule (5), second alternative],
(6) Y = *<factor>* *<multiply operator>* *<factor>* →
(7) Y = *<variable>* *<multiply operator>* *<factor>* →
(8) Y = A*<multiply operator>* *<factor>* →
(9) Y = A * *<factor>* →
(10) Y = A * *<term>* → [rule (5) applied ''backward'']
(11) Y = A * *<arithmetic expression>* → [rule 4, applied ''backward'']
(12) Y = A * *<arithmetic expression>* *<add operator>* *<term>* → [rule 4]
(13) Y = A * *<term>* *<add operator>* *<term>* → [rule 4]
(14) Y = A * *<factor>* *<add operator>* *<factor>* → [rule 5]
(15) Y = A * *<variable>* *<add operator>* *<variable>* →
(16) Y = A * B + C

But that is incorrect since step (9) shows that the string B + C derives from *<factor>*. But B + C is not a variable, an integer, or an expression *enclosed in parentheses* [see rule (6)]. The inconsistent result has been obtained by rewriting rule (5), in step (10), in a right-to-left transformation in an otherwise left-to-right (top-down) derivation. Thus, although individual rules can be used to rewrite either way, rules with more than one alternative must be applied in a manner consistent with the overall direction of the derivation to avoid attributing different structures to the same component of a string.

As another example, the sentence

5 = A

is incorrect, since a bottom-up parsing produces

5 = A → *<digit>* = *<variable>* → *<integer>* = *<variable>*
→ *<factor>* = *<factor>* → *<term>* = *<term>*
→ *<arithmetic expression>* = *<arithmetic expression>*
→ ?

At this point (level 3), we cannot rewrite in a bottom-up manner any further, and *no other alternative path exists* to proceed to the starting symbol *<sentence>* . Thus the sentence

```
5 = A
```

is rejected as syntactically unacceptable by the previous set of productions.

There are *other ways of specifying syntax* aside from BNF. For example, a set of braces {} can be used to indicate a choice of forms, as in

<name> ↔ *<letter>* < ∗ > { *<letter>* | *<digit>* }

where < ∗ > indicates successive repetition *n* times ($n = 0, 1, 2, \ldots$) of the symbols within the right-adjacent pair of braces. In this case the construction indicates that a *<name>* may be a *<letter>* followed by *n* *<letter>*s or *<digit>*s in any order.

Another notation might be

<from 1 > ↔ **FROM** *<variable>* = *<expression>* $\left\{\begin{array}{c}\texttt{TO}\\ \texttt{UNTIL}\end{array}\right\}$
<expression>

An example of such a structure consisting of terminal symbols might be

```
FROM i = x + y TO p + 5
```

A set of brackets [] can be used to indicate that the symbols within the [] are optional, for example,

<from 2> ↔ **FROM** *<variable >* = *<expression>* **[BY**
<expression> **]**
$\left\{\begin{array}{c}\texttt{TO}\\ \texttt{UNTIL}\end{array}\right\}$ [*<variable>* *<boolean operator>*] *<expression>*

where a concrete example might be

```
FROM j = A + B BY z + e UNTIL k> a + b
```

The rule for *<from 1>* is redundant since it is just a restricted case of *<from 2>* .

Languages can be classified according to the type of production rules that define the structure of acceptable sentences in each language. A classification scheme that is usually attributed to Chomsky separates languages into four classes.

Class-0 languages have no restrictions other than they must be *phrase-structure languages.* Formally, a phrase-structure language L can be defined as

$$L(V_N, V_T, P, S) = \{s \mid s \in V^*_T, V_T \subset V, S \in V_N, \text{ and } S \overset{*}{\rightarrow} s\}$$

where {} means "set of," | means "for which," $\in$ means "element of," $\subset$ means "subset of," and $\stackrel{*}{\rightarrow}$ means "generates" or "derives"

s is a string of the language and an acceptable sentence of the language if its structure is consistent with the set P

V_N is the set of nonterminal words of the metalanguage

V_T is the set of the terminal symbols of the language

V^*_T is the set of strings formed as sequences consisting only of terminal symbols

P is the set of production or rewriting rules, where each rule may contain elements from V_N, V_T, or both

S is the "starting" metalinguistic symbol (which would be <*program*> for a conventional computer language)

V is the total vocabulary of the language and includes both the terminal and nonterminal words. Here the term *language* is used in the special sense that the language of *actual* sentences is augmented by the possibly nonunique metalinguistic symbols

Thus the definition may be read: The phrase-structure language L is the set of such sentences s for which s is an element of that set made up of strings of words, such that each one is a terminal word in the vocabulary V_T, and the set V_T is a subset of the complete vocabulary V; S is the starting symbol and is a metalinguistic variable; and for every sentence s, S will generate the particular s by applying the production rules P. For a given language, that is, a given set of sentences, it is possible that more than one set of production rules may exist that will generate that set of sentences from the starting symbol S.

Class-1 languages are phrase-structure languages where at least one production is of the form

```
uAv ↔ uBv
```

where $u,v \in V^*_N$ (that is, u or v is either empty or sequences of metalinguistic symbols, $A \in V_N$, and B may be a string made up of either terminals or metalinguistic symbols or both). Languages constructed from these types of production rules are called *context-*

sensitive languages. The production rule means that the symbol A is rewritten as the string B only in the context of u...v.

Class-2 languages are distinguished by production rules that are restricted to the form

```
A ↔ B
```

where A is a single metalinguistic variable and B is a string made up of words from the terminal or metalinguistic vocabulary sets. Since the rewriting of symbols is independent of the context, that is, not dependent on what appears before or after the symbol, this type of language can be characterized as *context-free. Most conventional programming languages are approximately context-free*. The deviations from the context-free model are usually handled by ad hoc techniques.

It can be shown that the set of productions for any context-free language can be generated by an equivalent set such that all its productions are in the *normal forms*

```
A ↔ BC
A ↔ t
```

where A,B,C are nonterminals and t is a terminal symbol. *Another normal form* would be that where all productions are of the form

```
A ↔ tμ
```

where t is a terminal symbol and μ is a string of metalinguistic symbols, possibly empty.

Class-3 languages are generated by production rules such that

```
A ↔ t
A ↔ tC
```

where t is a terminal symbol and both A and C are single metalinguistic symbols. Sets of production rules of this type are also called *regular grammars*.

In general, the BNF notation is adequate for describing the rewriting rules of conventional context-free computer languages subject to augmentation by ad hoc techniques to deal with particular language constraints by the use of so-called informal descriptions, or by relatively simple formal extensions to handle *limited* context sensitivity. For example, that a number not exceed a certain value is a constraint not easily expressed in straightforward BNF form. Unfortunately, there is currently no adequate theory or formalism to deal with languages that are *essentially* context-dependent and where the syntactical and semantic aspects are strongly linked. It is likely, however, that such languages will become increasingly important in future user-oriented computer systems. Certainly, the formal problems involved with context-dependent computer languages are not equal to, and certainly not greater than, those involved with the resolution of context dependency and semantic linkage in natural languages. For the case of natural language where there exists no *adequate* theory or formalism, one can nonetheless adequately resolve ambiguity in many instances. For the case of context-dependent computer languages, one has no choice but to rely on a strategy where ad hoc and heuristic techniques attempt to resolve possible contextual ambiguity. If the use of context dependency in future computer languages is to be managed successfully, then we would anticipate that the solution lies in the direction of adopting those techniques that have played central roles in the field of artificial intelligence. We believe that the future expansion of user-oriented languages lies in taking advantage of many of the discoveries of artificial intelligence, particularly those that apply to the analysis and translation of natural languages or "naturallike" subsets.

It is appropriate to point out that for natural languages, the concept of phrase structure is at best a simplification of the nature of language and at worst may be an obfuscation of the essential role of language. In its very essence, language is the articulation and communication of information, ideas, perceptions, and *states of feeling*. To regard any specific set of productions as a set of rules that are implicit in a language and that can function as a mechanism for generating all possible sentences in that language is to oversimplify what is a rich, complex, and perhaps infinite domain of possibilities.

The prime purpose in exercising a language is to transmit meaning, and any syntactical structure, while not unimportant, is highly subsidiary to that purpose. The only concrete manifestation of language is the set of terminal words. The set of metalinguistic variables, the set of rewriting rules, and the starting symbol for those rules are mental constructs imposed on the concrete manifestations of languages and certainly are not unique to a language of any depth of complexity. Natural languages are permeated by the *semantic* quality of context dependency, but the concept of phrase structure, while it admits a restricted definition of context sensitivity (for example, class-1 languages), is simply an inadequate abstraction to reflect the richness of context dependencies and associated semantics as they occur in natural languages. Conventional computer languages are, *by design,* limited in the flexibility of their structures and the simplicity of their semantics. Even here, the concept of phrase structure is strained to take account of, *in a formal way,* all the various pragmatic considerations associated with the actual use of a language.

In our opinion, much of the current emphasis in computer languages on *formal* models of syntax and associated semantic considerations reflects a confusion between adequate *theory* and *mathematically interesting notational structures.* In the history of the physical sciences, with some exceptions, *theory* preceded the evolution of an associated formal or notational model. This is so because the range of mathematically interesting formalisms or notations is usually very large, while theory, if it is to be adequate, must be consistent with phenomena in the real world. Thus, in the areas of natural language or complex computer language where no adequate theoretical model currently exists, attempts at the construction of purely formal models or notations are strained, inconsistent, or inadequate to describe all the aspects associated with natural language or complex computer language.

Chapter 3

The Assignment Statement

Simple Assignment

In application areas such as scientific and engineering problem programming, mathematical modeling and simulation, financial and econometric modeling, operations research, actuarial computations, and statistical applications, programs are generally characterized as having structures and associated execution times that are heavily weighted toward the numerical computation of results. There is relatively minor concern with those programming structures and execution times involved with the input of data, the manipulation of databases, and the output of results. For that generic type of program, the most important programming construct, in terms of frequency of occurrence and the amount of execution time associated with its evaluation, is the assignment statement.

The purpose of an assignment statement is to carry out a computational procedure, that is, to compute a numerical value and to "assign" that value to a name. For a conventional computer architecture, the assignment of a value to a name can be considered equivalent to storing that value at a location corresponding to that particular name. Put another way, the act of assignment stores a value arrived at by computation at a particular address in the hardware memory. A name corresponds to the particular address, and that name appears on the left side of the assignment statement. The right side of the assignment statement is, in fact, a computational procedure to produce that particular value. In its simplest form, an assignment statement can be represented as

$$y = f$$

or

$$y := f$$

or

$$y \leftarrow f$$

The symbols =, :=, and ← are equivalent to each other and are used in different languages. The symbol ← is sometimes more convenient, since the simple = symbol can cause ambiguity in those languages where it is used both to separate the left and right sides of the assignment statement and as the symbol for a boolean test for equality *and* where the language design is such that the ambiguity is not resolved implicitly in all cases. The symbol := avoids that ambiguity as a pure sign, but it does not aid in emphasizing that the relationship between the left side and the right side of an assignment statement is essentially asymmetric. To the nonprogrammer, the statement

$$A = A + 1$$

is a mathematical inconsistency, since subtracting A from both sides of the equal sign leaves the statement $0 = 1$. The statement $A := A + 1$ is somewhat more appropriate, since, to the nonprogrammer, the use of the := symbol might spark at least a thought that the symbol was not equivalent to that ordinarily used in mathematical formulas. The ← seems the most appropriate, since by its very nature as a sign it implies that there is a transfer from the right side to the left side of the statement. However, as we will indicate, the overall pragmatics of the current programming environment favor the = symbol for assignments embedded in a very high-level user-oriented language. We must also distinguish assignment from the case of *definition,* for example, $\pi = 3.14159$, where assignment of a new value to π is not permitted and where π may be redefined only if it is not treated as a "reserved word" of the language. In the language PASCAL, definition is explicit, as in *const e* = 2.71828. In a language such as APL, evaluation of f is possible without the use of assignment. That is equivalent to evaluating f when it appears as an argument of a PRINT statement.

In the simple assignment statement $y \leftarrow f$, the left side, y, could be a single scalar variable or a symbol representing sequences of components of multidimensional variables such as vectors or matrices. More generally, the left side could contain operators to extract what would be an admissible name to be assigned to the value(s) generated by the right side. For example, if (L) is a list (a,b,c,d,e) and operator HEAD extracts the first element of a list, then HEAD (L) = 10 would assign the value 10 to a. (L) would then be $(10,b,c,d,e)$. The language SETL expands the concept of left-side expression and assignment statements to encompass operations on sets. We will assume, however, that the left side of the assignment statement is either a symbol name representing a scalar variable or a subscripted name representing a component of a multidimensioned variable. Thus the simple assignment statement, in its general form, can be written as

$$y_{i,j,k,\ldots} \leftarrow f(x_1, x_2, x_3, \ldots, a_1, a_2, a_3, \ldots, i, j, k, \ldots)$$

where y stands for a name and f represents a *formula,* in the sense that the right side of the assignment statement is a prescription to compute a value as a function of x_1, x_2, $x_3, \ldots$, which ordinarily represents variables whose values are real numbers; a_1, a_2, $a_3, \ldots$ are constants; and $i, j, k, \ldots$ are the indices for subscripts that tag the component $Y_{i,j,k,\ldots}$ of the name y.

An equivalent form of the previous statement would be

$$\texttt{COMPUTE}\ y_{i,j,k,\ldots} \leftarrow f(x_1, x_2, x_3, \ldots, a_1, a_2, a_3, \ldots, i, j, k, \ldots)$$

which more directly points out that the assignment statement is a command to compute a formula and to assign the resulting value to the name given by the left side of the assignment statement. We might also emphasize that, despite current convention, it is not necessary to associate the name with a particular hardware manifestation, that is, an address in hardware memory. In fact, for a user-oriented programming language, it is more feasible simply to consider the name of the variable in its most abstract sense and to consider the assignment statement as simply associating the value with the name. How such an association is made concrete is an *implementation* problem that can be solved in various ways for different computer languages and different machine architectures. The literal interpretation or association of a name with a hardware location can lead to ambiguous interpretation for some languages. Such ambiguity would occur when the same location is linked to different names during the process of storage reallocation or when data at different locations are linked to the same name at different levels of recursive procedure calls.

It is important to note that for the application areas mentioned at the beginning of this chapter, the original specification of the problem may contain formulas that range from the very simple to the very complex. By *very simple,* we mean a small number of variables essentially related in a linear fashion (that is, written as a linear string in the original specification). By *very complex,* we mean those formulas that contain many variables, particularly those standing in a nonlinear relationship to each other (for example, continued fractions or other nested numerators within denominators). Complex formulas also contain operators other than those that can be characterized as simple arithmetic—for example, operators that perform integration, summation, or multiplication of more than two variables or act over an extended range of subscripted variables.

The complexity of the formulas in the original specification of a problem is a function, very specifically, of a particular application field. For some fields, formulas tend to have a simple form, while for other fields, they are more complicated. Even if the formulas consist of a simple linear string of additive terms, they may contain a large number of different variables. Thus it is inappropriate to talk about the *average* complexity of formulas in original problem-solution specifications. It is important to emphasize this point, since there is currently a widespread view that expressions on the right side of an assignment statement are generally trivial, that is, generally no more complex than <*variable*> + <*constant*>. That view is based on the interpretation of experimental surveys of actual programs that found assignment statements in a language such as FORTRAN to be trivially simple. Those experimental observations do not imply that the original formulas in the problem-solution specification are at the same trivial level of simplicity.

The prevailing conception arises from ignoring or minimizing the very strong effects of computer-language design in producing programming-language structures that, in terms of complexity, are not directly related to the complexity of the original specification. The historical FORTRAN translation and linearization process is so prone to error that programmers quickly learn to break up complex formulas into simple parts as an aid toward error prevention and detection. Such simplification applies to most conventional computer languages. For FORTRAN it is particularly dominant, because of the card-image character of the historical FORTRAN statement and, in its early day, the need to handle individual cards to detect and correct errors. Put more simply, it is easier to change a simple form on a single card than to change a more lengthy form on several continuation cards—or continuation lines. (In a more modern version of FORTRAN, such as F77, source statements are line-oriented but still retain the flavor of the original card-image. The FORTRAN version F90 moves even farther away from the historical card-image.) The linearization process of FORTRAN also constrains the programmer to impose a large number of parentheses levels when translating a formula of moderate numerator/denominator complexity to a linear form. Because the omission of a single parenthesis would make the entire statement on a single card incorrect, it is more appropriate to break up lengthy statements into simple substatements that can be entered without parenthesization.

Thus the general experimental observation that the right sides of assignment statements are simple should be taken, not as an indication of the level of complexity of problem-solution specifications, but rather as a symptom of the psychological constraints that conventional language design imposes on programmers. A language that deals with the original form of the problem-solution specification would avoid many of the problems associated with conventional languages that are a consequence of the constraints imposed by historically available input devices.

For example, a moderately complex solution specification involving the computation from formulas (in this case, the solution of simultaneous sets of linear algebraic equations) might be

n is the number of equations with constant coefficients. A_{ij} (j = 1 to n, i = 1 to n) and constants C_i (i = 1 to n) for equations of the form $\sum_j A_{ij}X_j = C_i$.

{ To compute the roots X_i } INPUT n. INPUT A_{ij} FROM j = 1 TO n, i = 1 TO n. INPUT C_i FROM i = 1 TO n.

If i ≧ j THEN $a_{ij} = A_{ij} - \sum_{k=1}^{j-1} a_{ik}a_{kj}$ OTHERWISE $a_{ij} =$

$$\frac{A_{ij} - \sum_{k=1}^{i-1} a_{ik}a_{kj}}{a_{ii}}$$ FOR j = 1 TO n and i = 1 TO n.

FROM i = 1 TO n COMPUTE $g_i = \dfrac{C_i - \sum_{k=1}^{i-1} a_{ik}g_k}{a_{ii}}$.

FROM i = n BY −1 UNTIL i<1 COMPUTE $X_i = g_i - \sum_{k=i+1}^{n} a_{ik}x_k$.

OUTPUT X_i FOR i=1, 2, ..., n. { (Note that $\sum_{l}^{u} = 0$ IF l >u.) }

The specification does not seem to be encompassed by the structure of a *simple* assignment statement defined as

> *<simple assignment statement>* ↔ *<name>* = *<simple arithmetic expression>*

where we can informally define *<simple arithmetic expression>* as a sequence of names or numbers that are *appropriately* connected by arithmetic operators.

Note that the computational statements in the preceding specification are terminated by periods. Also note that in the part of the statement that comprises a computational formula, the right side of the formula is connected to the left side by the = symbol rather than the ← symbol. In this case, the use of the = symbol instead of the assignment operator ← creates no particular ambiguity. If for a particular computer language, the use of the = symbol for both assignment and boolean equality created no ambiguity over a wide range of structural forms, that would be a strong argument for preferring the = symbol to the ← symbol, since the = symbol is more consistent with prevailing mathematical notation for formulas.

More important, the preceding specification statements contain structural forms that are serious departures from the structure of the simple assignment statement. In particular, the statements contain FOR or FROM clauses, which cause the formulas to cycle through computations for sequences of values of j and i. The function of these FOR or (the equivalent) FROM clauses is to set up a loop, that is, to take the body of the formula and iterate it for the specified range of values of the indices j and i. Similarly, the token IF distinguishes between the two cases $i \geq j$ and $i < j$. Thus, if we regard the specification statements as *sentences,* then the tokens FOR, FROM, IF, THEN, and OTHERWISE play the syntactic role of *modifiers* of the formulas within the statement in the sense that they specify the range of the formula over various values of indices of which the formula is a function. What distinguishes those specification statement structures from the equivalent translations to a conventional language such as FORTRAN or ALGOL is that they do not contain any particular specialized notation like semicolons or colons, nor do they contain key words such as DO, BEGIN, or END, which are inherent to the syntax of these languages. If, indeed, these tokens were necessary, it would not be possible to regard the statement specifications as computable forms. But there is, in fact, nothing to suggest that they are not computable! A human being can, *in a precisely mechanical way,* interpret the previous specification statements as computational prescriptions and compute the quantities on the right side of all formulas step by step, given appropriate input. It therefore follows quite directly that *a machine should be able to follow this computational prescription when such statement specifications are input in exactly the form in which they have previously appeared.*

As we shall show in Chap. 8, ambiguities that may arise from the use of implicit multiplication, such as in the multiplication of the terms a_{ik} and a_{kj}, and the use of subscripts like ik without commas, can be resolved pragmatically. Thus, even for much more complex forms, there is no pressing reason to use a computer language that breaks up such specification statements into highly artificial subunits with arbitrary notational artifacts and structural relationships requiring close analysis for their correct translation.

What characterizes the preceding solution specification statements, which would not be present in an equivalent translation into a conventional computer language, is that they are understandable to those professionals who have a degree of mathematical literacy appropriate to the application area but no specific knowledge of a programming language. A statement that is understandable does not require documentation and therefore possesses the desirable quality of being self-documenting. A computer language whose structure is essentially identical to the specification statement would, by definition, be self-documenting. The documentation that does appear in the previous specification consists of the introductory comments that set the *context* of the formulas in identifying the class of variables and constants with which the formulas deal. Thus, for certain application areas, the concept of a *programming* language is redundant if the specification of the problem is well formed and computable as it stands. Indeed, many of the problem-solution specifications in the areas indicated at the beginning of this chapter are well formed or *nearly* well formed and can easily be cast into computable prescriptions using prevailing mathematical structures and notational devices.

In application areas such as scientific and engineering numerical computation, the conventional programming languages oriented toward those areas, such as FORTRAN and ALGOL, have played a retrogressive role historically. They have taken basically straightforward problem-solution specifications written in the prevailing mathematical notation and structure and transformed them into highly segmented syntactical forms that pose, simply by the artifact of their translation to these forms, substantial problems in proving correctness and even in understanding the semantics of a specific program. The historical reasons for this state of affairs are not primarily technical. The historical evolution of many contemporary programming languages has been governed by the economic milieu associated with the development of computers and by what might be called the "sociology of computing." Equally important may be the psychological motivations of those involved in using computers and designing computer languages.

Multiple Assignment

The use of multiple assignment operators is consistent with the goal of conciseness when the structure is used to replace a set of single assignments, such as in initialization

$$
\begin{aligned}
i &= 1 \\
j &= 1 \\
k &= 1 \\
l &= 1
\end{aligned}
$$

or the set

$$
\begin{aligned}
i &= E \\
j &= E \\
k &= E \\
l &= E
\end{aligned}
$$

where E evaluates to a numerical value at the time of the execution of the simple assignment statements. For such sets, we can use the multiple assignment structure

$$i = j = k = l = 1$$

or

$$i = j = k = l = E$$

As long as the semantics of the structure is restricted, as noted previously, there cannot be any ambiguity. But although the form $y = E$ may appear to be a simple assignment statement, it has no meaning as an assignment statement unless the right side, E, can be evaluated to a value at the time of execution. This does not mean, however, that we cannot give such statements a different interpretation. For example, we might interpret that statement to mean that any occurrence of the symbol y is to be replaced by the symbol E throughout the program or vice versa. Whether this makes any sense depends on the semantic structure of a particular programming language. In any case, such a construction associated with such semantics is not an assignment statement in the sense that we use the term.

In some languages, the structural forms (syntax) used cause ambiguity when the = symbol is used both for the assignment operator ← and as the boolean symbol of comparison of equality =. For example, in PL/1, the statements

$$X = Z$$
$$Y = Z$$

could be replaced by the multiple assignment

X,Y = Z

However, if the PL/1 program used the form

X = Y = Z

then the term $Y = Z$ would be interpreted as a boolean test of equality with the boolean value of either 0 or 1 for the value of the term. Thus the final value of X would be set equal to only one of two values, 0 or 1. The apparent semantic ambiguity here arises from the structure of PL/1 syntax and, in this particular case, could be resolved by using two distinct symbols, one for the assignment statement and one for boolean equality. Such distinction between symbols is not a necessary condition for semantic preciseness in language design, but is rather a function of the detailed nature of the syntax chosen for a particular language.

Another form that also falls within the spirit of multiple assignment might be

$$L_1, L_2, L_3, \ldots = 5, 43, 7 \ldots$$

which would have the associated interpretation that the elements in the *list* on the left side of the assignment statement are to be given the values, respectively, specified on the right side.

Another type of ambiguity can arise from the use of multiple assignment structures. Such ambiguity may be inherent; that is, it may not be resolved by a more adequate syntactical form. For example, one might write

$$k = 1$$
$$Y_k = Y_{k+1} = k = k + 1$$

where the value of k is equal to 1 before execution of the multiple assignment. If the execution is carried out from right to left in the manner previously defined for multiple assignment statements as an equivalent set of single assignment statements, then

$$Y_1 = 2$$
$$Y_2 = 2$$
$$k = 2$$

A different implementation, however, might assign the value of $k + 1$, which is equal to 2 after execution, as a new value for subscript k. We would then have

$$k = 2$$
$$Y_2 = k + 1 = 3$$
$$Y_3 = 3$$

These *inherently ambiguous* structures can be resolved only by adopting pragmatic or semantic rules that, in this case, interpret the way such assignments are actually executed. We consider these forms to be inherently ambiguous in the sense that the ambiguity cannot be resolved by a different set of syntactic structures or by analysis of local or global context.

Other Aspects of Assignment

For those languages that allow structures of the form

$$\mathbf{A} = \mathbf{B}$$

where **A** and **B** stand for arrays, the left side of the assignment statement can be interpreted as an array of names linked (or bound) to a structure in hardware memory. Likewise, the right side of the assignment statement can be considered to be the values in the corresponding locations linked to the array name **B.** Of course, the assignment statement would not be consistent in the sense of assigning the value of every element of **B** to a corresponding element of **A**, unless the dimensions of array **A** were equal to array **B.** Thus the statement

$$\mathbf{A}_i = 10$$

would be interpreted as assigning the value 10 to the location associated with the *i* element of the array **A.** From a more general point of view, it is better to ignore the association of a name with a specific location and simply consider that the name on the left side can associate with a value and assume that an implementation will be consistent with the type of data structure associated with that particular name.

It is also possible to design idiosyncratic variations of simple assignment statements. For example, instead of the statement

$$A = A + X$$

one could design the variant

$$A \mathrel{+}= X$$

When *A* is a name of a simple variable, the two forms can be regarded as identical. However, for those languages where *A* can be an expression that reduces to a *location,* the first form requires two evaluations of the location associated with the expression *A*. The second form requires only one evaluation of the expression *A* to extract the value at its corresponding location before adding the value associated with the expression *X*. In certain cases, that may lead to different final values associated with the location *A*. For that reason, such idiosyncratic variations of the basic simple-assignment form are not recommended if the goal is to design a language that is clear and not subject to unanticipated side effects.

In some programming languages, assignment statements may be treated like expressions, because the value of the expression is the value associated with the name of the left side of the assignment statement. This allows assignments to be embedded in other syntactic forms and, while playing the role of generating a value, at the same time will update the location in hardware memory associated with the name on the left side of the assignment statement. This feature, which can be used to reduce the incidence of redundant expressions in complex assignment statements, is illustrated in the next section.

It is also possible to use the assignment-statement form for *pointer variables,* which, in a language such as PASCAL, can be used to manipulate linked data structures where storage locations contain references or links to other storage locations. While the use of such artifacts may be justified for languages primarily designed for systems-programming applications, they tend to be highly error-prone. Such programs are also difficult to document or verify as correct. Certainly, for languages designed to be facile for the nonprofessional programmer/user, one should use other devices to accomplish the same end, even if there is a degradation in execution or storage efficiency. Historically, many complex programming structures were justified because hardware memory was a scarce commodity and needed to be conserved in the execution of relatively large programs. In the current generation of hardware, however, memory is a cheap, if not no-cost, commodity. Therefore it is not necessary to use structures that optimize the utilization of storage. Execution speeds associated with hardware have also increased. While execution time is certainly a serious consideration for programs characterized by large numbers of cycles through their core computation, even there the pressure for small increases in execution speed have been lessened. The decreased actual cost of hardware has given greater relative value to the time spent by human beings in translating problem-solution specifications into computer programs.

Another Example of the Assignment-Statement Form

Even simple assignment statements may contain many variables on their right sides, some of which may be repetitions of common subexpressions. For example,

$$X = e^{-at} \sum_{n=1}^{30} ((-1)^n \sin(2\pi t - n\pi T/2)(1 - \frac{|2\pi t - n\pi T/2| - (2\pi t - n\pi T/2)}{2(2\pi t - n\pi T/2)}))$$

That statement can be simplified by removing the common subexpression and, prior to evaluation of the main assignment statement, evaluating the subexpression as an assignment statement:

$$S = 2\pi t - n\pi T/2$$

$$X = e^{-at} \sum_{n=1}^{30} ((-1)^n \sin (S) (1 - \frac{|S| - S}{2S}))$$

When the original assignment statement is modified by structures that cause looping through various values of the variables, it may be more convenient to actually insert the assignment statement for the evaluation of S directly into the original statement. Thus the original statement would become

$$X = e^{-at} \sum_{n=1}^{30} ((-1)^n \sin (S = 2\pi t - n\pi T/2) (1 - \frac{|S| - S}{2S}))$$

Of course, implementing that statement on a conventional machine architecture would mean treating the left side of the subexpression S the same as the left side of any simple assignment statement. In other words, a value would be generated from the right side, stored in a location linked to the name S, and then updated when the right-side expression is cycled to different values of its variables. From a purely linguistic point of view, we can regard S simply as a name and need not associate it with an implementation object since it functions simply as a temporary variable and is not output. If one designs a language from this viewpoint (or as close to this viewpoint as is practical), one leaves open implementation designs for unconventional architecture that, in the future, may prove more desirable than the classical von Neuman machine.

Symbolic Equations

We do not consider in this book the area of symbolic manipulation of equations (or expressions) where the = symbol is neither an assignment nor a boolean operator. Rather, the equality symbol functions as a connective, and the names within that equality are true mathematical variables independent of the semantics associated with numerical computation. For example, the statement

$$y = \int_0^3 x \, dx$$

is an assignment statement that will assign the value 4.5 to y, whereas

$$y = \int x \, dx$$

will result in $y = x^2/2$ as a symbolic relationship in the same sense that

$$\int x \, dx = x^2/2$$

In this context, we could not assign a specific numerical value to the (dummy) variable x without first specifying the value associated with the lower limit of the integral (or specifying a value for the implied constant of indefinite integration).

Equalities between symbolic expressions belong to the domain of specialized symbol manipulation systems, which are languages in a very restricted sense.

Summary

The gist of the discussion in this chapter has been an attempt to show the linguistic clarity, over other forms, of an assignment statement cast into a flexible, sentencelike, multiline structure that admits qualifying phrases that cause cycling through various values of variables and that allows testing of expressions for their boolean values to determine which one of alternative expressions to compute. Other forms, while computationally equivalent, break up the calculation into an *ordered* list of subphrases, use unnecessary notational devices, and thus increase the difficulty in comprehending the flow of the computation. In the previous example of sentences constituting general types of assignment statements, we have used a period to delimit the end of a sentence (and thus the limit in scope of the qualifiers to assignment).

The location of the clauses that qualify the cycling involved in the calculation may be placed at any appropriate point of the sentence. That is, a FROM clause may be at the beginning or the end of the sentence, or at any point that makes comprehension of the statement easier. The location of the FROM clause is immaterial because, regardless of its position, it governs the range and values of those variables that are to be cycled through the computation. The only material point with respect to the placement of the FROM clause is its relationship to other, nested FROM clauses. It is a matter of arbitrary decision whether the last-mentioned FROM or FOR clause is to be cycled first or last. In most conventional languages, the last-mentioned loop variable is cycled first in reading the structure from top to bottom or from left to right. That is an arbitrary choice, however, and all that is required for a sensible interpretation of output is for the language designer to simply make the choice known to the user. Phrases such as IF should be located where they make *semantic* sense, in that they test the boolean condition prior to making a choice of alternative computational forms. The *scope* (see Chap. 6) of any particular control clause may be limited, within a sentence, by enclosing the clause(s) within parentheses.

The reasons for preferring the sentencelike forms outlined in this chapter are essentially psychological. That is, they are more psychologically assimilable to most people, professional or nonprofessional programmers/users, than what may appear to be the highly constrained and esoteric forms of many conventional languages. We stress that these are not *logical* reasons, and the whole topic reduces to a case of *de gustibus non est disputandum,* which can be roughly translated as "taste is not debatable." One cannot objectively resolve a dispute about programming style, which, in the context of our discussion, can be interpreted to mean programming-language-design style. As in all matters of taste, the only rational solution is a consensus of choice. However, what has been historically lacking is the existence of just that—*choice.*

Objective resolution between different language-design styles is possible if there is agreement on a measurable product of program activity. Possible metrics could be the length of time expended to translate a specification into a program, level of correctness, and the level of expertise necessary to use a language. While agreement on a common measurement would permit objective resolution among computer languages, the very large variance associated with individual programming capability makes practical differentiation difficult except for those languages that are markedly different in terms of the selected metric.

Chapter

4

Basic Control Structures

Simple Sequencing

A conventional computer program, being a *written* construct, consists of a sequence of program sentences, statements, or units. In the simplest form of program flow, unit_1 would be executed before unit_2, if indeed unit_2 follows unit_1. That is normal for written communication, where one processes information in a sequential-time-ordered flow, unlike the different sort of processing that may take place when information is presented in a visual, three-dimensional framework or when multiple-sensory information is presented to the human processor.

In the architecture of the conventional stored-program computer, the flow of execution control in the simplest case proceeds from a program stored in the sequentially addressed memory locations of the hardware. The decoding mechanism of the processor takes its first instruction from what is designated as the initial address of the program, its next instruction from the next address (usually by incrementing the address by 1), the next instruction from the next address, and so on. Thus the core of program control in most conventional computer languages is governed by a simple sequential flow. This stems from conventional memory architecture, which is basically *linear* in its organization. Because addresses can be described by a single positive integer, in a geometric sense, locating an instruction stored in a computer has only half a degree of freedom since negative address values are not permitted. Also, the input stream of data essentially must be in a time-ordered fashion. That is, if one were "reading" the stream, one could read only from left to right in the sense of increasing time. We point this out since this does not quite conform to other means humans use to assimilate information. For example, when we look at the usual television screen, we are presented with in excess of a million bits of possibly redundant information per second.

Obviously, one could not process even a fraction of that information in a linear manner, so there must be another physiological mechanism in operation that is not comparable to the half-linear sequential processing capability of an individual hardware processor.

The units (or subunits) of a program can be related to each other in different ways. Unit_i may be independent of unit_j in the sense that it does not depend on any result that follows from the execution of unit_j and therefore can be executed independently of the prior, subsequent, or simultaneous execution of unit_j. For statements that meet these conditions, over some particular *segment* of the program, unit_i and unit_j can be executed by independent machine processors. In more common parlance, that would be called a parallel or concurrent process. If, however, unit_i is independent of unit_j, then whether unit_j is done parallel to unit_i is not particularly relevant, since unit_j can be done *before* the execution of unit_i. Of course, in practice, cases of complete independence are rarely so simple. Depending on the complexity of the definition of the basic program unit (or subunit), units can be characterized as independent only to a certain point in the execution of any one of them. They may have to wait until another unit is partially processed to supply the output of data they need to proceed. The situation can be complicated if a graph representing the flow of program execution, instead of being simply sequential (that is, on the completion of one process, the next process listed on the graph is executed), contains branches to units not next in order to the current process.

In some languages, sequential execution is implicit. For example, in FORTRAN the statements are not separated by any explicit symbols, since historical FORTRAN is card-oriented. In modern FORTRAN, which is line-oriented, separation is achieved by an end-of-line (return) code, but this is not a language-*explicit* symbol. The separation and sequencing are accomplished simply by the physical sequence of two card images (or lines), each containing a statement, or two sets of continuation cards (or lines), each set containing a statement. In some other languages, a specific symbol is used. For example, the ; symbol *explicitly* indicates that in the statement A is to be executed first, then B. In other languages, the semicolon may simply be used as a *terminator* of a statement rather than a command to execute the subsequent statement. The distinction between the latter two alternatives can be clarified by the following examples. For the case where the semicolon serves as a sequential operator, we might write the statement

$$A = i;B = j$$

Where the semicolon is used as a statement terminator, we would write this program segment as

$$A = i;B = j;$$

Note that the latter form contains two semicolons. PASCAL, ALGOL, and C use the semicolon as an explicit sequencing operator; PL/1 uses the semicolon as a statement terminator. For languages that indicate the limits of a program's *regions* with the bracketing symbols BEGIN and END, those delimiters indicate the beginning and end of that program region and thus can be considered to function as *both* explicit terminators and implicit sequencing operators.

Within statements of a program, however, that may be defined for most languages, parentheses can also be used as explicit sequence control operators. Parentheses act as an explicit sequence control because the structure enclosed by the innermost set of parentheses is executed *before* the structure in the next innermost set of parentheses. For example, this type of explicit notational device can resolve various types of nesting problems that arise in nested IF...THEN...ELSE...forms. For simple arithmetic expressions or boolean expressions, nested parentheses can resolve ambiguity by interpreting the nesting level of the parentheses as indicating the order of execution. The use of simple parentheses can be a powerful notational device to resolve ambiguity in all sorts of complex statements.

When parentheses are used as notational devices to achieve that particular end, then on the level of actual programming-language text, there usually is no substantive purpose to be gained by discriminating among ordinary parentheses pairs, such as (), [], and {}. For two-dimensional languages of the sort illustrated in Chap. 8, the size of any particular parenthesis symbol makes no semantic difference. The different kinds of parenthesis symbols and the different relative sizes are employed simply to make such statements more readable and to clarify the contextual relationships among subunits of the statement. Nonetheless, some conventional languages, for example, ALGOL, require that brackets [] enclose the arguments of an array, while parentheses () are used for other purposes, such as enclosing the parameters of a procedure or enclosing an expression. The distinctions are usually made for implementation reasons in the hope that the lexical phase of compilation or interpretation will be more efficient. The efficiency gains are minor, however, compared with the probability of errors arising from programmer failure to pick the *correct* pair of brackets or parentheses in a particular situation. Language designers historically have overestimated the difficulties associated with implementation and thus have tended to select language designs that they (mistakenly) assume will simplify implementation. Because of that, programmer/users have been passive receptors of the most obtuse computer-language artifices.

In principle, one could assign varying properties to different types of parentheses to handle esoteric situations, if the use of such esoteric operators could be judged to be of greater value than the additional artificiality introduced by making such distinctions.

There may be implicit effects in essentially sequential structures that are controlled by other structures, causing cycling through various values of a variable. For example, in the LOOP structure (discussed subsequently) for most languages that allow nested loop structures, the innermost loop, or last-mentioned looping structure, is the sequence that is exercised first, in the sense of ranging through the various allowed values. Thus, for most conventional languages that can be characterized by the form $\text{LOOP}_1 \ldots \text{LOOP}_2 \ldots \text{LOOP}_3$ (body of statement), then, aside from the initialization of LOOP_1 LOOP_2 LOOP_3, control passes to the last-mentioned structure LOOP_3 and is not passed back (up) to LOOP_2 until LOOP_3 has ranged through the complete set of values it controls. The point here is purely aesthetic, but on that basis it does seem to violate the overall consistency of simple sequencing control.

Within arithmetic expressions, sequence control as pertaining to the order of arithmetic operators can be resolved by the use of parentheses, as noted previously, implicit precedence relationships among arithmetic operators, or normal mathematical notation in its two-dimensional form. An exception to this is in the programming language APL, which has no implicit precedence among operators and which evaluates expressions from right to left. Thus the assignment $Y \leftarrow A + B/C * D - E$ would yield the y value of -5 by FORTRAN precedence, and the value 0.75 by APL evaluation order if *A, B, C, D, E,* have the input values 1, 2, 4, 8, 10, respectively.

The Unconditional Branch

If programs were strictly sequential, it would take longer to write a program than to execute the process manually. One of the important control structures that allow programs to reexecute portions of themselves, as the data may require, is the unconditional branch, most commonly of the form

```
GOTO L
```

which refers to the textual point in the program where the symbol L appears. When that instruction is executed, program flow transfers to that particular point. L itself need not be interpreted as a statement label in the sense it need not associate with the subsequent statement. L is literally the point in the program text at which to begin processing.

From a purely abstract point of view, the "statement" L is in itself a *null-operation* operator. Of course, in a particular implementation, L may stand for a specific machine address or be interpreted as a label (symbolic or numeric) that tags (references) the subsequent statement or program unit. Thinking of it simply as a "mark" in the program text avoids some of the ambiguity associated with the esoteric interpretation of statement labels. In one specific language, SNOBOL, each statement may carry with it a notation that is, in effect, equivalent to an unconditional branch. In other words, the statement itself can specify its own successor. This is somewhat like the machine language associated with ancient hardware (such as the IBM 650) whose primary memory was a revolving magnetic drum. To optimize program execution, the programmer writing a machine-language instruction would, as part of that instruction, specify the address of the next instruction. The idea was to pick up the next address to be the position that would appear under the drum read device just as the current instruction processing finished. For that architecture, it was normal for the machine-language instruction to have a GOTO component as an integral part.

An example of a trivially simple program that uses a GOTO type instruction might be

```
L  READ DATA
   PRINT DATA
   GOTO L
```

In an appropriate programming language, this will cause the reading of single data items until the supply of data in the input file is exhausted. While that may be an unorthodox way of terminating a loop, it nonetheless can be a highly practical procedure for certain types of data processing where the number of input data is unknown, where the exact format that would indicate a termination of that data string is unknown, or where it is not possible to insist on the insertion into the data stream of some symbol that would act as a terminator to the calculation. When the input data stream is exhausted, many input devices send a terminating signal to the hardware processor. If the language designer has had the foresight to include a control structure that tests on such a signal, then the programmer can allow an *automatic* resumption of the main flow of the program.

The use of a simple GOTO may cause rather complex side effects if the unconditional branch is out of or into a loop structure or out of or into a "block" (as will be discussed later). This may cause erasure or otherwise affect the current status of various variables computed within that loop or block.

In an uncomplicated case of a control structure for the calling of subroutines, where only one copy exists and various executions use that particular single copy, then the program structure

```
[CALL [SUBROUTINE]] <name>
```

is functionally a special type of unconditional GOTO. It not only causes the machine program to go to the label (address) associated with the name of a particular subroutine, it also evaluates its own address. It then stores that address at some prespecified location so that upon completion of the execution of the named subroutine, a return can be made to the next statement of the main program after the call. If the machine architecture does not admit such a GOTO, then it would not be possible to have "closed" subroutines that exist in only one copy, even though used several times in the program. Such an omission in the basic machine architecture would force the use of "open" ("macro") subroutines, where every time the named procedure is to be used, it is entered (copied) in-line into the main program.

Because that is not practical for higher-level languages, the special "call goto" is indispensable to high-level programs. Of course, whether the actual word CALL (or a synonym) is explicitly used is of minor importance, as long as there is no ambiguity associated with the occasion of a name representing a procedure that appears in a program. From this point of view, if the mention of a procedure name is sufficient to cause the execution of that procedure, then the word CALL (or an equivalent synonym) can be regarded simply as a *noise word* for the language. In fact, for clarity, it might be appropriate to use the statement

```
[DO][PROCEDURE] <name>
```

instead of

```
[CALL][PROCEDURE] <name>
```

or some equivalent synonym. An alternative to [DO] might be the more informative word [EXECUTE].

An alternative to an explicit GOTO would be a statement of the form

```
EXIT (i)
```

which has the purpose of terminating i nested loops, where $i = 1, 2, \ldots$ The EXIT (i) normally would be placed somewhere within the computational stream of the enclosing loops, and the value of i would indicate that the i-enclosing loops be terminated when the EXIT statement is reached. Functionally, the use of that type of exit statement is equivalent to a GOTO statement, which transfers control to the statement following the loop(s) affected by the EXIT (i) command. But the EXIT statement, defined this way, has a somewhat different semantic definition than the standard GOTO and therefore cannot be regarded as a synonym. From the point of view of semantic clarity, its use in a user-oriented environment is somewhat dubious. A similar control statement would be the loop-control statement

```
CYCLE (i)
```

where $i = 1, 2, \ldots$ The execution of this command causes the ith enclosing loop to be reexecuted. Essentially, that is functionally equivalent to a GOTO L, where L would be the point at which the referred loop begins. The advantage of the explicit GOTO L over a CYCLE i type of statement is that the former requires that a physically explicit label L be placed in the program text, which makes the program flow explicitly clear.

During the past decade, there has been intense discussion as to the validity of permitting unconditional branches (that is, the GOTO) in programs for various reasons that have to do with programming clarity, error frequency, and the difficulty in proving program correctness. Chapter 9 discusses these considerations.

Conditional Structures

The purpose of a conditional structure is to be able to exercise alternative computations depending on whether a particular condition is true. A simple modification of the basic GOTO is the computed GOTO of FORTRAN, which is essentially an n-branch decision or switch that directs execution to a specified label depending on the value of a variable that can have only positive integer values. The general form of the computed GOTO is

GOTO $(L_1, L_2 \ldots L_n), I$

where if I has the value 3, when the command GOTO is executed, then program flow will branch to label L_3 and so on for other values of $I = 1, 2, \ldots, n$. (Of course, in FORTRAN, the labels would be statement numbers attached to particular statements according to FORTRAN card-image—or line—convention.) The computed GOTO is a special case of the general IF statement, to be discussed later.

Another structure for additional branching is the CASE statement, which is relatively rigid. For various languages, the CASE statement may have somewhat different syntactical forms and semantic interpretations. One formulation of the CASE statement, which reveals its heritage to the more general IF statement, is

CASE <*expression*>
  IF <*value*$_1$> **THEN** <*executable statement*$_1$>
  IF <*value*$_2$> **THEN** <*executable statement*$_2$>
  ...
  IF <*value*$_n$> **THEN** <*executable statement*$_n$>
  OTHERWISE <*executable statement*>

For this type of structure, the usual assumptions are that all the conditions are mutually exclusive to avoid inconsistency, that the order of evaluation is strictly sequential, and that there is an explicit "otherwise" exit for a semantically acceptable transfer in normal sequencing if none of the conditions is satisfied. Nonetheless, CASE-like statements have been designed that violate one or more of the previous criteria.

In the preceding formulation of the CASE statement, when the value of <*expression*> is equal to one of the <*value*$_i$>, then the corresponding <*executable statement*$_i$> is executed. For specific variants of the CASE structure, the actual tokens used may be WHEN instead of IF and some other symbol instead of THEN. Also, the form <*expression*> could include objects such as arithmetic operators, for example, and the form <*value*$_i$> could include specific instances of such operators, for example, the symbol +. A simple example of the use of the CASE statement in PASCAL would be

```
VAR ALPHA: INTEGER
BEGIN
  CASE ALPHA OF
    1:Z:= 3;
    4:Z:= 7;
    . . .
    10:Z:= X + 5
  END;
END.
```

For PASCAL, the values preceding the executable statement may consist of a sequence of values separated by commas, any one of which, if true, would cause the execution of the corresponding statement.

In any of its forms, the CASE statement can be regarded as a special case of the IF statement. As such, it is not a *necessary* construct in the design of a programming language; if introduced, it should be formulated in as general a form as possible. Any restrictions as to the nature of <*expression*> and <*value*> should be precisely defined, and an ELSE or OTHERWISE option for cases not specifically listed should be included. For this structure to fit in the general orientation of a user-oriented approach, the language designer must specify that the compiler implementation automatically check for any restrictions on the values attributed to <*expression*> or <*value*> and forward any appropriate analysis or error message to the user when the program is either compiled or executed.

In the list-processing language LISP, the conditional structure analogous to the CASE statement is the list expression

$$\text{(COND } (p_1e_1)\ (p_2e_2) \ldots (p_ne_n))$$

where the symbols p_i are LISP expressions whose values are either *true* or *false* and the e_i are LISP expressions. The value of the LISP conditional structure (COND...) is the value of the expression e_i that is paired to the *first* p_i that is true. Evaluation is not continued after the first true p_i is found.

A selection structure, similar to the CASE statement, is the "guarded" statement. An example of this conditional structure is

```
IF <boolean expression_1> → <statement_1>
! <boolean expression_2> → <statement_2>
   ...
! <boolean expression_n> → <statement_n>FI
```

where <*statement*$_i$> is either a single statement or a sequence of single statements separated by semicolons. The boolean expression on the left side of the arrow is called a *guard.* Only if that boolean expression is true is the sequence of statements on the right side of the arrow executed. If, when it is time to execute the guarded command set, none of the guards is true, then the program will abort. This type of construct differs radically from the usual conditional structure in that, when two or more guards are true, then the corresponding statement is selected in a nondeterministic manner. It is nondeterministic in the sense that when more than one guard is true, which of the corresponding statements will be executed is undefined. The use of a nondeterministic construct can be useful in certain esoteric cases or for languages designed for parallel processing. Otherwise, the concept of a guard is basically a formal notational device that may be of interest for proving the correctness of programs. As a *language construct,* however, a guard does not appear to be a particularly valuable tool since it can be simulated easily by more basic constructs.

An example illustrating the caution that must be exercised in using the nondeterministic feature of the guarded command set might be the program

```
x = 0
boolean = TRUE
LOOP IF boolean → x = x + 1
! boolean → boolean = FALSE ENDLOOP
```

where a statement whose guard is true is executed until its guard is no longer true. If more than one guard is true, then the choice is nondeterministic. The loop terminates when none of the guards is true.

One possible path in this program would be to always choose to execute the first statement of the loop. In that case, the loop computation would never terminate. Of course, at a certain point the value assumed by x would "overflow" the arithmetic register or that hardware location chosen to store the current value of x. While the specification that maps into the specific program would be acceptable in a mathematical sense, the program, when executed, might not fulfill the abstract implications of the original specification. Another example would be

```
B1 = TRUE
B2 = TRUE
IF B1 → y = a + b1 + b2 + b3 + b4 + ... + bn
! B2 → y = b1 + b2 + b3 + b4 + ... + bn + a FI
```

Execution of the first assignment statement may not give the same results as execution of the second assignment statement, assuming that the sequence of b_i is the same in each case. If the value of each b_i is *very much smaller* than a, then in the first guarded command, addition of each b_i *after* a has been entered into the arithmetic accumulator may result in a "shifting loss" (because of the finite size of the arithmetic accumulator and the necessity of aligning decimal points for addition). That may generate a substantially different result than the arithmetically equivalent second guarded command.

The IF Structure for Selecting Alternatives

We prefer an IF-type conditional structure of the form

```
IF <complex Boolean expression>
THEN <sequence of executable statements>

[{ ELSE      } { <sequence of executable statements>
 { OTHERWISE }
|CONTINUE}]
```

An example of a *<complex boolean expression>* might be the instance

```
IF E < F < G OR (K = SINΘ AND H < ω) . . .
```

where parentheses associate the contents of an expression and resolve ambiguity. A *<sequence of executable statements>* may itself contain IF statements as well as any other form of executable statements, as long as the semantics are consistent. Those statements may include the "no-op" CONTINUE, which would simply cause normal sequencing. However, omission of the ELSE/OTHERWISE phrase implies normal sequencing, thus making an explicit CONTINUE unnecessary. Ambiguity relating to nested IFs is resolved by the use of parentheses to delimit the range of any instance of an IF statement. The parentheses are optional, but their omission may lead to ambiguity in terms of the program semantics unless there is an associated precedence rule. An example might be

```
  Read B,i,j,m,n,r,Θ.
  T = 999.
1 COMPUTE A = B + 2, (IF i = j THEN (IF m = n THEN
  T = r SINΘ) OTHERWISE T = r COSΘ) AND PRINT T,A.
2 COMPUTE A = B + 2, (IF i = j THEN (IF m = n THEN
  T = r SINΘ OTHERWISE T = r COSΘ)) AND PRINT T,A.
```

In case (1) $T = r \sin \Theta$ if $i = j$ and $m = n$, and $T = r \cos \Theta$ when $i \neq j$. The prior value of T is not changed when $i = j$ and $m \neq n$. In case (2),

$T = r \sin \Theta$ when $i = j$ *and* $m = n$, and $T = r \cos \Theta$ when $i = j$ and $m \neq n$. The prior value of T is not changed when $i \neq j$.

In the preceding example, the parentheses resolve any ambiguity without restricting the form of statements possible for either the THEN or the ELSE clauses. They also eliminate the necessity of specifying precise precedence rules that would connect ELSE clauses with specific IF constructs. The IF structure, as given in the preceding definition, can be considered itself a statement or part of a complex "sentence" where it modifies the actual computational flow. From another point of view, the IF structure can be viewed as a modifier or qualifier within the generalized assignment statement discussed in Chap. 3.

Historically, conventional languages have used more restricted forms of the IF structure. The arithmetic IF statement of FORTRAN can be characterized as

IF (<*arithmetic expression*>) N_1, N_2, N_3

where <*expression*> is a simple arithmetic expression and N_1, N_2, and N_3 are the statement numbers corresponding to associated FORTRAN statements. If the value of <*expression*> is negative, then there is a branch to that statement associated with N_1. If the value of <*expression*> is equal to zero, then statement N_2 is executed. If <*expression*> is positive, the jump is to the statement labeled N_3, which is then executed. The FORTRAN logical IF can be defined as

IF *(<logical expression>) <statement>*

where <*statement*> cannot be another logical IF or a DO type of statement. The <*logical expression*> is essentially equivalent to what was illustrated previously as a complex boolean expression, except that the relational operators are .LT., .LE., .EQ., .NE., .GT., .GE., .AND., .OR., and .NOT. instead of the usual mathematical symbols used to express relations between variables, and bracketing periods are used to enclose a relational or logical operator. FORTRAN 77 permits a simple form of the IF...THEN...ELSE....

For ALGOL-like languages, the IF structure is comparable to the first example given in this section. Ambiguity is resolved by restricting the type of statements that may appear in the THEN or ELSE clauses, by using BEGIN/END pairs as brackets to associate the contents of a particular clause, or by using a FI as the right bracket to an associated IF, which plays the role of a left bracket. The use of the symbol ENDIF plays a similar role as a right bracket to the left-bracket BEGINIF. In some languages, ambiguity is resolved by matching an ELSE clause to the closest IF phrase not containing an ELSE. Functionally, there is no difference between nested parentheses and alternative symbols such as BEGIN/END, IF/FI, and

BEGINIF/ENDIF. The language designer must make that choice on the basis of program clarity. The major advantage of parentheses as a nesting notation to resolve ambiguity is that they have been used historically for that purpose in mathematical notation. Furthermore, nested sets of parentheses can alternate among (), [], {}, and any other available parenthetical symbol to increase program clarity. For two-dimensional languages, parentheses can be further differentiated by their size. In fact, the notion of indentation for complex statements, widely introduced for the use of ALGOL 60, was a limited attempt to impose a two-dimensional linguistic structure on what is essentially a one-dimensional string of symbols to enhance program readability, even though in ALGOL-like languages indentation has no semantic interpretation.

In constructing the IF construct, some languages, such as PL/1, require punctuation symbols, for example, semicolons, at points in the linguistic structure where they perform no functional purpose. For particular structures, elimination of such excess punctuation would create no difference in the semantic interpretation of the structure. An example might be

```
IF...THEN...;ELSE...
```

The semicolon before the ELSE symbol is redundant because it does not add to the semantic interpretation. One could make the distinction that there are two lexical symbols, one being the symbol ;ELSE and the other the symbol ELSE. Aside from that, the lexical analyzer of the program would recognize the ELSE symbol as the sign that starts the ELSE clause and would regard the semicolon as simply noise once it detected the subsequent ELSE.

The <*complex boolean expression*> in the general form IF <*complex boolean expression*> ... may have a TRUE/FALSE value supplied by the "interrupt" feature of the hardware processor, by the operating system software, or even internally by the program. Conditions that would trigger that feature would include the overflow of a result beyond the magnitude of an arithmetic register, the attempt to divide by a value equal to zero, or the detection of the end of a physical file stored in some hardware unit. The ON <*condition*> structure of PL/1 plays this sort of role. In most cases, this sort of function can be simulated by basic program constructs.

We should also note that an IF structure can be used not only as a modifier for a complex "sentence," but also as an arithmetic expression, yielding a value. For example, consider the assignment statement

```
X = IF Y > 0 THEN 26 ELSE 55.
```

Or an IF structure can be used to generate the value of a boolean variable, as in

```
B = IF g > 2.3 THEN TRUE ELSE FALSE.
```

The IF structure can also be used as an object for the GOTO command. For example,

GOTO (IF X > 25 THEN STATEMENT_1 ELSE STATEMENT_2).

The parentheses enclosing the IF structure are optional and are solely for program clarity. STATEMENT_1 and STATEMENT_2 are physical points in the program that, while literally no-op operators, mark the relevant program point at which program flow is to continue.

Decision Tables

A decision table can be thought of as a two-dimensional array consisting of rows and columns. The array is separated into two parts—the rows that constitute the upper part and the rows that constitute the bottom part. The upper rows of the first column are boolean expressions; that is, they evaluate to either TRUE or FALSE. The bottom rows of the first column are executable statements called *actions*. The boolean expressions in the upper rows of the first column are also called *conditions* or *tests*. If the array **A** represents the decision table, then the element $A_{i,j}$ ($j \neq 1$) contains a symbol indicating TRUE or FALSE, for example, Y or N, for all $i <$ LOW, where LOW is the number of the row that starts the lower part of a column. The entries $A_{i,j}$($j \neq 1, i \geqq$ LOW), which represent the entries in the lower rows corresponding to the actions in the lower part of the first column, may have a value that consists of a symbol, for example, an x mark, to indicate whether that action is to be executed. Decision tables, as a language structure, can be highly useful in restricted or specialized application situations. Their use in a general programming language is dubious, however, since each column in a decision table ($j \neq 1$) is essentially a restricted case of the structure

IF *<complex boolean expression>* **THEN** *<sequence of executable statements>*

The *<complex boolean expression>* is the sequence of Ys and Ns in the upper part of a specific column. If this sequence is TRUE, then those actions indicated by x's in the lower part of that column are executed. There is no ELSE clause, because if the boolean conditions are not satisfied in the current column, then the next column is examined. The entries of the table corresponding to specific upper-row conditions can consist of not only TRUE/FALSE entries but also the entry DONTCARE. Figure 4.1 is an example of a decision table.

```
miles driven ≤ 7500              Y N    YY    . . .   . . .
miles driven > 7500                Y          . . .   . . .
single                           NYNYYY       . . .   . . .
married                          Y Y     YYY. . .
male                             N NNYYYYY. . .
age ≤ 25                         NYNNYYY      . . .
age > 25                         YNYYNNNYY. . .
only driven non-work             YNYYNNYNN. . .
work < 10 miles                   N    YN  Y  . . .
work > 10 miles                   Y    NY  NY. . .
no driving violations            YNYYNNNNN. . .
no major violations               N    YNY    . . .
no accidents past 10 years       YYYYYNNY   . . .
accidents | 3 in 5 years         NNNNNYNNY. . .
student                          NNNNYNYNY. . .     . . .
economy car                      YNYYYNNYN. . .     . . .
licensed over 5 years            YNYYNNYNN. . .     . . .
none of the above fits                                  Y
----------------------------------------------------------
Rate # 1                         x
Rate # 2                          x                    x
Rate # 3                           x
.......                                                x
.......                                               x
.......
                                          x           x
                                           x
                                         x
                                                        x
.......                              x
.......
.......
ADD SURCHARGE                           x
PROBATION                               x
REJECT                               x
INVESTIGATE                             xx            x
SEE SUPERVISOR                                         x
```

{ Note: A blank indicates a "don't-care" or redundant condition. }

Figure 4.1 Example of a decision table.

Loop Qualifiers

LOOP (or REPEAT or CYCLE) structures are the most important structures for those programs that are characterized by relatively little data input and output but that spend most of their time in computation. For such programs, nearly all of the program-execution time is spent executing those statements controlled by the LOOP structure. What distinguishes so-called *computational* programs from *data-processing* programs is that in a computational program most of the execution time is spent "within" a loop; that is, a relatively small section of the problem text is repetitively executed.

It is not uncommon for FORTRAN compilers to be extremely inefficient when compiling machine code for statements relating to FORTRAN input and output, resulting in excessive execution time for relatively small amounts of input/output. A computational program that is not compiled inefficiently and that does not expend a predominant part of its execution time under the control of a LOOP structure is probably a *trivial* program, in the sense that it might take less time to compute it manually. Of course, there are exceptions to this statement, but they usually involve the real-time monitoring of input data. For those programs that are essentially data processing (that is, which deal with the transformation of lengthy streams of input data and complex manipulation of internal files) or fall in the category of "systems programming," the LOOP structure is of lesser importance because it consumes a relatively small portion of program execution time. Of course, there are in-between cases.

FORTRAN enables the programming of a fixed number of iterations over a sequence of statements by making the first statement preceding the body of the loop the DO statement. For example, a specific FORTRAN loop might be

```
      DO 13 I = 1,31,2
      ...
      ...
      (body of the loop)
      ...
      ...
   13 CONTINUE
```

The body of the loop contains a sequence of FORTRAN statements, any one of which may itself be a DO statement. The integer value following the DO specifies the *range* of the loop; that is, in the program segment above, all statements up to and including statement number 13 are to be executed. The symbol CONTINUE is a no-op instruction. The integer variable before the equal sign in the DO statement, in this case, I, can be considered the *index* or the *loop-control variable* of the DO statement. For the above example, I starts with the *initial value* 1, and the body of the loop is executed for that particular value of I. On the next cycle, the value I is *incremented* by the value 2, and the body of the loop is then executed with the new value of I = 3, and so on, until I reaches the *terminating* value I = 31. At that point, the body of the loop is executed for the last time. In classical (pre-1977) FORTRAN, the initial, the incrementing, and the terminating values of I must be *positive* integers. A further restriction is that those values cannot exceed a specific positive integer value.

Those restrictions were introduced by the original designers of FORTRAN because of implementation and efficiency considerations connected with the then-current architecture of IBM machines. However, there is no substantial implementation difficulty in generalizing the DO statement so that the initial, the incremental, and the final entities associated with the index of the loop are generalized expressions whose values are real numbers, either positive or negative. If the index variable of the loop also appears as a subscript within the body of the loop (for example, if a statement contains the array element $A_{I\ldots}$), then if I has a noninteger or negative value at that point in the execution, the semantics of the specific programming-language design should specify precisely the action to be taken.

For the case of noninteger but positive values of I, a plausible action would be either to truncate the value of I or to take the integer nearest to its real value. Likewise, when the array subscript I assumes a negative value, it would be plausible to abort that section of the calculation, emit an appropriate error message, and continue on with the first statement that is a successor to the aborted loop. If the subsequent computation requires as input those values that have been aborted because of the negative subscript values, then, of course, the subsequent computation itself must be terminated with the appropriate error messages to the user. (However, some modern languages—or their implementations—violate this caution.)

For a DO-type structure, synonyms to the capitalized DO might be DO TO, REPEAT, REPEAT TO, CYCLE, CYCLE TO, DO UNTIL, or similar variants. The decision as to whether to permit the termination of more than one loop structure at the same point of the physical text, that is, the same statement number, is a language-design choice that is essentially implementation-dependent and that need not concern us at this time.

A variation of the DO structure might be

```
WHILE <complex boolean expression> DO
  BEGIN
  ...
  ...
  (body of the loop)
  ...
  ...
  END
```

For this structure, it is possible that the loop may never be traversed if no instance of the boolean expression is true. It is also possible that the loop may not terminate, which is a risk in using this type of construct. Thus this can be regarded as an *unlimited* DO-type structure. Similarly, one can construct another type of unlimited DO-like structure, such as

```
REPEAT
...
...
(body of the loop)
...
...
UNTIL <complex boolean expression>
```

For this case, the loop makes at least one traversal, regardless of the value of the boolean expression, and may not terminate unless the boolean expression assumes the value TRUE.

Whether or not there are restrictions on branching (GOTO) out of or into a specified point of a (nested) loop is a somewhat arbitrary choice for the language designer. Our point of view is that the user should not be restricted in constructing the program flow, even though this may lead to difficult-to-comprehend programs. The obscurity here, if any, lies with the resulting *logic* of the program flow, not with the clarity of the linguistic structure of the program sentence. Similar considerations apply to whether the loop index and the expressions for the increment and terminating condition may be modified within the loop body. We would opt for the less restricted alternatives. The less restricted alternatives may make the compiler construction somewhat more complex (though not onerously so), but they would not significantly affect the time expended during execution. A basic question here is whether the language designer wishes to force the user into what appears to be simpler forms of program flow. Chapter 9 discusses the concept of structured programming, but we might note here that attempts to enforce simple program flow sometimes lead to more complex and more-difficult-to-understand programs. (The sentence structure of the application language discussed in Chap. 8 avoids many of these problems.)

In the case of terminating a loop on an exception, the necessity of using a reference point for the GOTO can be avoided by an EXIT-type instruction that simply terminates that particular loop or, if so specified by the language design, all enclosing loops. In the latter case, the program proceeds to the next sequential statement.

One could also admit a structure such as

```
REPEAT n TIMES STATEMENT 1, STATEMENT 2,...
STATEMENT k.
```

where *n* assumes integer values. Or one could also admit an iterative structure illustrated by

```
⎧ LOOP    ⎫
⎨ REPEAT  ⎬ n TIMES
⎩ PERFORM ⎭

. . .
. . .
(body of loop)
. . .
. . .
ENDLOOP
```

In the first structure, the STATEMENT k is either explicit statement numbers (referencing the associated statement) or points in the program text that implicitly refer to the next sentence of the program. Thus *nonsuccessive* statements can be "looped."

A loop-qualifier structure, which is general, powerful, and an aid to program clarity for those programming languages where the basic computational unit is a sentence, might be expressed in the syntactical specification

```
{ FOR  } <name>  = { <expression> | <list> } [BY <expression> ]
{ FROM }

⎧ TO    ⎫
⎨ UNTIL ⎬ [ <expression> <boolean operator> ] <expression>
⎩ WHILE ⎭

[{ WHILE } <complex boolean expression> ]
 { UNTIL }
```

Here, *<expression>* is any expression that executes to a value consistent with assignment. In the more general sense, it could be a definite integration or other process more complex than a simple arithmetic evaluation. *<list>* is here meant to be a list of numerical values, names, or arithmetic expressions separated by some appropriate notational device, for example, commas, ands, or, more simply, blanks. The key word UNTIL is to be interpreted as specifying the *terminating* condition for the loop; that is, the loop is not executed when the condition specified by the UNTIL clause is true.

For example, the phrase

```
FROM i = 2 TO 10...
```

would cause *i* to assume the values 2, 3, 4, 5, 6, 7, 8, 9, 10. However, the phrase

```
FROM i = 2 UNTIL 10
```

would cause i to assume the values 2, 3, 4, 5, 6, 7, 8, 9. Other specific instances of this syntactical form may be

1. From i = x + y TO z − Q... (sequence of computable statements, including additional FROM or FOR phrases)
2. FROM j = m BY 2.345 UNTIL a + b... (sequence of computable statements, including additional FROM or FOR phrases)
3. FROM a = b + 5 BY 2 UNTIL q > 20... (sequence of computable statements, including additional FROM or FOR phrases)
4. FROM k = d/e TO INFINITY... (sequence of computable statements, including additional FROM or FOR phrases) The key word INFINITY means that k should not terminate; however, exit from the loop may be caused by some other condition becoming true.
5. FROM gamma = 2k + 3 BY .01tau UNTIL w > 5800... (sequence of computable statements, including additional FROM or FOR phrases)
6. FROM i = a + b BY c + d UNTIL e + f < g/h... (sequence of computable statements, including additional FROM or FOR phrases)
7. FROM i = a BY c TO 100 WHILE k < g... (sequence of computable statements, including additional FROM or FOR phrases)
8. From alpha = a + b BY c/d TO p − q WHILE z < 10 AND y = 20... (sequence of computable statements, including additional FROM or FOR statements) Brackets can be inserted to delimit the argument of the WHILE clause to resolve any possible ambiguity.
9. FROM I = 1 TO 20, 25 BY 0.5 TO 30, 40 BY 2 TO 60...
10. FROM J = 10 BY 4 TO 50 AND 51 TO 70...
11. FROM K = 2, 7, 9, 13, 17 BY 3 TO 47, 55, 73...

When the BY expression is omitted, the increment value is assumed to be +1 unless the initial value is greater than the final value. In that case, the increment is assumed to be −1.

We also consider additional FOR-type structures, which are semantically equivalent to special cases of the FROM phrase structure. Strictly speaking, the FOR structures are logically redundant, since they can be accomplished by the use of the more general FROM form. In our opinion, however, they add to program clarity since they mimic conventional mathematical notation. In fact, FROM and FOR can be treated as synonyms. Additionally, it is supportive of user-oriented design if key words such as FROM or FOR may be represented in lowercase or uppercase or mixed upper- and lowercase characters. Thus the "F" in FOR or FROM may be capitalized if this key word is placed at the beginning of a computational statement.

Specific instances of the FOR structure are

1. FOR i = 1,2,...,12 (followed by a sequence of executable statements that may contain additional FROM or FOR forms) The difference between the two values of the list, before the ellipsis, specifies the increment.
2. FOR i = 3,7,12,13,19 (followed by a sequence of executable statements which may contain additional FROM or FOR forms)
3. FOR i = 5(10)55 (followed by a sequence of executable statements that may contain additional FROM or FOR forms) Here the increment is the value enclosed in parentheses.
4. FOR i = 0,5,...7.5 (followed by a sequence of executable statements that may contain additional FROM or FOR forms) This is structurally identical to the FOR in number 1, except that i assumes some noninteger values.

These variations of the FROM/FOR clause may be written in any combination as a list to specify the values to be assumed by the index variable. For example,

FOR i = 2 BY 3 TO 13,17,19,23,27(2)37,49,54,79,83,...,205,346 BY 3.5 WHILE Z <2034 COMPUTE *<sequence of executable statements>*

We emphasize that the FROM/FOR clauses act as qualifiers for what can be regarded in the programming language as a "sentence." In this sense, the loop is simply a *sentence* controlled by a set of FROM or FOR qualifiers. From this point of view, the value assigned to the control value as the loop iterates may change not only as specified by the arguments within the FROM or FOR clauses but also as an outcome of the values assumed by those arguments that result as statements are executed within the overall sentence. Restrictions in that regard might make program flow simpler, but not necessarily clearer, if the application is sufficiently complex to warrant a more general approach to loop control. That, it seems to us, is a decision that the programmer, not the language designer, should make. The language designer's function is to provide the most powerful expressions, subject to linguistic and notational clarity, within the limits of feasible implementation.

For nested or multiple FROM phrases within a single sentence, FROM can be replaced by WITHIN or AND, where AND can also play the dual role as a connective even where its successor is an explicit FROM phrase. (In addition, a comma may also play the role of a connective by replacing the successive use of the term AND after the first FOR or FROM in a nested loop.) For example,

FOR $i = 1(1)50$ AND $k = 0$ BY 2 UNTIL $y > 2000$ READ X_{ik}, COMPUTE $y = 2X_{i,k}$ AND PRINT y.

FROM $i = 1$ TO 500 READ X_i, If $X_i \neq 10$ COMPUTE $y = y + X_i$, $n = n + 2$ OTHERWISE GO TO STATEMENT 1.

If $a > k$ COMPUTE $x = \sqrt{(a-k)d}$, $Y = B_{ij}x + C_0T$ AND PRINT Y, a, T, k, OTHERWISE COMPUTE $x = 2ak$, $Y = B_{ij}x + C_0Td$ AND PRINT Y, a, T, k FROM $a = 1$ to n WITHIN $T = 2$ BY 0.1 UNTIL 3 AND FOR $k = 0(5)90$.

FROM $i = 1$ TO 10 AND $j = 1$ TO 10 READ A_{ij}, COMPUTE $B_{ij} = A_{ij} + X_i + Y_j$ AND PRINT A_{ij}, B_{ij}, X_i, Y_j, i, j.

FOR $r = 1, 2, \ldots, 10$ AND FOR $\Theta = -P(.01)P$ COMPUTE $S_r = r\text{SIN}2t$, $C_r = r\cos^{-1}t$, $A = T_r = \sum_{P=1}^{30} \text{TAN}(.1Pt)$,

$$V_r = \prod_{i=1}^{25} \frac{\text{LOG}_2 i}{A + \dfrac{i}{tC + \dfrac{DEF}{G}}}$$ AND PRINT r, t, V_r, A.

IF ($X \geq Y$ AND $g > 0$) OR $|42 - g/e| > (X - Y)^2$ THEN COMPUTE $T_{XY} = g\left(\frac{X}{Y}\right)^2$ AND $W = YT_{XY}$ AND PRINT W, T_{XY}, X, g FROM $g = 2k + 3$ BY .01t UNTIL $W > 5800$ AND FROM $X = 1$ TO 100 OTHERWISE GO TO STATEMENT 2.

Some of the notation in the preceding examples is not possible within the domain of conventional computer languages, which have been designed within the framework of obsolete input devices. Such notation is possible, however, and highly desirable for reasons of program clarity, by using either hard-copy terminals that have that notational capability or CRT terminals that allow such notational flexibility because of their graphic and character-generation capabilities. The use of such notational structures is one of the principal features of a two-dimensional language discussed in detail in Chap. 8.

As the preceding examples indicate, the relative positions of the FROM or FOR clauses are not restricted to the beginning of the sentence. They may also appear at the end of the sentence or anywhere within the sentence if the position adds to the clarity of the sentence structure. However, any possible ambiguity is removed if the scope of FOR/FROM clauses that do not appear at the beginning or the end of a sentence is noted by parentheses enclosing the clauses and that part of the sentence which they control. The flexibility of placement of FOR/FROM clauses does not generally interfere with semantic clarity, nor does it add significantly to implementation complexity. It has no significant effect, if properly implemented, on execution efficiency.

Other Considerations

Various levels of indentation, "esoteric" forms such as the FI to terminate an IF phrase, and the DO/OD brackets or EXITLOOP are common to ALGOL-like languages. In such languages, the indentation and associated punctuation symbols such as the comma, the colon, and the assignment symbol (:=) must assume specific textual positions, depending on the specific phrase structure of a construct. The other specific rules limiting their occurrence tend to detract from rather than add to program clarity. In ALGOL-like languages, indentations have no semantic meaning, since they do not affect the translation into executable code. For those languages, the entire program *is* the sentence, in the sense that the entire program can be construed as a single linear string of lexicographically recognizable symbols.

In the preceding examples, we have attempted to construct forms that are comprehensible to readers who are mathematically literate, even though they may not have other than a superficial acquaintance with a conventional programming language. These considerations are in the realm of the psychology of computer programming, as well as in the realm of human-factors design (see Chap. 9). Another characteristic of the examples is that they allow for alternative syntactical forms even if one particular form is general enough to encompass a broad range of applications.

Of course, all of the iterative structures and even more complex variants of those in this chapter can be simulated by the use of GOTO and IF-type statements. The use of an explicit GOTO is held in disfavor by some advocates of good programming style. Chapter 9 summarizes the arguments for and against the use of the GOTO as an option in a programming language. The selection of a particular language structure is a function of the programmer, however, not the language designer. Nonetheless, some designers of computer languages have attempted to enforce the nonuse of certain structures that they regard as "harmful." This is analogous to trying to pass a law to require that people speak and write only those sentences that can be parsed into forms no more complex than

<*subject*> <*verb*> <*object*>

based on the theory that (1) all language can be reduced to such simple forms and (2) use of such simple forms makes communications of meaning simpler. An adequate examination of that thesis would have to distinguish whether we are in the realm of logic, language, or psychology.

Chapter 5

Input and Output

Introduction

It is possible for a program not to have any input of external data and yet be a meaningful program. For example, a program designed to compute the sequence of prime numbers does not need any external data. This would be an example of a program that is a pure computation, rather than a program characterized as being in the realm of *data processing*. However, if a program, upon termination, does not or has not output any data, then such a program cannot be regarded as meaningful as either pure computation or data processing. It is meaningless from a pure computation or data-processing point of view because whether or not the program has been run makes no difference. Without the output of data, a program cannot have any effect on the external environment and therefore cannot be considered as having a semantic effect. The only meaning that such an "outputless" program might have would stem from the side effects of running it on physical hardware. For example, most computer hardware has various control lights and other visual indicators that signal the states of various registers. If one wanted to present the *appearance* of a computer actively running programs, rather than it being in an unused state, then any simple nonterminating program would achieve that end. The blinking of the visual indicators would give the appearance of a piece of hardware in an active state. Similarly, if the architecture of the hardware system is such that one central processor controls a set of auxiliary devices that are assigned priority levels as far as their access to the central processor, then the frequency of the on/off states displayed by the visual indicators will indicate if any auxiliary device is blocking the processing, or if processing on the central processor is slow because one auxiliary device with superior priority is dominating access to the central processor. In this pragmatic sense, the frequency of the central processor's console indicators may say something about the *quality* of the program insofar as signifying cleverness in the interweaving of requests from the entire set of auxiliary processors so that the execution efficiency of the central processor is maximized. One important exception to these considerations is the program that is an *operating system* and whose purpose is to manage other programs. A minor exception, undesirable as programming practice, is the interpretation of no output as an indication of the program's failure to find or to compute an item with specified properties.

In the vast majority of application contexts, the manner in which data are input and the manner in which results are output are of the most fundamental pragmatic importance for the overall efficiency of computer usage. From the view of programming-language design, the manner of inputting data is a question of the *format* style for a particular language. The format mechanism to describe the manner in which results are to be output is also a function of specific language design.

Although it is our opinion that the manner in which input and output of a program are carried out is of the highest pragmatic importance, this has not been the historical view. For example, the official definition of ALGOL 60 does not contain any reference to statements or structures connected with input or output. The reason generally given for this strange omission is that ALGOL was designed to be independent of the particular characteristics of any specific computer. It was therefore left up to the individual compiler writer of an ALGOL compiler for a specific computer to invent the necessary input language forms, formats, and restrictions. Justification for that position lay in the assertion that different machines have widely different input and output devices, and therefore the specification of input and output language structures would not be appropriate.

Of course, such an argument is obvious nonsense. Prior to the 1980s, the period in which most of the current conventional higher-level languages were developed, the range of input devices associated with various computers of different manufacturers was very limited. The principal manual input device was the keyboard, or card punch, connected to a CRT-type display or directly into some auxiliary storage medium such as a magnetic tape/disk/card. In general, keyboard input devices were distinguished by the fact that they produced linear input, that is, a string of codes corresponding to specific characters, in a timewise-ordered fashion, that is, from left to right. The character set available to the various keyboard-entry devices was very limited, usually consisting of the uppercase English alphabet and a small set of special symbols, more recently augmented by the lowercase English alphabet and perhaps a special set of auxiliary function keys. The historical picture thus has been one of limited, rather than wide-range, capability for input as data to a program. Given the historical context, we can interpret the previously mentioned omission on the part of the designers of ALGOL as indicating a lack of concern about certain aspects of problem solving in the real world. Certainly it is a point of view that we would regard as being antithetical to the purposes of user-oriented design.

The Problem of Input/Output in FORTRAN

Unlike ALGOL 60, FORTRAN, which was the first widely used high-level language, did specify rigorously the structure of input to FORTRAN programs and output from such programs. The actual design, however, was such as to almost guarantee errors in those programs that required data to be input in various forms and output according to desired display rules.

The syntax of the conventional FORTRAN input/output statements can be represented as

```
   READ (<readernumber> , <formatlinenumber>) <name> , < * >
   <name>,
   WRITE (<printernumber> , <formatlinenumber>) <name> ,
   < * > <name> ,
L FORMAT ([ '<carriage-control character>',] <format
          specification> , < * > <format specification > ,)
          { where L↔<formatlinenumber> and the last comma
          is omitted}
```

An example of a FORTRAN input statement would be

```
READ (5,10) X,Y,Z
```

An example of a FORTRAN output statement would be

```
WRITE (6,11) P,R
```

In the READ statement, the number 5 identifies the particular reading device, which, for FORTRAN, has historically been a card reader. The reason why a particular number, such as 5, is used has to do with the configuration of the IBM computers that were available when FORTRAN was invented. The number 6, which appears in the FORTRAN WRITE statement, has its historical origins in the architectural configuration of the early IBM machines. The number 10 in the READ statement specifies the line number associated with the FORMAT that will control the layout of data. Likewise, the number 11 in the FORTRAN WRITE statement references the FORMAT that specifies the form and spacing of output results as they appear on a line printer or other output device. The first character, if present, in the

FORMAT specification also controls the spacing between lines for line-printer output, as well as the skipping to the top of the next page.

For instance, if the carriage-control character is a +, the paper will not advance, thus making it possible to overprint characters on the same printing line. If the carriage-control character is not present, then printing will proceed in normal single-line spacing. If the carriage-control character is a 0, then double-line spacing will result; if the carriage-control character is a 1, then the paper will skip to the top of the next page before printing the next line of output.

For integers, the format specification would be *Iw,* where *w* indicates the number of columns on the card image (or the number of printer columns) allocated to the integer right-justified in the field *w*. For example, the following statements in historic FORTRAN

```
  READ (5,7) A,B,C
7 FORMAT (I7,I4,I6)
```

will cause the reading of the three values for A, B, and C from a card (or line) image. If in this instance A has the value equal to 35, then the digit 3 must be in the sixth column of the card image and the digit 5 must be in the seventh column of the card image to satisfy the criteria of right-justification in the field. Likewise, if in this instance B has a value equal to 245, then the digit 2 must be placed in column 9 of the card image, the digit 4 in column 10, and the digit 5 in column 11. The value assumed for C in this instance would be treated similarly. The symbol for positive integers (+) may be omitted, but if the negative symbol (−) is desired, then the space used by it must be taken into account. If the data values are not in the proper right-justified positions of the field, then either extra zeros will be added to the value that is input to the computer or digits of the actual data may be ignored or transferred to other input variables. If a set of data must be distributed among a sequential set of *n* data fields, and each data field requires a separate input format because of the intrinsic structure of the data set, the data-preparation task is not only difficult, but highly error-prone. This becomes even more difficult for the other allowed format specifications.

A real number requires the specification *Fw.d,* where *w* indicates the number of columns allocated to the entire field of that number. The value of *d* indicates the number of columns allocated for digits *after* the decimal point. Blanks, sign, and the column for the decimal point must be counted into the value assumed by *w*. If an actual decimal point is not put in the appropriate place when the data is read, then a decimal point will be inserted into the real-number value input to the program. The decimal point appears to the left of the last *d* digits of the field *w* allocated to the real data value. Of course, the last digit of the data value must be in the rightmost column of the field allocated to that real number, or the value input to the program may not be correct.

For most FORTRAN compilers, if a decimal point is explicitly placed in the data value, then the value of *d* in the format specification will be ignored. When used to control a WRITE statement, the format specification *Fw.d* will cause the appropriate real number to be printed right-justified in a field with a total width of *w* print columns and with the decimal point appearing just to the left of the rightmost *d* columns of the print field. Thus spacing between values can be controlled by picking a value for *w* larger than necessary for the associated value of the output variable. For floating-point numbers of the form 0.12345678E-03, the format specification *Ew.d* may be used, where *w* specifies the number of columns of the *entire* field devoted to this numerical value, including the columns used to print or read the decimal point, both signs, and the E. If no decimal point is recorded within the appropriate field, it is assumed to be just to the left of the rightmost string of *d* digits, which are to the left of the E of the data value. On output, the E will appear explicitly, before the positive or negative integer denoting the value of the exponent associated with the floating-point number (the + may be omitted). The decimal point will appear just to the left of the *d*-digit string. In practice, however, most implementations of FORTRAN ignore this restriction and will print a floating-point number with a leading 0, then a decimal point, and then follow it by *d* digits. Thus the actual practice is to regard *d* as specifying the number of significant digits to be printed for a floating-point value.

In calculating the value of *w*, the programmer must take into account the columns needed for the sign of the number, the sign of the exponent, the column necessary for the leading 0, the decimal point, the character E, and two (or three) columns for the exponent. The I, F, E format specifications, if preceded by an integer *n*, indicate that format structure is to be repeated *n* times. The printing of literal values can be accomplished by the specification *wH*, which indicates a Hollerith constant. The value of *w* indicates the number of characters (including blanks) following the *H* in the format specification that are to be printed literally in the appropriate field in the sequence of the format statement. For example, the statements

```
   WRITE (6,22)
22 FORMAT ('1',20H RESULTS FOR CASE A )
```

will cause the printer to skip to the top of a new page and print the legend RESULTS FOR CASE A (with a blank on either side).

In many implementations of FORTRAN, the use of the *wH* format specification can be avoided by enclosing literals, meant to be output, in single quote marks ('). A literal may include blank spaces at the beginning, in between, and at the end. The format specifications *wX* can be used to indicate that *w* blanks are desired in the appropriate column positions when printing output. Usually there is also an *Aw* specification to control the input and output of alphanumeric information. The details associated with this specification vary from one implementation to another. Thus an example of a relatively uncomplicated FORTRAN format statement might be

```
525 FORMAT (4X,I3,2HD=, F10.2,2X,F6.0,1X,E14.7,E13.4)
```

where each format statement must have a statement number preceding it.

FORTRAN, in formulations after the initial design, evolved a READ statement that was an implied loop. For example,

```
READ (5,100) (B(J),J = 1,10)
```

will cause the reading of 10 values of the data specified by the associated FORMAT statement as the first 10 values of the one-dimension array B.

More recent dialects of FORTRAN, such as WATFIV, have liberalized the FORTRAN READ statement so that one can simply program

```
READ A,B,C,D
```

and not specify any particular format. Controlling the layout of the results computed by a FORTRAN program can still be considered highly onerous unless one opts for some simple standard form of data layout varying with the specific FORTRAN dialect. If the requirement is for complex or "fancy" layout, requiring different columns for different sets of result output, interspersed with headings and literals in any particular line, then the programming of sets of different format statements becomes highly error-prone and forces the programmer into such strategems as using graph paper to lay out the fields controlled by different format structures. Even then, a miscount for any particular field may cause a misalignment in the output set of results. Change in one of the values of *w* or *d* in one of the field specifications will shift the entire line over from that point. Because of the difficulties associated with FORTRAN output, programmers working in application areas where FORTRAN is predominant tend to minimize the need for and the value of clear and easily assimilable output. *Thus the inherent linguistic structure of FORTRAN has not only produced the difficult-to-understand programs characteristic of the language, it also often generates results that require auxiliary documentation for minimum comprehensibility.*

The irony of the situation is that such technically elaborate input specifications are neither necessary nor justifiable for reasons based on machine architecture, execution efficiency, implementation difficulty, or any other pragmatic reason. The situation can be illustrated quite clearly by a case where data is restricted to an arbitrary sequence of numerical values that are integers, fixed-point numbers (that is, real numbers with explicit decimal points), or floating-point numbers (that is, real numbers or integers with an explicit E followed by an exponent). From an implementation point of view, it is a simple matter in an arbitrary sequence of values to distinguish which value is an integer, which value is a fixed-point number, and which value must be interpreted as a floating-point number. The only structural specification for the input of numerical values need be simply that the termination of each value be signaled by a character code. The most convenient, and most user-oriented (user-friendly), character code would simply be that representing a blank space! The actual number of blank spaces between values can be arbitrary (as long as there is at least one blank space). A comma as a value terminator would also introduce no additional difficulty. The number of values per input file also can be arbitrary and need not be specified in advance by the programmer. This mode of input is now known as *free-field input* and is used in many relatively recent implementations of various conventional programming languages. Not only is there no particular negative consideration involved with the implementation of free-field input, but generally, given a competent compiler writer, it is usually processed much faster than the execution time consumed by most FORTRAN compilers in dealing with formatted input. The reasons for this inefficiency are probably inherent not in the structure of the FORTRAN FORMAT statement, but rather in the historical method of dealing with formatted input (and output) by FORTRAN compilers, which may use interpretation rather than direct compilation. Nonetheless, the main objection to the FORTRAN format structure is not the execution inefficiency that may be associated with any particular FORTRAN implementation, but rather the horrendous burden placed on the programmer.

While the problem of numerical input admits of a relatively simple and efficient solution by the use of free-field input, and alphanumeric input can also be handled easily, the case of output, especially where there are complex display requirements, requires more ingenuity from the language designer.

COBOL Input/Output

In COBOL, the basic READ and WRITE statements appear to have a simple structure. That is accomplished by associating a format with each variable that can be changed by exercise of the MOVE operator. An example of a format description for a name might be

```
SIZE IS 6 CHARACTERS; CLASS NUMERIC; POINT LOCATION IS
LEFT 1; SIGNED.
```

A more convenient way to describe the format of a data item is by the use of the PICTURE clause, for example,

```
PICTURE IS 999
PICTURE IS 99999V9
PICTURE IS SVP999
PICTURE IS AAAAA
PICTURE IS XXXX
PICTURE IS 9X999
PICTURE IS A99
PICTURE IS X99
PICTURE IS AXXX
```

where a 9 in the PICTURE argument indicates that the character position is to be filled by a numerical decimal digit, a V indicates the location of an implied decimal point (the decimal point is not part of the actual data), the symbol S indicates that the data item has a sign, and the symbol P indicates that the assumed decimal point exists outside the actual storage data. In this sense, a PICTURE clause is meant to be equivalent in function to a POINT clause. A POINT clause specifies how many positions to the right or left of the least significant position of a datum the decimal point is to be located.

In COBOL, a *numeric* cannot contain an actual decimal point. The use of a string of As as the argument of the PICTURE clause indicates that the associated variable is entirely alphabetic. The number of As gives the number of characters in the datum. Alphanumeric data are indicated by sequences of Xs. It is also possible to combine combinations of the symbols 9, A, and X within the argument of one picture. The PICTURE argument may also contain the character Z to indicate that suppression of leading zeros is desired. A *$* indicates that an actual $ should be placed in the datum at the particular position when it is output. There are additional symbols to influence the structure of the final edited data item for output. While the intent of the PICTURE device is laudable, its basic simplicity is obscured by the relatively large set of symbols to differentiate among alphabetic, alphanumeric, and numeric characters; signs; decimal position; zero suppression; blank suppression; the insertion of symbols like the $, the comma, or special credit or debit symbols; and the various rules restricting the successors and predecessors of particular format symbols.

PL/1 Input/Output

PL/1 has complex structures for the input and output of data such as files and strings, together with various formatting structures such that the entire input/output process of PL/1 can be regarded as being heavily influenced by both FORTRAN and COBOL practice. Any merit ascribable to the PL/1 approach lies in the wide range of options available for input/output. The particulars of format control, however, are inept and do not recommend themselves to a user-oriented approach. One of the interesting options available with PL/1 is the output command, an example of which is

```
PUT SKIP DATA (X,Y,Z);
```

where the values for X, Y, and Z are, respectively, 10, 20, 30 prior to the execution of the output statement. The actual output as a result of this statement would be

X = 10   Y = 20   Z = 30;

The word PUT means print; the sequence PUT SKIP means to start the printing at the start of a new line. One must wonder about the etymology of the words PUT SKIP when the equivalent *print newline* would have performed the same function and would have been self-explanatory. Symptoms such as that, evidenced in conventional language design, should make an analyst consider whether such design contains an element of psychopathology. In all fairness, we must mention that PL/1 also has key words READ and WRITE, where GET/PUT are used for what PL/1 terms to be *stream* input/output and *record* input/output. In our opinion, however, this does not resolve the obtuseness associated with PL/1 input/output language design.

It should also be noted that the simple PL/1 statement PUT LIST (X) will cause the printing of the value associated with the name *X* at the next "tab" position of the current print line. This sort of statement is highly dependent on the vagaries of the particular output device. The location of the tab positions may also be an implementation-defined characteristic; that is, different PL/1 compilers may use different columnar positions or may even include a language device to adjust the position of the tabs.

Another input capability available in PL/1 is that of identifying input data regardless of its actual sequence. For example, the statement

```
GET DATA (X,Y,Z);
```

would allow the input of data presented as X = 10, Y = 20, Z = 30 in any arbitrary order. The command

```
GET DATA;
```

will also have the same effect if the input stream is the same.

In general, for ALGOL-like languages, the input/output facilities are implementation-dependent, and "built-in" commands are usually primitive in the sense that READ will cause the inputting of the next character from the input device. Similarly, PRINT will cause the printing of one character on the output device. More versatile input/output commands are left to user-defined procedures (subroutines).

The historical attitude among some language designers toward input/output-format representation is that they regarded such considerations as outside the purview of programming languages. That attitude stems in part from a confusion between the format of *internal* blocks of data as recorded in main memory and auxiliary memory, such as magnetic tapes or magnetic disks. This confusion has given rise to the distinction, within a computer language structure, between *logical* records and so-called *physical* records. From our point of view, the actual internal formatting of data is not a concern to be addressed in any substantive sense in the language-design process. If anything, it is an implementation concern. For language designers, what is of importance is only whether their language designs are implementable in a reasonably efficient way. What we mean by input is the concrete manifestation of data prior to entry into the computer. Normally, that would mean data punched on cards (a medium now used infrequently), keyed into a keyboard device associated with a CRT, or directed into some auxiliary storage medium such as a magnetic tape or magnetic disk.

We are not concerned with the actual coding representation of data keyed into a CRT terminal or auxiliary storage device. Our concern is toward how the actual "keying in" is physically accomplished or, what is equivalent, how an image of that action may be represented so it can be treated as a *linguistic* object. With respect to output formatting, we are concerned with how the results of a computation and added information can be displayed so that they are clear, informative, and self-explanatory. From a language-design point of view, in the context of user-oriented criteria, the linguistic solution must be such as to minimize the artifice employed by the programmer. As far as possible, the linguistic format prescriptions should be consistent with the underlying specification language for a range of relevant application areas.

The problem here is somewhat akin to the concerns of some language designers in specifying how arrays are to be stored within internal memory, that is, whether they are to be stored rowwise or columnwise for two-dimensional arrays. Of course, n-dimensioned arrays for $n > 2$ present more complex representation problems, but that actually should be of no concern in the design of the language. The only aspect relevant to language design is the *order* in which specific elements are output or input, regardless of the actual storage implementation.

A User-Oriented Approach to Input/Output

As previously noted, the user should not be burdened with overspecification of the characteristics of the input. Rather, input should be of free-field format, where the decision as to what classification or type to allocate for incoming data can usually be made automatically in an implementation-efficient manner. Thus a language oriented toward numerical computation (this does not exclude dealing with names whose associated values may be alphanumeric strings) might allow the simple statement

```
READ A,B,C,D,E,F,G.
```

Directions to read a specific input device might take such forms as

READ FILE *<information associated with the number of elements to be read from the file, the name to be associated with this information, the number of the input device if relevant>*

Alternative READ statements that would be admissible are

```
READ Aᵢ FROM i = 1 UNTIL Aᵢ > 15.
READ Aᵢ,Bᵢ₊₁ FROM i = <expression> UNTIL Aᵢ = 45.16.
FROM i = 1 TO 10 READ Xᵢ.
FOR i = 1(1)50 AND k=0 BY 2 UNTIL Y>5000 READ Xᵢₖ, . . .
COMPUTE Y = 2Xᵢ,ₖ AND READ Q.
FROM i = 1 TO INFINITY READ Xᵢ, IF Xᵢ ≠ 10 THEN COMPUTE
Y = Y + Xᵢ, n = n + 2 OTHERWISE GO TO STATEMENT 1.
```

For individual data that lie outside the range of integer, fixed-point, floating-point, or alphanumeric strings, there should be little difficulty in defining analogous commands for appropriate application-oriented languages. Similarly, directions to process "files" can be engineered in a similar spirit that preserves the clarity and obvious meaning of those linguistic structures. However, for output, where display is an important consideration, there should be a range of output commands that give the programmer sufficient flexibility while still retaining the goal of clarity and *simplicity* of structure.

A simple (formatless) output statement is

```
PRINT A,X + Y,C,D.
```

or

```
PRINT X,y,Yi,SIN(Ti + Yi^2) FOR i = 1,2, . . . , N.
```

For a language designed for application areas that are dominated by numerical computations, it is convenient (but not necessary) to regard all internal numerical values as being in floating-point form. Therefore the preceding simple output statements would cause the output associated with the names that follow the PRINT command to be output in the same sequence as that accompanying the "print list," where the number of columns allocated to each floating-point datum across a line could either be specified by the language designer or be implementation-dependent for the actual output device. In any case, the advantage here for the programmer is a simple formatless output command. (We should also note in passing that the PRINT command may be replaced, as appropriate, by commands such as WRITE FILE.) Additional relatively simple output commands would be

```
PRINT x + y/z,a - b*c{I.F},p*q - d + e{I}.
```

or

$$\text{PRINT} \int_1^{10} \frac{\text{SINx}}{\text{x}}\,\text{dx}.$$

For these forms, each floating-point value associated with a name in the print list will again be output in prespecified fields (columns) of the line. However, those names succeeded by a set of braces of the form {I}, {I.F} will be printed as fixed-point numbers. The value input for the dummy parameter I indicates the number of places to the left of the decimal point of the fixed value associated with the preceding name (that is, the integer part). The value of the dummy parameter F indicates the number of places to the right of the decimal point for the value associated with the preceding name. A pair of braces containing only an I will cause printing of the integer nearest to the actual value. If it is considered desirable to retain the prespecified field width, the total value of I + F would not exceed a maximum value.

It is also understood that leading zeros would be suppressed. An alternative formalism might be *{f.d}* where *f* specifies the maximum field width of the output datum and *d* the number of digits (if any) to the right of the decimal point. The maximum number of names or expressions in a PRINT statement and the maximum width of the print field for each datum would be, of course, a function of the particular output device. The programmer must take into account the characteristics of the real world. The field of computing, in contradistinction to mathematics, cannot divorce itself from the concrete limitations of available machine architectures and the characteristics of available input/output devices. Certain output devices simply are not suitable for complex format display. For example, if the programmed output exceeds the normal line width of a printer, some printers will "wrap around" the excess output so that it appears on the next line, but other printers will simply *omit* the excess output with no warning indication whatsoever.

For applications requiring the output of columns of numerical results, it is convenient to print a heading. That could be done by using the aforementioned simplest form of the preceding PRINT statements, where the names in the print list have values that are the desired alphanumeric headings. An alternative capability would be given by a statement such as

```
PRINT LABEL NUMBER, A,X - Y + 1, SIGN A(J), STANDARD
DEV.
```

where the literals that occur after the key word LABEL will be printed in print-line fields corresponding to those of the previous print list. Again, the actual characters permitted, the maximum number of labels per statement, and the number of alphanumeric characters in a single literal string would be restricted by the capabilities of the actual output device. Acceptable synonyms for the key words PRINT LABEL would be

```
PRINT LABEL ≡ LABEL ≡ HEADING ≡ PRINT HEADING
```

We will discuss the advantages and disadvantages of using synonyms as key words in Chap. 8.

Complete control of the printing of a line representing a sequence of computed values and *program-specified* literals is given by

PRINT FORMAT <*label*> < * > { <*name*> | <*expression*> }
FORMAT <*label*> <*b*> < * > { <*placeholder*> | <*alphanumeric string*> }

The symbol <*b*> is one blank space. The symbol <*alphanumeric string*> includes any printable character (except a placeholder) *and* any blanks. As for the placeholder, since the use of CRT displays for programming is now almost universal, it is convenient to choose the "reverse-video" mode, that is, *white* characters on a *black* background for four special characters. We would choose the *reverse-video* characters: d . ± e

d . ± e

The symbol <*placeholder*> is a string containing only these possible characters. Thus the placeholder dddd (in reverse video) means that we want to print an integer not exceeding four digits at the *identical place* occupied in the format statement. The placeholder d.dd (in reverse video) means we want to print a fixed-point number allocating one digit to the left of the decimal point and two significant digits to the right of the decimal point at the *actual point* relative to the beginning of the format field, that is, one space after the <*label*>. The occurrence of the reverse-video e at the end of a placeholder field indicates that we want to output an *exponent* character of the exponent value of the floating-point value at that placeholder position. A reverse-video ± means that we want an *explicit* + or − symbol printed at that particular spot, preceding the value or its exponent.

An example of such a PRINT FORMAT sentence and its associated FORMAT sentence is shown in Fig. 5.1.

b=6.21 .

Print format 1 $a+b^2$, 2a, a^3b^4, a for a=2 to 7.

Format 1 a+b*b=dd.ddd and 2a=±ddd and a*a*a*b*b*b*b=±d.dddddeeee for a=dd .

Figure 5.1 Example of PRINT FORMAT command and linear format specification.

We have used a simple two-dimensional notation, principally exponents in the superscript position and implied multiplication, for the expressions in the PRINT FORMAT sentence. However, the FORMAT sentence is strictly linear. (We will subsequently illustrate a full-blown two-dimensional format structure called an IMAGE.)

The output of Fig. 5.1 is given in Fig. 5.2.

```
a+b*b=40.564 and 2a= +4. and a*a*a*b*b*b*b=+1.18975E+04 for a=2.
a+b*b=41.564 and 2a= +6. and a*a*a*b*b*b*b=+4.01541E+04 for a=3.
a+b*b=42.564 and 2a= +8. and a*a*a*b*b*b*b=+9.51801E+04 for a=4.
a+b*b=43.564 and 2a=+10. and a*a*a*b*b*b*b=+1.85899E+05 for a=5.
a+b*b=44.564 and 2a=+12. and a*a*a*b*b*b*b=+3.21233E+05 for a=6.
a+b*b=45.564 and 2a=+14. and a*a*a*b*b*b*b=+5.10106E+05 for a=7.
```

Figure 5.2 Output of the program of Fig. 5.1.

The first-occurring <*placeholder*> (string of reverse-video characters) controls the placement of the value of the first-mentioned name or expression in the PRINT FORMAT statement. The *n*th placeholder controls the placement of the value of the *n*th-mentioned name or expression in the referenced PRINT FORMAT statement. Each placeholder should be preceded by one extra reverse-video *d* if there is the possibility that the numerical value might be negative. However, if we have inserted a reverse-video ± as the first character of the placeholder, this extra reverse-video d is not necessary. Similarly, if there is a possibility that an exponent might be negative, we would use a reverse-video ± or an extra reverse-video e of the exponent placeholder.

We emphasize that *what will appear in the output will be exactly what appears in the program statements.* All literals will appear in the exact column position as they appear in the format statement relative to the beginning of the format field; all values will appear in exactly the columns designated by the reverse-video string of symbols. In the FORMAT illustrated in Fig. 5.1, the placeholder designating integer output contains an extra reverse-video d. This is forced because the output shown in Fig. 5.2 is produced by the two-dimensional programming system discussed in Chap. 8. This system translates acceptable two-dimensional text into FORTRAN as an intermediate stage. The implementation specifics of this translation interact with the FORTRAN compiler format protocol to cause a decimal point to be printed after an integer value. This idiosyncrasy for *linear* format specifications may be avoided by using the two-dimensional IMAGE format, which we will subsequently illustrate.

Consider a case where we want to display results grouped in sets of *n* lines, where each line requires a different format, that is, different literal strings and different placement of computed output values. Such a format would be relatively difficult to program on first try in a conventional language. Adopting the approach that we have suggested, however, the set of *n differing* output lines could be represented by *n* format statements, where the *last digit* of each format number is horizontally aligned as follows:

```
FORMAT 1  <format field>
FORMAT 2  <format field>
FORMAT 3  <format field>
 . . .
 . . .
 . . .
FORMAT n  <format field>
```

The initial point of each format field is aligned with all the others. When output, the strings of alphanumeric characters that represent the literals in each numbered format would have *exactly* the same relative position they have in the program proper. Likewise, computed values as called for in the PRINT FORMAT statements corresponding to each numbered FORMAT statement would appear, on output, in exactly the same position they do in the FORMAT statements marked by placeholders. *Thus there cannot be any programming error for the display of output. The debugging problem has been reduced to a matter of proofreading.* If the set of format statements (and associated print format statements) are *seen* to be correct, then (unless there is a system-implementation error or a hardware failure) there cannot be any error in the output display. We think that this is a striking example of how certain aspects of program correctness can be reduced, by proper language design, to an almost trivial consideration. This indicates that other innovations in language design can substantially reduce the problems of program incorrectness.

We submit the notion that a great deal of what is called the "software problem," in appropriate application domains, can be reduced and in certain cases eliminated by using those program structures that mimic the conventional structure and notation normally associated with specifications in a particular application area. This removes the burden from the programmer/user and puts it where it belongs—on the language designer and the programming-language system implementer. Essentially, our approach, given the considerations specific to an application area and taking the broadest possible view, is to *automate* the programming process by using appropriate linguistic structures and notational forms. Of course, in a philosophical vein, we admit that mathematical perfection is not possible in the real world of computing. It is appropriate to adopt a pragmatic view and hope to approach as closely as possible the limit of perfection, given real-world constraints.

A program that illustrates these points in more detail is shown in Fig. 5.3*a* and *b*.

The associated FORMAT *n* templates are also illustrated in Fig. 5.3; the corresponding output is shown in Fig. 5.4.

Of course, the prior PRINT FORMAT statement, if qualified by one of the FROM or FOR phrases, will cause sequential line printing controlled by the loop index. Also, the list of PRINT statements given could have been combined into *one* sentence by substituting a comma or the key word AND for all periods except the last. We listed only one sentence per line for pedagogic clarity, but more than one sentence (or fragment of a sentence) per line would interpret to the same program semantics and might be more convenient.

The concept of format spaceholders can be generalized for two-dimensional languages that allow two-dimensional input and output via hard-copy devices or CRT terminals. An example of a 2-D format is shown in Fig. 5.5. The first 2-D statement in Fig. 5.5 is analogous to the linear PRINT FORMAT statement, except that it is a PRINT IMAGE statement to indicate that it is a 2-D form. Essentially it iterates the computation for the values i = 2,3,4. The computational expression embedded in the PRINT IMAGE statement first computes the

Read EN, M, D, Y. Read a_i, b_i, c_i for i= 1 to 4 .
Read t, p, d. Read events, particles, mean2, variance2, calibration, mean5, variance5, Emean, Evariance, plate, reg. Read A_i for i=1 to 7 .

Print format 1 EN, M, D, Y. Skip 1 line.
Print format 2. Skip 1 line.
Print format 3 a_1, a_2, a_3, a_4.
Print format 4 b_1, b_2, b_3, b_4.
Print format 5 c_1, c_2, c_3, c_4.
Print format 6 t, p, d. Skip 1 line.
Print format 7. Skip 1 line.
Print format 8.
Print format 9.
Print format 10 EN.
Print format 11. Skip 1 line.
Print format 12 events.
Print format 13 particles.
Print format 14 mean2.
Print format 15 variance2.
Print format 16 calibration.
Print format 17 mean5.
Print format 18 variance5. Skip 1 line.
Print format 19 Emean.
Print format 20 Evariance. Skip 2 lines.
Print format 21 plate.
Print format 22 reg.
Print format 23 A_1, A_2, A_3, A_4, A_5, A_6, A_7.

Figure 5.3*a* First part of a linear format program.

```
Format  1            EXPERIMENT NUMBER:±ddd  DATE:±ddd/±ddd/±ddd .
Format  2                   INPUTS(CLASS PARAMETERS).
Format  3 INPUTS FOR ALPHA1=±ddd, ALPHA2=±ddd, ALPHA3=±ddd, ALPHA4=±ddd.
Format  4 INPUTS FOR  BETA1=±ddd,  BETA2=±ddd,  BETA3=±ddd,  BETA4=±ddd.
Format  5 INPUTS FOR GAMMA1=±ddd, GAMMA2=±ddd, GAMMA3=±ddd, GAMMA4=±ddd.
Format  6 THETA=±d.dddddd          PHI=±ddd         DELTA=±d.ddddddeeee.
Format  7                          OUTPUTS.
Format  8 (note that an asterisk   indicates that the calculation.
Format  9  may not be meaningful for the particular set of data).
Format 10 see separate data input list for experiment number ±ddd.
Format 11                     --------------------- .
Format 12         NUMBER OF EVENTS DETECTED=±ddddd .
Format 13                 DIFFERENT PARTICLES=  ±ddd .
Format 14 THE MEAN OF THE FIRST 200 EVENTS WAS ±d.ddddeeee .
Format 15 WITH A VARIANCE EQUAL TO ±d.ddeeee .
Format 16 (instrument calibration=±d.dd) .
Format 17 THE MEAN OF THE FIRST 500 EVENTS WAS ±d.ddddeeee .
Format 18 WITH A VARIANCE EQUAL TO ±d.ddddeeee .
Format 19 THE MEAN OF ALL EVENT WAS ±d.ddddeeee .
Format 20 WITH AN ASSOCIATED VARIANCE OF ±d.ddeeee .
Format 21               PLATE NUMBER ±ddd  .
Format 22               REG: ±ddddd  .
Format 23               ARRAY LIST ±ddd ±ddd ±ddd ±ddd ±ddd ±ddd ±ddd .
```

Figure 5.3*b* Second part of the linear format program, illustrating format alignment.

```
          EXPERIMENT NUMBER:15.  DATE:10./16./90.

               INPUTS(CLASS PARAMETERS)

INPUTS FOR ALPHA1=34., ALPHA2=39., ALPHA3=30., ALPHA4=35.
INPUTS FOR  BETA1=23.,  BETA2=24.,  BETA3=26.,  BETA4=27.
INPUTS FOR GAMMA1=54., GAMMA2=48., GAMMA3=40., GAMMA4=42.
THETA=1.936534            PHI=17.          DELTA=+7.81347E+05

                           OUTPUTS

(note that an asterisk   indicates that the calculation
 may not be meaningful for the particular set of data)
see separate data input list for experiment number 15.
                 -------------------

       NUMBER OF EVENTS DETECTED=4965.
             DIFFERENT PARTICLES=  14.
THE MEAN OF THE FIRST 200 EVENTS WAS +4.5238E+04
WITH A VARIANCE EQUAL TO +1.32E+02
(instrument calibration=11.45)
THE MEAN OF THE FIRST 500 EVENTS WAS +4.6003E+04
WITH A VARIANCE EQUAL TO +1.2945E+02

THE MEAN OF ALL EVENT WAS +4.5789E+04
WITH AN ASSOCIATED VARIANCE OF +1.30E+02


            PLATE NUMBER 49.
            REG: 4984.
            ARRAY LIST 45. 38. 23. 67. 45. 56. 48.
```

Figure 5.4 Output of the program of Fig. 5.3.

for i:=2 to 4 print image 1,i,i, $\int_0^i \frac{e^{-iz}\mathrm{SINH}^{-1}\frac{z}{2}}{z^5+\frac{1}{2}}dz$,i,i, $\sum_{r=1}^{i} r^i$,i, $\sqrt{i}$

----- -----

image 1 $\int_0^{\#} \frac{e^{-\#z}\ \mathrm{SINH}^{-1}\frac{z}{2}}{z^5+\frac{1}{2}}dz = \#.dddddd \quad \sum_{r=1}^{\#} r^{\#} = ddd \quad \sqrt{\#} = \#.ddd*10^3$

Figure 5.5 A two-dimensional PRINT IMAGE and its IMAGE template.

(same) value of *i* twice, then it computes the same value of *i* as the upper limit of the specified integral in the figure.

The expression then computes again the (same) value of *i* in the exponent of e, then *i* twice again, *i* again as the upper limit of the summation, again the value of *i* as the exponent of *r*, *i* again, and finally *i* as the argument of the square root. In this figure, the subsequent statement is the *format statement* (template) designated as IMAGE 1, analogous to the linear FORMAT 1 statement. What follows in that 2-D construction, which is the field of the IMAGE statement, are not expressions, assignment statements, or computational imperatives. Rather, they are *pictures* or, perhaps more appropriately, *images*. Embedded in these pictures, in various places, are strings of reverse-video d's (or single occurrences of same) with reverse-video decimal points either omitted or located within or at the boundaries of a string of reverse-video d's. The reverse-video d's serve the identical function of placeholders as they did in the previous linear FORMAT statements. The major difference here is that they are related to each other not just in a left-to-right manner, but also in terms of their *vertical* spacing. They indicate where the values computed in the 2-D list following the key words PRINT IMAGE are to be placed, where the priority of placement of a computed value—in the case where two different placeholders occupy the same horizontal position but different vertical positions—is to be given to the uppermost placeholder. Otherwise, the sequence precedence is the same as that for the linear FORMAT statement. The constructions noted in Fig. 5.6 are the *output* of the previous (2-D) program. The associated values of *i* and the computed values of the names given in the field of the PRINT IMAGE statement are placed within each picture at the place signified by the placeholders in the IMAGE statement. Since the PRINT IMAGE statement is controlled by the loop qualifier FROM i = 2 to 4, the picture is repeated three times. In each repetition of the picture, different values are output as the computation cycles through the appropriate values of *i*. Exponent values are output exactly where the reverse-video e's were placed in the IMAGE template.

Figure 5.7 illustrates the *same* PRINT IMAGE sentence and its *different* IMAGE template. Figure 5.8 is the output of that program. These figures emphasize the concept that the IMAGE template is a "picture," or two-dimensional format, which may be output repetitively under the control of a FOR loop. In other words, the integral symbols of Fig. 5.5 are *operators* but the integral symbols of Fig. 5.6 are *pictures* of integrals, not operators. This point is stressed by Fig. 5.7, which uses a different IMAGE template *for the same computation*. Each picture contains a different set of computed values correspond-

----- -----

$$\int_0^2 \frac{e^{-2z}\,\mathrm{SINH}^{-1}\frac{z}{2}}{z^5+\frac{1}{2}}\,dz = .12922 \qquad \sum_{r=1}^{2} r^2 = 5 \qquad \sqrt{2} = 1.414{*}10^0$$

----- -----

$$\int_0^3 \frac{e^{-3z}\,\mathrm{SINH}^{-1}\frac{z}{2}}{z^5+\frac{1}{2}}\,dz = .07884 \qquad \sum_{r=1}^{3} r^3 = 36 \qquad \sqrt{3} = 1.732{*}10^0$$

----- -----

$$\int_0^4 \frac{e^{-4z}\,\mathrm{SINH}^{-1}\frac{z}{2}}{z^5+\frac{1}{2}}\,dz = .05161 \qquad \sum_{r=1}^{4} r^4 = 354 \qquad \sqrt{4} = 2.000{*}10^0$$

Figure 5.6 Output of the program of Fig. 5.5.

for i:=2 to 4 print image 1,i,i, $\int_0^i \frac{e^{-iz}\mathrm{SINH}^{-1}\frac{z}{2}}{z^5+\frac{1}{2}}\,dz$,i,i, $\sum_{r=1}^{i} r^i$,i, $\sqrt{i}$.

Image 1

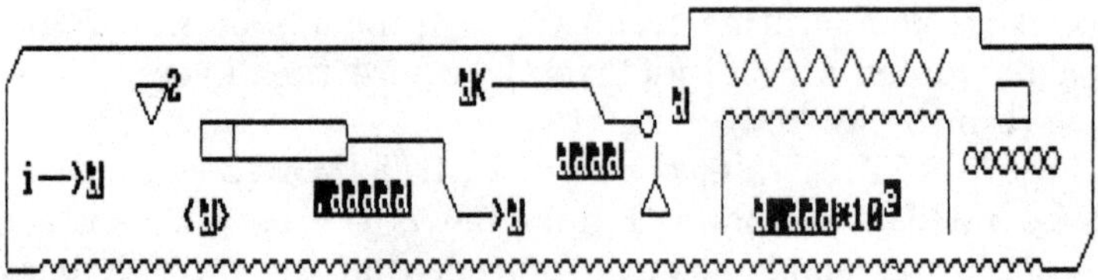

i—>

K

dddd

.dddddd

dddd*10

Figure 5.7 The same PRINT IMAGE as in Fig. 5.5, but using a different IMAGE template.

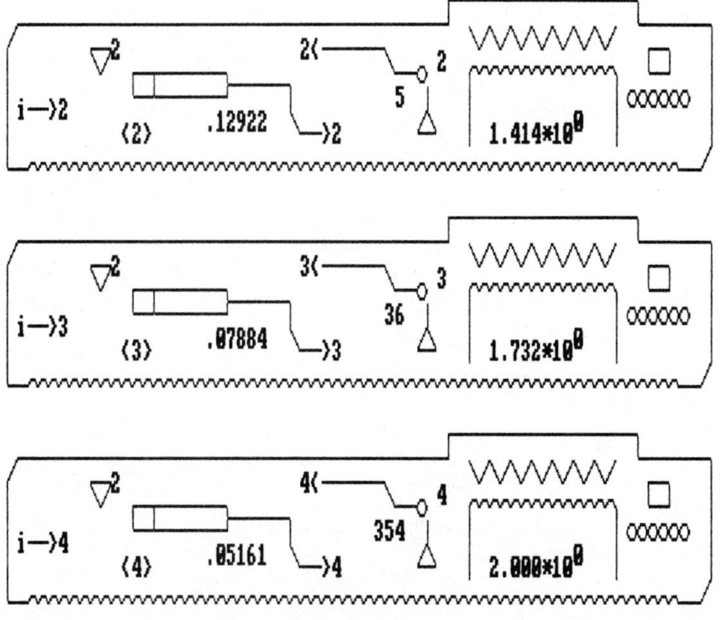

Figure 5.8 Output of the program of Fig. 5.7.

ing to the values of the variables/expressions that are executed in each cycle of the PRINT IMAGE clause.

Given the versatility now available from commercial hard-copy input/output devices and CRT-type terminals with programmable character generators, program-format structures of the form we have illustrated are not only appropriate, they are extremely powerful for the generation of complex output displays. As we shall indicate in Chap. 8, these 2-D formatting techniques can be extended for the editing of complex 2-D programs or complex mathematical text and also used for the automatic typesetting of nonlinearized mathematical text. More importantly, they permit the entering of programs using conventional (textbook) mathematical notation. For specifications dominated by numerical computation, this permits the direct *copying* of a mathematical formula straight from a textbook—lessening, to a major extent, the need for explicit applications programming.

Chapter

6

Declarations, Types, and Scopes

Many linguistic mechanisms have been used in the design of computer languages. One cannot evaluate the usefulness of the different mechanisms unless one has an explicit goal for the usage of a computer language. Our viewpoint is that the goal of programming, using a computer language, is to reduce the given (well-formulated) solution specification of a problem to a program, that is, to a form executable by the hardware-software machine. Since programming is a human activity, regarded as work in the economic sense, the evaluation must be based on minimizing the extent of work. In terms of time or cost expended, that involves translation from a solution specification to a program in computer language, the indirect costs ascribable to the activity of the machine used to translate the program from the computer-language text into its computationally equivalent machine-language text (if there is a difference between texts), and the cost of the execution of that program by the machine. For the case of a software-hardware machine that *efficiently* processes the input computer language text and *efficiently* executes the input program, the concept of work minimization applies principally to the process of translating the solution specification into a computer-language program. Thus the automation of programming is the primary goal of language design, except in those instances where the indirect costs associated with translation-software implementation and necessarily inefficient machine execution counteract that goal.

Historically, automation of programming has not been the prevailing goal of language design. Rather, the design of many conventional languages has been influenced by the desire to achieve a practical or theoretical simplicity of compiler or interpreter implementation. Additionally, there has been an emphasis on efficiency of compiler translation or interpreter execution for some languages, as a function of specific machine architecture. The desire for theoretical completeness has also played a role when the language has been considered in terms of a mathematical model. Underlying many of these considerations, although not always explicitly expressed, has been the aesthetic assumption that programming is in itself a rewarding intellectual experience and that certain linguistic forms and programming procedures can be considered more "beautiful" than others. The rôle of aesthetics in the historical design of languages should not be discounted or minimized, nor should the advocacy of programming style as an aesthetic criterion be overlooked. Our point of view is primarily from an engineering perspective in that it is concerned with those economic metrics relevant to user efficiency.

Specific languages differ widely in terms of their levels, ranging from low level (for example, machine language) to high level (for example, Ada), and may have sharply different goals (for example, system-programming capability, as in the language C, or simplicity, as in BASIC). In this chapter, we will discuss declarations, storage, type, binding, and scope as used for various languages and examine their utility and consistency specifically as design criteria for user-oriented languages. It is not our purpose to consider these concepts as universal truths applicable to all languages or to a universal language. We consider language design to be a strong function of the application domain and the class characteristics of the set of intended users.

Storage Declarations

In most programming languages, various sorts of "declarations" are required. A declaration is a program statement that does not directly result in executable machine code. Instead, it gives the compiler information to use, either to structure the machine-code representation of the translated program or for internal "housekeeping." The housekeeping arrangements are those associated with the management of storage space for data and the manipulation of various sorts of tables that are adjunct to the translation and compilation process and with the checking of "type," as discussed in the next section. A common kind of declaration is that associated with the reservation of storage for data. One of the characteristics of FORTRAN-like languages is that they perform storage allocation during the compilation process and not during execution of the program.

ALGOL-like languages defer storage allocation to when the program is run so that storage for variables and other program attributes can be allocated and reallocated during actual execution of the program. As a somewhat related consideration, ALGOL normally requires that declarations appear at the beginning of a block. However, it is interesting that the official revised report of ALGOL 60 states that "(4.4.1 Syntax) *<program>* :: = *<block>* | *<compound statement>*" and the associated syntax and examples for compound statements indicate that declarations need not be included.

COBOL also requires that declarations associated with data attributes appear in the "Data Division" of the COBOL program.

In FORTRAN, the naming of a simple variable (that is, an unsubscripted variable name) does not require a specific declaration. Storage is automatically reserved and associated with that name. The naming of a subscripted variable, however, requires a prior declaration explicitly indicating how much storage should be reserved for that *array* name. For example, if there is a variable $a_{i,j}$, where $i = 1, 2, \ldots, 10$ and $j = 1, 2, \ldots, 40$, FORTRAN would require the statement

```
DIMENSION A (10,40)
```

to appear prior to the first appearance of the variable *A* (*I, J*). This causes the compiler to reserve 400 units of storage for the variable *A* (*I, J*) and also assigns to the variable *A* the *type value* of *array*. Whether the assignment of a type value is an operationally distinct aspect of the compiler implementation depends on the prominence assigned to type distinctions by a specific language.

The restrictions on DIMENSION-like declarations are specific to the particular language. For example, in FORTRAN the declaration

```
DIMENSION X(Y)
```

limits *Y* to be an explicit integer in some dialects and a single character variable name, with additional restrictions, in other dialects. When *Y* is used as a variable name, it must be known at compile time. However, when *Z* is a *subscript* in a *reference* to *X*(*Z*), the *Z* is limited to the form $A * I \pm B$, where *A* and *B* are explicit integers and *I* is a variable of *type* integer. ALGOL permits expressions for the array (dimension) declaration bounds, as well as unrestricted linear expressions for subscripts.

In certain dialects of FORTRAN, the commitment to "appropriate" programming style is emphasized by the stricture that not only should there be a DIMENSION declaration appearing before the first occurrence of the array variable name, but also that this declaration should appear at the beginning of the program, before any other statements. For instance, in the FORTRAN dialect WATFIV, the use of a DIMENSION declaration somewhere in the middle of a program, prior to the first textual reference to the argument of the DIMENSION declaration, would, in many implementations, result in a message to the user that a stylistic error has occurred, because all DIMENSION declarations should appear at the beginning of the program. From an implementation point of view, whether a DIMENSION statement appears at the beginning of the program or somewhat later, as long as it is prior to the first instance of its referenced argument, is of little matter in terms of efficiency or ease. All storage assignment is done before the actual program is executed, and many efficient techniques exist for the extension of storage as various portions of the program are compiled. Thus this is an example of a rule that has no purpose other than to force an aesthetic criterion on the programmer. For someone who tends to program intuitively, that is, develop a program without a prior outline, that rule is not only an unnecessary burden, but one that makes the programming process more prone to error. (Of course, an intuitive programming style is not currently in favor.) In any case, our position leads us to ask two questions:

1. Are declarations of array storage necessary for the case of *static* storage allocation, where storage is assigned prior to the execution of the program?
2. Are they desirable for compilation efficiency in the mode of static assignment of storage prior to program run time?

We can deal with the answer to question 1 in the following way. For a static program, that is, a program where all the data that will influence the amount of storage necessary for the program is known, one can write an explicit DIMENSION statement such as DIMENSION A (10,20) because somewhere in the program there is a statement indicating that the subscripts associated with the array variable A run from 1 through 10 and from 1 through 20.

In a FORTRAN-like language, one could not have the program fragment

```
READ N
DIMENSION A(N)
```

since the amount of storage necessary for the array variable A will not be known until the program is actually executed and the value of N is input (although this stricture is relaxed in FORTRAN 90). That requires *dynamic* storage allocation and is not considered in this discussion. All languages that require the static allocation of storage prior to execution and that require declarations to assign the relevant amount of storage assume that such information is contained within the program. That is equivalent to saying that the DIMENSION declaration, for any specific variable, is determined by the explicit textual structure of the program. If this were not so, that is, if the range of each subscript associated with a specific array variable was not explicitly given within the program text, then that program would be either inconsistent or incomplete.

The designers of such languages historically have assigned to the programmer the task of specifying the relevant DIMENSION declaration statement after examining the specific program-text flow. Since the determination of such a DIMENSION declaration depends specifically on an examination of the specific range allocated to subscripts, it would appear that insertion of DIMENSION statements within a program is not a necessary task of programming. Since the process of constructing DIMENSION declarations can be visualized as an algorithmic process, there is no reason why that process cannot be automated and assigned to the compiler as an additional housekeeping task in the compilation process.

Our second question about declaration of array storage concerns whether such an automated process, operating within the compilation process, can be done efficiently without excess economic expense. It turns out that for languages that require explicit specification of the subscript range (certainly this is a requirement of all conventional languages that are bound to static storage allocation), the automatic production of DIMENSION declarations can be done in a straightforward and efficient manner. The gist of the method is to use continuously updated tables of all names used with subscripts and all subscripts used as indices within explicit or implicit loops of the program. This housekeeping function can be done simultaneously with the other processes necessary for compilation, accommodates the goal of one-pass compilation, and does not add substantially to the cost of compilation.

The case of storage allocation for the same index i used as a subscript for different array names, for example, A_i, B_i, C_i, does not offer any special difficulty in the assignment of appropriate storage with respect to each array variable, when the range of the index i changes during the program-text development. For example, consider the FORTRAN loop

```
   DO 25 I = 1,10
25 A(I)  = I**2
```

From a straightforward scan of the program segment, it is quite clear that at this point the amount of storage space reserved for the array variable A must be at least 10 locations associated with the variables A (1), A (2),..., A (10). At later points in the program text, the amount of storage associated with the variable A may be increased if its loop index ranges beyond the previous maximum of 10. While most conventional languages have made the design decision to *require* an explicit DIMENSION-like declaration for the mode of static storage allocation, such a decision cannot be justified on the basis of either necessity or implementation efficiency and thus must be grounded in other considerations. But we should add a note of caution: It may be possible to construct *specific* linguistic structures, usually low level, where *straightforward* local analysis may not yield an unambiguous storage allocation. In such cases, a compiler-initiated request for more information is appropriate, or detailed program-flow analysis may be initiated. Aside from such exceptional cases, we can conclude that the generation of storage declarations can be automated, thus making such declarations largely unnecessary for programming using a very high level language.

Type Declarations

The other major use of declarations is to associate a discrete type value with a name. These type values may be a predefined set of values of the computer language or associated with a name as defined by the user. Thus, in PASCAL the declaration

```
var x: integer;
```

will cause the allocation of storage for the name *x,* as well as an implementation appropriate to variable values that are integers. In a PASCAL program, every variable occurring in a statement must be declared, and the declaration must precede the first instance of the variable in the text and must be accompanied by a type specification. In PASCAL, predefined data types are boolean, integer, real, and char (character). An entity of type boolean can assume one of only two values, *false,* or *true.* The values assumed by entities of type char would be the characters available for any particular implementation, usually the alphabetic characters, the digits 0 through 9, and the character for a blank. An example of a user-defined *scalar* type might be

```
type color = (white, red, blue, yellow, black);
```

While PASCAL allows new types to be defined by declaration and their sets of allowed values to be explicitly enumerated, as in the preceding example, these values cannot be read or written directly. Instead, they must, on input, be represented by values of one of the primitive types, such as boolean, integer, real, or char, and then converted internally. In the example, the values enumerated in the type declaration, "white," "red," and so on, are regarded as identifiers that denote the values of the *ordered* set associated with the type color. ALGOL 68 also allows both user-defined and language-defined *type* declarations. It makes a distinction between the type of *values* that may be assigned to a variable and the type characteristic of the name of a variable in its role as a *reference* to a data object in memory of that type. References are also used to construct pointers, which are new types. This results in programs that may contain type errors due to abstruse referencing and dereferencing rules.

Data types in PASCAL can be quite complex, but they must be built up from standard scalar types (for example, integer, real, boolean, or char) or from simple (unstructured) types defined by the programmer. *Structured types* are composed of other simpler scalar types and are functions of the type(s) of the components of the structure and the way the entity is composed. For example, an array is a structured type that consists of a fixed number of components, each of which is of the same type. Each array component may be addressed by the array name and its subscripts, that are of type *index*. Other structured types are *record* types, *set* types, *file* types, and *pointer* types.

The usual rationale given for such complex typing attributes in a programming language (for example, Ada) is that the specification of type

1. Simplifies the implementation of the program
2. Allows the compiler to check the type compatibility of operators and arguments before the program is executed
3. Improves the program readability and assures the correctness of the program by enforcing a stylistic discipline on the programmer
4. Makes program maintenance easier, since proper typing enhances program self-documentation

Unfortunately, there is at present no substantial experimental verification for such claims. Nor do the claims appear to be plausible. The requirements for *detailed* typing (for example, integer, real, floating point, fixed point) divided into subtypes or mutually exclusive types and the requirement for *complete* and *explicit* declarations for all program variables enforce a large set of constraints on any moderately complex program. In principle, the consistency of such constraints, *if applied correctly,* will enforce some aspects of program correctness. But the process of *constructing* a program, in the sense that such construction is a mental process, will be hindered by the psychological difficulty of constructing program elements consistent with such detailed distinctions. The little that is known about the psychology of programming would lead us to believe that minimizing the distinction between program elements is psychologically less error-prone than a mental process that must continuously enforce a rigid consistency in a complex way as the program text is being written. The use of highly detailed typing along with complete declarations would seem to put an unnecessary burden on the programmer when the same goals can be accomplished more efficiently with techniques that automate programming at little sacrifice in compilation or run-time costs. Of course, the ultimate resolution between the two approaches must come from the accumulation of more experimental evidence bearing on the desirability of each programming style.

The notion that everything must be declared is based on the view that program semantics can be completely encompassed by an abstract model that is consistent and complete. Thus the explicit declaration of the existence of a program variable is also an explicit linkage (reference) of the name of the variable to a location that itself is linked to a value that may be stored at that location. While the concepts of "location" and "value" can be defined abstractly, their utility lies in the connection to the underlying assumptions of conventional machine architecture. In our opinion, however, these concepts will prove to be abstruse for forthcoming architectures that are not conventional.

Another argument advanced for the necessity of complete, explicit declarations is that they avoid spelling errors. This is an example of an occurrence that can be regarded as pathological being substituted for what is normal. It is equivalent to saying that if something can happen, then it *will* happen. Such reasoning is inappropriate without empirical evidence to show that the frequency of the predicted occurrence is not negligible. Of course, such evidence would depend not only on the particular language but also on the entire programming environment. Similarly, one of the arguments for obligatory declarations of type for all program variables is that, for the case of static typing, errors can be detected during program compilation. The implicit basis for that argument is the assumption that type errors and operations on inconsistent types are frequent and important. But again, there is no substantial empirical evidence to support such an assumption. Highly detailed type-specification requirements in a programming language raise the level of technical competency necessary for the programming process and, as argued previously, may increase programming error. As an illustration, suppose we declare

```
REAL X, Y, Z, A
INTEGER I, J
```

for a language that forbids mixing types in expressions on the right side of assignments. Suppose

```
X = 0.992
Y = 21.623
I = 5
```

just before the execution of the assignment

```
Z = X + Y + I
```

in some program fragment. Clearly such an assignment is "illegal" or "incorrect" under the language type rules we have assumed. Seriousness about the type characteristics would require that the compiler reject this program fragment as incorrect. However, FORTRAN languages, while encompassing explicit or implicit type differentiation for numerical data, will usually resolve such type inconsistencies by rules of conversion specific to the context. For example, the assignment

```
A = I
```

would give A the value 5.0, whereas the assignment

```
J = X
```

would give J the value 0, since FORTRAN truncates a real number when converting to an integer-type number. Further, consider the program

```
INTEGER I, J, K, L
I = 9
J = 5
K = 45
L = I/J * K
```

A FORTRAN program would assign the value 45 to L, since integer division results in truncation of the real result. ALGOL distinguishes between / and ÷ . The former operator specifies that division always yields a real-type value irrespective of the operand type, while the latter is equivalent to integer division in the FORTRAN sense. Also, the diadic operators +, −, and *, will yield a value of *real* type if both of their operands are not integers. Conversion from *real* type to *integer* type is accomplished by the standard function *entier* (E), which assigns a value that is the largest integer not greater than the value of E.

The difficulty is clear in the case of assigning type attributes to numerical values. Historically, there has been an implementation advantage for distinguishing between integers and real numbers, which were further distinguished by fixed-point type (real numbers not in floating point) and floating-point type values that explicitly carried the value of the exponents used to increase the range of the number by multiplying the number by some numerical base (for example, 10) raised to that exponent. Current hardware speeds and advances in understanding implementation techniques make such distinctions less justifiable in accepting a relatively small increase in run-time efficiency in the interest of decreased type complexity. Certainly, in the previous example, there is nothing wrong with forming the sum

$$Z = 0.992 + 21.623 + 5$$

as an assignment. Yet some have argued that the first plus operator is distinct from the second plus operator, because the first plus symbol adds two real numbers and the second plus symbol adds a real number to an integer. Such a distinction makes no pragmatic difference. If one were to take this distinction seriously, one would have to have one kind of add operator for integers, a different operator symbol for real numbers, and a third for operands of different types. One could also argue that an operator for fixed-point values should be different from that for floating-point values. (FORTRAN does make this distinction between fixed point and floating point for input/output data.) The symbol - is commonly used both as a monadic *negation* operator (as in $y = -a$) and as a diadic *subtraction* operator (as in $y = a - b$) without causing ambiguity. However, a consistent application of the philosophy of complete typing might require that different symbols be used for what are different operators.

For numerical types, one possible solution to the problem is to regard all numerical values as being of the same type. After all, from a theoretical standpoint, integers are a subset of the reals, and the difference between fixed point and floating point is really not one of type (although so treated in FORTRAN-like languages), but rather one of *representation,* which need appear only on the level of input or output. As indicated in Chap. 5, there is no substantive problem in the representation of values as integer, fixed point, or floating point, to a specified precision on the program levels of input and output. For implementation, one could, in principle, do *all* arithmetic operations in floating point, with appropriate conversion for input/output representations or for specific internal evaluations such as for values used as subscripts. With modern hardware, the decrease in execution efficiency would be more than compensated for by the large increase in program simplicity. And with future hardware architectures, we foresee the tradeoff of execution efficiency for program simplicity to be even more narrow. Of course, declarations are required where multiple-precision arithmetic operations are desirable. But this is not a question of data-type declarations functioning as a language classification. Execution of multiple-precision operations are much less efficient timewise than single-precision arithmetic, unless performed by specific hardware designed for efficient floating-point arithmetic.

In this case, there is a pragmatically justified reason for making a distinction as to specifically how the arithmetic operation should be implemented, but there is no distinction as to type because the data values belong to a different set. The distinction between multiple precision and single precision is more like different subroutine calls than different type declarations. For example, let

```
A = 1234
```

```
B = 5673
C = A*B  = 7000482
D = 4321
E = 1620
F = D*E  = 7000020
G = C - F = 462
```

If this calculation is done in single precision, floating point on hardware where single precision, floating point is equivalent to a four-decimal digit representation, the result for G would be 0. We have not changed type, but we have lost numerical precision because of the *subtraction* of two nearly equal numbers. A different set of input for A, B, D, and E might produce a result to the same degree of precision as the input values.

Another reason given for the necessity for explicit declarations is that full checking for consistency is possible only if all attributes of program entities are declared. Again, the underlying assumption is that software error is primarily due to type inconsistency, a dubious conclusion that is unsupported by any substantial empirical evidence.

It is also interesting to note that conventional architecture does not support the concept of type. Everything stored in memory, whether data or instructions, is a bit string. Operators can be classified as different types, such as fixed-point addition and floating-point addition, but that is saying no more than that different operators do different things. Thus, on the hardware level, instructions can be added to data and the result executed as an instruction. Whether this is useful depends on the specific context of the situation. (For example, the addition of data to instructions is sometimes used to simulate the operation of an index register.) Permitting such type mixing into a programming language, however, would destroy any possibility of a meaningful concept of data type.

More generally, a declaration provides the name of a program entity (the name of a variable is one such entity) and associates it with a set of attributes, such as required storage, or some type of classification that may assume either a predefined or user-defined set of values. The process of associating attributes with a program entity is known as *binding* that entity to its attributes. Type attributes can be bound not only to the names of variables, they can also be bound to operators, for example, boolean operators such as AND or OR. In the case of PASCAL, types can also be composite in the sense that a name can be declared to be both of type *array* and of type *boolean*. As we have indicated by previous example, however, conversion between types can add to semantic complexity, as in the conversion between *real* and *integer*. But binding need not be explicit. For example, in FORTRAN, explicit declarations of type can be avoided simply by the use of a particular form for a variable name. If the first character of a name, is I,

J, K, L, M, or N, then type INTEGER is assigned to it; otherwise, type REAL is assigned.

For PL/1, type is simply one of the many attributes associated with the name of a variable. PL/1 supports a default mechanism to supply attributes when they are not explicitly declared in a program. Default resolution thus tends to be complex in various PL/1 dialects, since the actual attributes assigned may be influenced by the context in which the variable appears or by the first letter of the name of the variable. For PL/1, the declaration of storage attributes is even more complicated. One can declare the attribute STATIC, which will reserve storage for a named variable during compilation. A declaration of AUTOMATIC will allocate storage for a named variable upon entry to the relevant block and free such storage on exit from the block. The declaration CONTROLLED allows programmer control over storage allocation. The program command ALLOCATE will assign storage to the named variable at that point of program flow, and the command FREE will free storage at that particular point of program flow, for the variables that are arguments of these commands. The actual effects of these commands, however, are linked to other attributes and their default rules. An example illustrating that declarations in PL/1 are more complex than just simple declarations of type is

```
DECLARE C CHARACTER (23) INITIAL ('THIRTEEN');
```

In the example, the first item after the key word DECLARE is the name of the variable, and the next attribute indicates that it is of type *character* and of length 23, with an initial value equal to the string 'THIRTEEN'.

For ALGOL-like languages, *declarations* such as

real x

imply that the name x references a storage location for real numbers. Thus, although declarations are usually said to be "nonexecutable," this type of declaration substantially affects the semantics of the executed program. Thus the *assignments*

```
A = 2
B = A
```

would associate the value 2 with the name A and the name B; that is, separate copies of the value 2 would be assigned as values to A and B. However, a language that also permitted a user-defined *definition*

```
B ≡ A
```

would cause the reference to storage of A and B to be the same and thus raise the possibility of type inconsistency between A and B. To avoid this, such languages have highly restrictive rules for the use of definitions. Consider the declarations

```
type x: character string
x = 3.1415927
```

While the assignment

```
z = 2 * x
```

appears simple, its meaning is ambiguous in a language that differentiates such types by explicit declaration. Similarly, consider a language where B is of type boolean, with implementable values being the one-bit string 0 or 1. While the assignment

```
x = x + B
```

may be simple, it is nonetheless ambiguous as a program statement.

The point we want to make is that in conventional languages that require explicit declarations of variables and particularly the explicit declaration of type, such differentiation acts to make a strong association between a name and the *reference* to the hardware storage of the values(s) to be associated with that name. In our own use of the term *name,* we avoid even an implicit linkage to a hardware reference, since we are concerned with language design that leaves open the possibility of implementation on other than von Neumann architectures.

The excess use of the typing mechanism in the explicit generation of attributes to be linked with names also constrains machines from being independent of language design. It should be recognized that a declaration such as *real X* is logically redundant if somewhere in the program there is an assignment of the form X = 2.3, since the right side of the assignment strongly implies that X is a "real variable." The set of statements

```
INTEGER X
X = 2.3
```

is, strictly speaking, a logical contradiction. Many programming languages, however, will execute the assignment by truncating 2.3 to the integer 2. Logically, the problem can be resolved by recognizing that the declaration INTEGER X has the actual semantics: "Truncate X to an integer if it is otherwise," assuming that there is no strong type distinction between integer and real values. Even in instances where type distinction is desired, explicit declarations may not be necessary, because the type can be inferred from the context or the implicit form of name.

Ambiguity can also be resolved by a default mechanism, such as in PL/1, that assumes a canonical form unless explicitly specified or there is feedback from the user/programmer in cases of inherent ambiguity. For example, in COBOL the type attributed to most elements is implicitly determined by their PICTURE specification, as noted in Chap. 5. For most languages, the definition of procedures, subroutines, or functions or the distinction between a MAIN program and a subprogram are, in effect, *declarations,* since they tell the compiler to process a particular program text segment in a special way that is reflected in a specific mode of execution at program run time. Treatises on programming languages are replete with statements regarding the enhancement of implementation efficiency through the use of explicit declarations. Many of these arguments assume only one relatively efficient implementation option, whereas there may, in fact, be many options that are equally, if not more, efficient.

The programming language Ada, sponsored by the U.S. Department of Defense, is characterized by a rich and complex set of declaration and type differentiations with stylistic similarity to PASCAL. Declarations are categorized as object declarations (which include variable declarations and constant declarations), number declarations, type declarations, subtype declarations, subprogram declarations, package declarations, task declarations, exception declarations, and renaming declarations. An example of a variable declaration is

```
ALPHA,BETA : INTEGER;
```

An example of a constant declaration is

```
BOUND : constant INTEGER := 5000;
```

A number declaration might be

```
PI : constant := 3.14159;
```

Ada emphasizes the notion of type. The language's philosophy interprets type as characterizing a set of values that objects of that type may assume and the set of operations that may be performed on them. It justifies the extensive and elaborate use of type declarations and concomitant restrictions as serving various important programming purposes. This philosophy stresses that the goal of program maintainability is substantially enhanced, because type declaration allows for the collection of knowledge about the common properties of objects; thus the type name can be used to refer to these common properties when program objects are declared. A change of properties has only to be effected at a single point of the program text, that is, by changing the type declaration. This view stresses that type characterization separates the abstract or external properties of programming objects and programming operations from the underlying internal implementation-dependent properties characterized by a specific machine architecture. The claim is that such separation aids in the programming of disjoint sections of program text that are produced and maintained by different programmers and separately compiled. The claim is also made that explicit typing enhances program reliability, readability, and security; the spirit motivating this approach depends heavily on the presumed experience with PASCAL.

Type and subtype declarations are further divided into several classes. *Scalar* types are types whose values have no components; they include types defined by enumeration of their values, integer types, and various kinds of real types. *Array* and *record* types are composites since their values consist of several component values. An *access* type is one whose values provide access to other data objects. There are also so-called *private* types, which are known to users only by name; *discriminants,* whose values distinguish alternative forms of values of these types; and the set of associated operations. The set of possible values of a *private* type is defined but not available to the user. The set of possible values of any object of a given type can be restricted by the use of a *constraint.* A value is restricted to a *subtype* of a given type if it is controlled by such a constraint. The given type is called the *base type* of the subtype. A type is also its own subtype and its own *base type.* Also, certain types may have *default initial values* defined either for the objects of the type or for some of their components. Examples of type and subtype declarations given by the Ada programming-language standard of 1980 are

```
type COLOR is (WHITE, RED, YELLOW, GREEN, BLUE, BROWN,
BLACK);
type COL_NUM is range 1 . . 72;
type TABLE is array (1 . . 10) of INTEGER;
subtype RAINBOW is COLOR range RED . . BLUE;
subtype RED_BLUE is RAINBOW;
subtype ZONE is COL_NUM range 1 . . 6;
```

In Ada, separate type definitions, even if textually identical, are treated as distinct types. For example, the declarations

```
A : array (1 . . 10) of BOOLEAN;
B : array (1 . . 10) of BOOLEAN;
```

define A and B as distinct types, while the declaration

```
C, D : array (1 . . 10) of BOOLEAN;
```

defines C and D as being of the same type.

Enumeration types define an ordered set of distinct values, as in

```
type DAY is (MONDAY, TUESDAY, WEDNESDAY, THURSDAY,
```

```
FRIDAY, SATURDAY, SUNDAY);
type HEXA is ('A', 'B', 'C', 'D', 'E', 'F');
subtype WEEKDAY is DAY range MONDAY . . FRIDAY;
```

Types can also have attributes such as successor values and predecessor values. A predefined enumeration type is that of BOOLEAN, which has the literal values FALSE and TRUE with the ordering relationship FALSE < TRUE. An example of an integer-type declaration would be

```
type PAGE_NUM is range 1 . . 2_000;
subtype SMALL_INT is INTEGER range - 10 . . 10;
```

Real numerical operations are divided into floating-point and fixed-point types. Floating-point declarations are defined on the level of FLOAT and LONG_FLOAT, with the minimum required number of decimal digits for the equivalent decimal mantissa specified, as well as the range constraint, as in

```
SUM: LONG_FLOAT;
```

or the user-defined

```
type MY_FLOAT is new LONG_FLOAT digits 8 range MIN . .
MAX;
```

An assignment statement could be formulated as

```
SUM:= SUM + LONG_FLOAT (X(I)) * LONG_FLOAT (Y(I));
```

Type declarations for fixed point contain a declaration of the error-bound *delta,* which is specified as an absolute value, together with the range, that is, the upper and lower bounds for the fixed-point values. There are also restrictions on the respective values of *delta* and range between a type and its subtype. The values for *delta* and the two range values must be known at compilation time.

The preceding brief commentary on typing capabilities in Ada should indicate that in this language type declarations play an important role, are subject to complex restrictions and textual specifications, and produce a program that may not be consistent with the declared goals of readability and maintainability.

Binding

The point at which various attributes, which include type attributes and storage attributes, are effectively linked with a program entity, such as the name of a variable, is called the *binding time.* The act of binding may be either static or dynamic. For most languages, the static binding of type to a variable is usually done by an explicit declaration, for example, INTEGER X,Y (FORTRAN) or *var* X,Y: integer; (PASCAL). In APL, SNOBOL 4, and the list-processing language LISP, binding of names to type is both implicit and dynamic. In the language APL, there are no explicit declarations of type; type is determined by local context, and the type attribute of a data object may change dynamically during execution. For example, at different points of the program flow, the same name may be (1) a scalar variable, for example, $x \leftarrow 25$; (2) a vector, for example, $x \leftarrow 3\ 5\ 7\ 11\ 17$; or (3) a literal, for example, $x \leftarrow$ 'C'. Thus what is considered to be a *crucial* characteristic for most conventional languages is simply omitted from the design of APL. In the language SNOBOL 4, there are no explicit type declarations, and data types are inferred from local context. In ALGOL, where type declarations are explicit, the type of a variable is static, and checking for type consistency is done during compile time. The type of a variable not declared in a procedure would be that of the type declared in the enclosing block of text, rather than that declared in other blocks that call the procedure at execution time.

The use of dynamic binding of variables to type attributes (occurring during program execution time) gives a program great flexibility but adds to the semantic, as well as the implementation, complexity of the program. The type characteristic of a name may change during execution, since the type is implicitly redefined by new use of the name during the context of the program flow. For assignments, the type of the expression on the right side of an assignment would determine the current type characteristic for the name on the left side of the assignment. Of course, this concept disrupts current schemes designed to prove program "correctness" and enhance "structured programming," because the type characteristic becomes dependent on the specific local context of program flow. For example, if in some region of program text there are several possible logical branches, the type characteristics of some named variable, for example, *Z*, at some successor region may have been defined by the *previous* flow through branch 1, branch 2,..., or branch *n*. It is unclear at a particular text occurrence of *Z* where it derived its current type. The resulting semantic complexity leaves open the possibility of confusion over the actual type at any particular point of the program flow, since, as indicated in the previous example, a named variable could be, at various points of programming flow, an integer, a sequence of values, or a character string. This dynamic aspect also forces the use of implementation schemes that are essentially interpretive and therefore incur a large penalty timewise during execution. While dynamic binding has certain benefits by increasing program flexibility, those benefits are more than overshadowed by the liabilities incurred in program comprehensibility and efficiency of implementation.

Particular binding rules and binding times are sometimes determined by a specific implementation on a specific hardware architecture. Thus, if a program is recompiled under a different compilation for the same program written in the same language, inconsistencies may result.

The mixing of types within a computation, whether in static or dynamic mode, poses consistency problems for many languages, with differing solutions. In a pragmatic sense, there may not be any problem whatsoever. The problem arises when formal methods are applied to the analysis of program flow and program consistency. From a pragmatic point of view, performing an arithmetic operation on an *instruction* may serve a feasible and desirable purpose. Similarly, arithmetic operations on mixed types, such as adding integers to literal strings, may, in the given context, also be both feasible and desirable. Such operations pose a problem, however, when attempts are made to model the programming process by formal models and abstract denotations. The failing here is not with engineering "tricks" (this does not mean that such pragmatic approaches are not treatable by consistent methodologies grounded in empirical experience); rather, it lies with the inadequacy of current formal attempts to model the programming process by oversimplified and inadequate abstractions. There also tends to be a confusion between the mathematical aspects of the programming process and the psychological determinants operating in the sphere of the individual programmer confronted by the problem specification. In many cases the problem specification is *not* well formulated, and the programmer has access only to inadequate software tools and inappropriate computer languages.

Both PASCAL and ALGOL 68 allow unchangeable binding of value by definition, as in the PASCAL construct

```
const e = 2.7182818
```

which cannot be changed later on in the text by simple reassignment. Thus the subsequent statement

```
e:= 5
```

would be an error, since a change in the value bound to e (which can be implicitly considered to be of type *constant*) can be accomplished only by a redefinition using the preceding programming construct.

The type MACRO (a higher-level operator) is implemented as an "open subroutine" in that the code representing the MACRO is substituted literally in the program text prior to execution. Thus the use of MACRO-type commands in a programming language requires that binding take place during compilation. However, entities of type *procedure* or *function* implemented as (closed) subroutine calls may postpone the binding of procedure or function parameters until actual execution time.

Scope

The scope of a binding is usually that region of program text or range of program instructions over which the binding of attributes and values to a program entity is effective and known. From the point of view of execution at run time, the scope is comparable to the "lifetime" when such binding is in effect during program flow. More precisely, scope is a property that applies to individual elements of the program and that may have a status that is not distinct from, but dependent on, the context of program flow. For example, in a language such as PASCAL, a label, which performs the function of being the reference point for a GOTO statement, must be defined by a label declaration (for example, *label 3* or *label 5*). The label must be declared before its first use. The scope of label *L* declared in block *B* is the entire text of block *B*. Only one statement in block *B* may be prefixed with the label *L*. Then a GOTO statement anywhere within block *B* may reference label *L*. A GOTO L would be incorrect, however, if it occurred outside the block in which the label was declared, or if it caused a jump from the outside to the inside of a structured statement, such as a *for* loop or a *while* structure. For example, the program fragments

```
for k: = 1 to 10 do
     begin STATEMENT1;
     3: STATEMENT2
     end;
goto 3
```

or

```
     procedure QUEUE;
     begin
 . . .
 . . .
 . . .
     5: STATEMENT3
end;
begin
 . . .
 . . .
 . . .
     goto 5
end.
```

contain illegal references to *label 3* and *label 5,* even though the label may have a scope within a block that includes these statements.

The concept of scope ranges from the very simple to the very complex. For the language COBOL, all variables are global. In ALGOL, variables are local within their enclosing blocks and global to some nested block within their enclosing blocks. PL/1, PASCAL, and Ada have extensive and complex scoping rules for their program entities. The idea of scope as an explicit concept is primarily due to the development of ALGOL 60 during that historical period when hardware memory was a scarce resource. The use of scoping rules for variables allowed the reallocation of memory when it was not needed at points during the program flow.

In large programs, there may be large numbers of unique identifiers (names). These names may be introduced by different programmers, thereby raising the possibility of the incompatible use of the same name in different sections of the large program. Scoping was seen as a solution to both the memory resource problem and the name inconsistency problem, since names would be limited to a specific region of program text defined by a given language's scoping rules. Of course, in the current environment, memory is increasingly less of a scarce resource for most conventional applications, and simpler solutions are available for name consistency. There is little pragmatic justification anymore for intricate scoping rules. Also, scoping rules are intimately joined with the concept of complex block structure in the design of a language and therefore would appear to be not as suitable to those languages that are not block-structured to any degree of complexity.

In ALGOL-like languages, the scope of a name is limited to the block where it is declared, and blocks are usually delimited by *begin/end.* The scope of a name also includes an interior nested block, unless such a name is redeclared within the subblock. Names declared inside block_i are local to block_i, whereas names declared in a block including block_i are global to block_i. Since the value of a variable declared in an ALGOL block is undefined upon exit from its block (and therefore the storage space for the values associated with this variable are relinquished), the declaration *own* preserves the value associated with the variable declared to be *own* for reentry to that block. In ALGOL 60, however, there are difficulties associated with *own* arrays, because the values of the subscripts specifying the size of the array may change *before* reentry to the subject block.

Additional scoping distinctions for ALGOL-like languages usually include the restriction that two different declarations of the same identifier name in the same block are unacceptable. Identical names declared in different blocks are acceptable, but they reference different data objects. While a name declared in an outer block retains validity in an inner (nested) block (unless redeclared), a name declared only in an inner block is undefined to an operation in an enclosing outer block. Declarations must be at the head (beginning) of the block. An exit from the block deallocates the storage assigned to the name declared in the block, even if the block is reentered at some subsequent point of execution. In that case, storage is again allocated independent of the previous execution, and the variable values are again initialized regardless of the history of the previous program flow. A GOTO that occurs outside a block may not go into the interior of the block except to the portion that constitutes the head of the block.

In FORTRAN, variables are normally local to the subprogram unit. The COMMON declaration, however, assigns two variables from two different subprograms to the same memory location or one variable in the main program and one in a subprogram to the same location. The COMMON declaration must explicitly appear in both scopes. There are specific rules regarding restrictions on the simultaneous use of EQUIVALENCE declarations (which assign two variables, both either in the main program or in a subprogram, to the same location) and DIMENSION declarations.

In PL/1, the scoping rules are not only complex, they are linked to an intricate set of default rules that affect the scope of attributes. A name declared to be INTERNAL has scope only in the block in which it is declared. A name declared to be EXTERNAL may have scope in several blocks but only if it is so declared, together with the same attributes, in all blocks and procedures in which it is intended that the scope of the variable should extend. Identifiers that are neither parameters in a procedure block nor appear in an explicit declaration in a begin/end block are considered to have a (global) scope extending outside the block.

The storage associated with names is independent of the scope attribute and is controlled by the STATIC, AUTOMATIC, and CONTROLLED attributes. The scope attributes and the storage attributes are linked by various default rules and restrictions; for example, if the storage attribute is declared AUTOMATIC, then the scope attribute must be INTERNAL. Thus there is an inherent inconsistency in the default scope associated with implicit declarations, as allowed in PL/1, where undeclared variables are treated globally within procedures and thus may conflict with the use of the same variable name in blocks nested within the procedure. Similarly, in a language such as ALGOL 68, where references (pointers) can be declared explicitly, there may be undefined values for reference variables (that is, variables whose value is a reference) where the scope of the reference is not the same as the scope of a variable defined in an inner block. The pointer mechanism in PASCAL is more restrictive and avoids scope conflicts by distinguishing between *static* variables, whose scope is limited to the block in which they are declared, and *dynamic* variables, which are referenced by pointers and created by a special procedure NEW that limits pointers to access only dynamic variables. Various dialects of PASCAL, however, enforce different implementation restrictions on that mechanism.

The language SETL (motivated by set theory) attempts to resolve the scoping problem by using a treelike, nested family of scopes. The philosophy here is to avoid unrestricted global use of names, since a name, if used once, becomes in effect a reserved word for other program sections, which one may wish to program independently. Another hope is to prevent conflicts between subroutine names for cases where large numbers of different subroutines are created. SETL was designed to avoid a scoping system where names would be local, unless declared specifically as global, since this would force large amounts of repetitive declaratory text for every potential namescope or subroutine name. The goal of SETL is to divide a potentially large collection of programs into a system of sublibraries to permit cross-referencing. Since all subroutine calls are recursive, it is desirable to define scoping rules for variables on various levels of nested calls. Similarly, because a procedure P_1 may access variables in P_2, one must know when a variable X in P_1 references the same name X in P_2. The scoping rule must also handle the case where P_1 wishes to reference the name X of P_2 but using a local name, for example, Y (in a word, "aliasing"). SETL also recognizes certain restrictions so that remote references will not introduce scoping errors. Also, namescopes enclosing *several* subroutines are allowed, and a single subroutine may contain several independent namescopes. Scope boundaries are considered to be equivalent to "logical brackets," which are described by *level numbers*. Each subroutine is a namescope of level 0 but can contain other scopes and be embedded in a larger scope. A scope declaration includes the (optional) level indicator and the scope name. For example,

```
1  scope 3 routine;
   . . .
   . . .
2  end routine;
```

where the text between 1 and 2 is the body of the scope. Scopes must have the names of their "parents" and each of their "siblings" (in nested scopes). Reference to each scope is made by *concatenating* the scope name with its parent, grandparent, and so on, where the variable name X is referred to as

`X.` *<scope name>* . *<parent scope name>* . *<grandparent scope name>* . < . . .

The rules for variables referencing the same data object, but by different names (aliasing), are somewhat complex. SETL uses explicit global declarations to achieve nested scoping similar to ALGOL; it also uses an *include* declaration similar to the spirit of FORTRAN's COMMON for nonadjacent, nonnested scopes. Global declarations use the concept of *global level* to limit the declared scope range (logical brackets). Use is also made of an explicit or implicit rule for an *owns* declaration, so that the current value of each variable *owned* by a procedure will be stacked when the procedure is entered and the value unstacked on a return from the procedure. There are also exceptions and complex restrictions governing applications of these rules.

The situation for the language Ada is also quite complex in the area of scoping. The goal of scoping rules in the design of Ada emphasizes the ability to introduce new names without the programmer having to be concerned about possible conflict with preexisting names. It also emphasizes the Ada facilities offered for separate compilations. The basic scope model is ALGOL-like in that, within a program unit, identifiers declared in an outer subprogram or block have scope within an inner-nested subprogram or block, unless an explicit scoping restriction is declared. The major difference between the rules of Ada and those of ALGOL 60 is that the Ada convention is applicable within a restricted program unit rather than throughout the entire program. Overlapping scopes of declarations with the same identifier can occur, and several meanings can be acceptable at a given point; the ambiguity is resolved by various rules of "overloading." The language specifications make a distinction between the *scope* of a declaration (the region of text over which a declaration has an effect) and the *visibility* of a declaration. The declaration of an entity represented by an identifier is said to be *visible* at a given point in the program text when an occurrence of the identifier at that point can reference the entity with an acceptable meaning. However, *visibility* may be dependent on the occurrence of some suitable context that in itself requires additional rules related to appropriate context. There are also somewhat complex conventions for the naming and renaming of the various entities permitted in Ada.

From the previous discussion, it would seem that many languages—outstanding examples of which are ALGOL 68, PL/1, and Ada—while intending to provide for different declaration, type, and scope rules that are mathematically elegant, have instead constructed elaborate, interconnected devices that are excessively complex in structure and interdependent and that may be replete with undesired side effects and undetected type and scope violations. It is our view that declarations for storage allocation, type, and scope, except where *logically* necessary or where there are substantive implementation reasons, tend to obscure rather than enhance the goals of program clarity and correctness. In particular, the use of highly detailed, explicit type declarations to detect type errors, either at compile or execution time, can be appropriately characterized as an attempt to elucidate and enumerate the errors generated by the programming process considered as an abstract, consistent, and complete process. This point of view, however, is not supported by any substantive empirical data that would indicate the frequency, and therefore the importance, of specific type errors. It reflects the notion that if something possibly *could* happen, then it *must* happen, and frequently! Such a viewpoint denies that, for a sufficiently complex program, it is grossly impractical to conjecture all *possible* errors and that the class of *important* errors is a matter for empirical determination.

The idea that scope rules are necessary because large programs have many different names and many different programmers, each working on a different section, can be disposed of in a relatively straightforward way without the necessity of *explicitly* invoking scope. Let's consider a program to be broken up into sections ("simple" blocks) of text, where a section is not necessarily any specific program construct (that is, it does not have any particular phrase structure) and is merely identified (explicitly "declared") with different author-programmers. Names then, particularly names of variables, may be implicitly tagged by section indicators, either as concatenated prefixes or suffixes. For example, for section *A* and variables *X, Y, Z, N, M,*..., we might (automatically) tag those variables as *AX, AY, AZ, AN, AM,*....For section 1, we could similarly tag variables as *X*1, *Y*1, *Z*1,..., using a suffix convention. For section 2, we might tag corresponding variables as *X*2, *Y*2, *Z*2,.... Or still using a suffix convention, we might have, as an alternative to the first set of forms for section *A*, the variables *XA, YA, ZA,*....For more elaborate subsectioning we could use tagged variables of the form

```
X&1&b&3
```

to denote the variable name *X* appearing in section 1.b.3, where & is any symbol not used as an operator or delimiter and acting as a section-denoting symbol. Thus, as long as each section indicator is unique, then straightforward (automatic) application of this simple rule will avoid scoping interference among names of program entities. Of course, we have assumed that names can be of indefinite length. Such an assumption poses no substantial implementation problems or any substantive degradation in execution efficiency. The use of naming conventions to indicate their local environment (that is, their occurrence in a particular subsection) can be facilitated by the use of subscripts and superscripts playing the role of section indicators after the automatic linking of independent sections into a composed program document where each variable is explicitly linked to its section-denoting symbol.

One *possible* way of avoiding the necessity of intricate scoping rules, in relating variables from different sections, is to consider that the entire program text consists of only two major categories. The first category is the central program, which, for administrative reasons, may be broken up into textual sections and subsections. All variables used throughout the central program, as long as they have distinct (explicit or implicit) names, are known throughout the program. That is, all distinctly named variables are global throughout the central program. All the variables used within the entire central program are also, in a certain sense, local to the entire central program, since they should not be known to the other major program category, which is simply the set of procedures (subprograms, subroutines, functions, and so on) that are called (implicitly or explicitly) by the central program. Any name used within a procedure is local to that procedure; that is, it is not known to any other procedure or to the central program. Names occurring in the central program are not known to any procedure and *must* be passed to a procedure as parameters, and similarity between procedures. (See Chap. 7 for a more detailed discussion of methods of passing parameters and methods of procedure calls.)

Thus an alternative option for dealing with different textual *sections* is to treat them as procedures. Of course, where it is desired that data objects have more than one name (as in relating names from different textual sections), explicit IDENTITY or EQUIVALENCE declarations would be required to indicate that the same value is associated with more than one name. Truly global names such as π and e should be *defined* (cautiously) and *not redefined* throughout the entire program, including "external" or "library" procedures. Recursion can be dealt with on the implementation level (not on the program text level) as a special case to resolve the use of the same name internal to a set of recursive procedure calls. These considerations imply that, for large programs and large numbers of author-programmers, the central program could be simply a sequence of procedure calls, where each procedure is associated with a specific author-programmer.

The preceding comments are simple but not simplistic. Modern computer hardware has increasingly liberated the programming process from the constraints of insufficient storage allocation and insufficient computation speed for a relatively large domain of applications. Simple schemes such as the automatic allocation of storage without the need of explicit declaration for cases where such allocation can be logically inferred from the program text, the minimizing of type distinctions, and the simplification of scope control of program entities tend to shift responsibility to the compiler-implementor rather than the author-programmer. Such an attitude is consistent with the general viewpoint of user-oriented computer-language design.

Chapter

7

Procedures and Parameters; Iteration and Recursion

Multiuse Subprograms

A multiuse subprogram is a program segment that defines a specific computation and that can be expected to be used many times in a program, usually operating on different sets of data. In general, there are two options. One option is to literally *copy* the subprogram at every point in the larger program where it is to be used, a tedious and inefficient method for the user-programmer unless the copying is done automatically. The second option is to *define* the subprogram by writing it out just once and then to *call* the subprogram either explicitly or implicitly. The first option, when done automatically, is sometimes termed a *macro call* and usually results in slightly faster execution at the expense of additional memory for each generated copy. The second option is more suitable for general use and program clarity and the one toward which our discussion is directed.

The simplest type of multiuse subprogram is where the subprogram can be used in a way that is equivalent to the use of a variable name in a program. For example, in the program fragment

```
Y = A + B/C + G
```

or

```
Y = A + 2 * B + F (NAME1, NAME2, NAME3, NAME4, . . . )
```

G and F are subprograms that result in single values when the subprogram fragment is executed, and *NAME1, NAME2,...* are the actual names of variables appearing elsewhere in the program, usually preceding the subprogram unit.

This type of subprogram is usually called a *function* and can be defined implicitly or explicitly. It is defined implicitly when its definition resides outside the program. In that case, it is usually called a *library function* or *library routine.* Examples of common library functions are the trigonometric functions, such as sine and cosine, and functions with names like SQRT (square root). Say that within a program there is the clause

```
Y = SIN (theta)
```

This usually would mean that the trigonometric function *sine* is to be applied to the current value of the variable with the name *theta* and the result assigned to the current value of the variable Y.

Functions can also be defined explicitly within a program. Specific definitions might take the forms:

```
FUNCTION pause = 1 + 2 + 3 + 4 + 5 + ... + 100.
```

or

```
FUNCTION F(a,b,c) = a + b/c.
```

or

```
FUNCTION testn(e,f,g) = if e > f THEN 5g else 7.
```

or

```
FUNCTION comp(a,b) = if a > b THEN comp = 6; else
comp = 1.
```

or

```
FUNCTION G = alpha + beta/gamma.
```

Whether the user should be required to use the key word FUNCTION explicitly when defining a function should be determined by the language designer, based on whether the omission of such an explicit declaration would give rise to syntactic or semantic ambiguity or introduce serious implementation difficulty. Similar considerations apply to the use of a special symbol to signal the end of the definition and the use of punctuation symbols if more than one phrase is permitted in the definition. Since a multiuse subprogram is an entity that is conceptually obvious to the user, we find no objection to requiring the explicit declaration of function definitions by the use of the key word FUNCTION. From the point of view of language design, the designer should take care that the definition form required for a function is as simple and consistent as possible. In general, there is no particular implementation difficulty that follows from allowing the value of the function to be determined by the values of n variables, defined in the program prior to the use of the function name, where n may be 0 (no names) or as many as practical for a specific implementation. The function definition may be restricted to a single sentence or single lines, or may be multisentenced or multilines. The separation between sentences or lines should be with some notation (for example, commas or periods) that the designer anticipates to be less error-prone for the psychological model of the user in the context of the application environment. Definition of functions should be terminated by an explicit symbol, which could be the usual period or a specialized symbol such as END. The general idea is to define the *use* of functions, the function *definition* convention, and the *naming* conventions so they are consistent with the idea that the function is a simple program that returns a single value. Thus the name of the function can be used in exactly the same way as the name of a variable.

More formally, we can define a function in the following ways:

```
FUNCTION { functionname (X,Y,Z,...) } . E. END.
         { functionname             }
```

or as

```
FUNCTION { <name> (< * > <parameter dummies> ,) }
         { <name>                                }
= {f(x1,x2,x3,...)| <expression> }.
```

where E constitutes the subprogram associated with the function definition and E may include previously defined functions. The identifiers X, Y, Z,...are *dummy variables* or *formal parameters* that are local to the function definition as explicated within the body of E. The second form for function definition is much simpler syntactically, resembling an assignment statement and requiring no special symbol such as END. As noted previously, the function can be used in the program by explicitly stating its name in the same way that any other variable name is used. For the case of the function that has arguments, the dummy variables used in the function definition are replaced by *actual names* (*actual parameters*) that have meaning in the previous segments of the program. By doing this, we essentially replace the list of dummy variables with an equivalently *ordered* list of actual parameters. Thus, when the function name is used in the program, an alternative method would be to explicitly associate the pair (formal parameter, actual parameter) as in

```
Y = name(X = a, Y = b, Z = c,...)
```

This latter method is appealing only when the list of formal parameters is long and the formal parameters can be expressed as mnemonic lexical items. For example, consider the definition

```
FUNCTION process (name, field size, department,...)
= ....
```

and the program segment

```
Q = process (name = ARRAY_I, field size = 32,
department = major,...)
```

Of course, the use of the equal symbol (=) can be replaced by a keyword lexical item such as *is, is equal to,* or whatever is appropriate for the particular application for which the language is designed.

In view of the above, defining (using the second function syntax)

```
FUNCTION Q(X) = X² + 1.
FUNCTION R(X,Y) = XY + Q(XY²).
FUNCTION H = A + B SINE t.
```

would permit the program phrase Z = Q(R(Q(π),H)).

The definition of the function H assumes that the names A, B, and t refer to variables found in the program. In other words, that sort of formulation assumes that variables within a function definition that do not play the role of formal parameters are to be considered global variables. Such a language-design option may be quite dangerous in terms of programming practice, since it can have all sorts of unintended effects. There may be specific application-language designs, however, where such a facility for subprogram usage does warrant inclusion of that capability. The problems here may be clarified by our subsequent discussion of the various methods of passing parameters and the use of recursive definitions. We also note that it is desirable, in the context of this category of subprogram definition, to permit phrases such as

$$C = \sum_{x=1}^{n} xQ(x) \quad \text{or} \quad D = \int_0^y Q(X)\, dX$$

where Q has been defined previously as a function.

It is also possible to define functions without specifying an explicit number of arguments (parameters). For example, one could have a program statement of the form

```
FORi = 1,...,n COMPUTE Dᵢ = MAX |Wᵢⱼ| where i≤j≤n
```

Upon execution of the program the function MAX will cause a particular value of W_{ij} to be assigned to the name D_i. The definition of the function MAX will be a subprogram that selects out the maximum value from the set W_{ij}, as determined by the limits specified for j.

We have used the symbol = in the definition form to mean definition or *is defined as* for FUNCTION, since any ambiguity between such use of this symbol and other interpretations is easily resolved by the context. If that is not the case in a particular application language, a unique symbol such as ≡ or :: = or any other symbol easily available from the character set can be used.

A more general type of multiuse subprogram is conventionally called a *subroutine* or a *procedure*. We will use both terms as synonyms. The major difference between a subroutine and a function, as defined previously, is that a subroutine does not have a value or type associated with its name. A subroutine has a list of parameters that can be divided into two different classes. For example, one might define the subroutine *sub* as

SUBROUTINE *sub*$(I_1, I_2, I_3, \ldots O_1, O_2, O_3, \ldots)$

where the dummy parameters (formal parameters) I_1,I_2,I_3 are placeholders for actual variable names (actual parameters) to be found in the program, with actual values before the subroutine is invoked. The dummies O_1,O_2,O_3...are placeholders for actual variables in the program, which will be given values computed by the subroutine when it is activated. More formally, we could define such a subprogram as

SUBROUTINE < *subroutine name*> (<*parameter list*>) . <*body*>
RETURN[.][< * > <*body*> **RETURN**[.]] [[<*body*>] [**END**
[<*subroutine name*>] **SUBROUTINE**]].

where < * > means that the succeeding expression may be repeated *n* times, where *n* equals 0, 1, 2, 3,... and SUBROUTINE ≡ PROCEDURE. <*body*> denotes the subprogram(s) associated with the definition of the subroutine. RETURN causes the passing of computed values back to the calling program.

Implementation of this form is simpler if the convention that all subroutine definitions are placed at the end of the program is followed. If that is not desirable for the specific application language, then implementation considerations can be eased by mandating that a unique lexical item begin and end a subroutine when it is embedded within a program. Here, the explicit use of the key word SUBROUTINE (or PROCEDURE) is sufficient to begin the definition. If more than one RETURN is permitted, the item END is sufficient to terminate the definition. If it is useful to specify that no more than one RETURN be used in a subroutine, then that key word can be the definition terminator.

The formal parameter list associated with a subroutine definition may contain "attributes" linked with each formal parameter either in pairs or by sequence. For example, the formal parameter list might be structured as

```
(x:INTEGER,y:REAL,...)
```

Of course, the actual explicit symbol linking the formal parameter to its attribute, or type, optimally depends on the available symbols for the particular language application.

As noted previously, there is less chance of ambiguity, unintended side effects, or inconsistency if the design of the language specifies that (1) all variables named within the subroutine definition are local to that definition and (2) dummy parameters can be replaced by actual names only through explicit exchange, on a one-to-one basis, when the subroutine is activated. However, if the particular application requires that the design of the language be such that all variables within the program are considered to be global, then it would be not only permissible but expeditious to allow global variables, which are not named on the actual parameter list, to be mentioned within the subroutine definition. In that case, explicit naming of output parameters is not necessary.

Where it is desirable to allow a definition of the procedure to contain global variables that refer to variables outside the procedure (this is sometimes referred to as *inheritance*), then the procedure is in an environment where the procedure uses variable names that have been given meaning outside the body of the procedure. These variables may be altered at the time the procedure executes. As we have noted, this sort of mixed-scope convention can lead to unanticipated side effects.

To specify the point at which a subroutine is to be exercised during normal program flow, one could use the phrase

. . . [CALL] [SUBROUTINE] <*subroutine name*> (<*parameter list*>) . . .

The key word CALL need not be explicitly mentioned at that relevant point of the program as long as the names of subroutines are reserved, that is, are not used in another context, such as naming a variable. Likewise, the lexical items SUBROUTINE and PROCEDURE are redundant as long as subroutine names are treated as reserved words throughout the program. Whether the subroutine "call" is used as an isolated statement within the program or simply as a phrase within a larger structure depends on the choice of syntactic flexibility for the particular application.

Of course, the most basic type of multiuse subprogram is simply a program section with no name and no parameters. This is activated, that is, called, by a GOSUB <*label*> command, where <*label*> serves to mark the place in the program where the subprogram text occurs. The specific subprogram begins with a unique label, such as a line number, and is terminated by a RETURN or an equivalent lexical symbol. Of course, this is possible only if all the variables within the subprogram are global. The problems that arise here do so because the subroutine is invoked via an unconditional branch, that is, a GOTO-type command. The subprogram may invoke other subprograms in a manner identical to its own invocation from the overall program, which often results in an unduly complex representation of program flow and adds to the difficulty in comprehending a program that has been designed to encompass a logically complex process. Used this way, the subprogram is simply a section of the entire program that happens to be referenced in this special way. Previously mentioned methods of defining and using subroutines or functions are, in general, far superior.

There is another possible variant of the multiuse subprogram. If a program were divided into sections and each section had a unique section name and explicit termination (END) symbol, then it would be possible to call any particular previous section of the program by simply stating at some point

CALL *<section name>*

Thus a section of the program could be executed in normal sequence as well as behave like a subroutine if called in the manner previously specified. The problem with this somewhat arcane convention is that the specification of parameters would not be straightforward and would require artificial procedures to indicate actual parameters for the instance of a particular program section activated as a subroutine.

We should also note, for the sake of completeness, that some languages use the term *function* but allow the return of more than one value, usually by allowing a sequence of values to be pushed onto a stack. There are also languages that allow the return value to have a structure such as arrays, bodies of other subprograms, or even pointers to memory locations. We will not comment further on this matter, since, in general, these more complicated functions have disturbing side effects that usually are not appropriate for a user-oriented approach. A possible exception to this would be a language intended for mathematical applications, where it might be appropriate to treat arrays and other higher-level mathematical structures as individual objects that could be returned as a result of the invocation of a procedure.

Passing Parameters

The definition of a subroutine or a function specifies a computational process on items that are symbolically represented by the (possibly empty) list of formal parameters. The formal parameters act as placeholders (dummy symbols) for actually named variables found at various instances of the program. For example, if X is a dummy variable in the formal parameter list, then at one invocation of the subroutine, X may be replaced by the name A. In a different invocation, however, X may be replaced by name B. An actual name, if it replaces a dummy symbol that is a placeholder for an input value, should have an actual value at the time of subprogram invocation. (Of course, for symbolic programming, the value can be a symbol rather than a numeric value.)

The technique of replacing dummy symbols with actual symbols is usually called *passing parameters*. But a problem arises here since different languages, and possibly even different implementations of the same language, use different techniques to pass parameters. These different techniques may not only cause the same definition of a subprogram to execute with different output results but also change the variables in the outside program in different ways. The broader implications are that the specification of an algorithmic process is not complete unless certain auxiliary assumptions are included in the algorithm's specification, either implicitly or explicitly. An illustration of other implicit assumptions would be considerations such as operator precedence, which are usually implicit to language use but which should be explicitly specified in the language design. Another consideration might be numerical significance. Precision may be implicit because of specific language design decisions, a function of implementation decisions as to methods of rounding or truncation, or based on "tolerance" criteria specified by the programmer. For example, a programmer writes IF A = 0 THEN....Does this mean A is 0 to perfect precision? Or is $A < \varepsilon$ where ε may be just large enough to encompass rounding or truncation errors arising from simple numerical-based conversions?

For parameter passing, because of its great potential for generating unintended results, and undesirable side effects, the methods used should be explicitly specified at the level of language design and prominent in any explication of specific language use. In other words, if the language is to be user-oriented, consequences of a particular passing technique should be made clear to the user-programmer on the most fundamental level of "how-to-program-in-this-language." The following sections discuss several of the most common techniques used for parameter passing.

Call by value

The *call-by-value* method is the simplest method of parameter passing and the least prone to misunderstanding or side effects. When a parameter is a call by value (or *pass by value*), the value of the actual parameter replacing the corresponding formal parameter *at the time of call* (invocation) becomes the initial value of that corresponding formal parameter that occurs in the definition of the subprogram. If the actual parameter is an expression, it is evaluated before being substituted for the formal parameter. Because of this method, the actual variables, as they enter the computation defined by the subprogram, act as variables purely local to the subprogram and will not cause a feedback of information to the calling program. In terms of implementation considerations, that means that the storage reserved for formal parameters is entirely distinct from the storage associated with any actual parameter.

Strictly speaking, the remarks in the preceding paragraph apply only to those formal parameters that play the role of placeholders for input values. When formal parameters are designated as placeholders for output values, the values achieved as a result of executing that particular subprogram are passed back to the program, and the actual parameters corresponding to the output formal parameters are assigned the computed values. Sometimes this latter technique, if it involves only what we have termed *output formal parameters,* is said to be *call by result.* Likewise, treating the input formal parameters and the output formal parameters as suggested previously can be termed *call by value-result.* It is not uncommon to group all three categories under the nomenclature *call by copy.*

For example, consider the following subprogram definition

```
SUBROUTINE exchange (I1,I2,O1,O2). T = I1, O1 = I2,
O2 = T.
END.
```

Suppose that in the program there was the phrase

```
CALL exchange (i,Ai,i,Ai)
```

and at the time that that call was invoked, i = 1 and A_1 = 7. A consistent implementation of the call-by-value mechanism would then initialize the formal parameters. The formal parameter I_1 would be set equal to 1. In effect, the location allocated to the *local* name I_1 would assume the value 1. Likewise, the formal input parameter I_2 would be set equal to 7, or, equivalently, the contents of the memory location linked to I_2 would be set equal to 7, where I_1 and I_2 are considered to be variables local to the particular subroutine. As part of the initialization process, the output parameter O_1 would be linked to the *name* of the "outside" variable i (but not its address), and the formal output parameter O_2 would be linked with the outside *name* A_1. Note that A_1 is the first value of the *set* A_i. O_1 and O_2 are variables local to the subroutine and have addresses associated with them. However, the linkages to outside variables are noted within the subroutine but separate from the addresses used to store temporary values for O_1 and O_2. In effect, when the subroutine terminates, the pair (*name* i, *value* O_1) and the pair (*name* A_1, *value* O_2) are transmitted back to the calling program. The addresses associated with i and A_1 in the program are then determined, and the respective values inserted at the corresponding memory locations. Thus, after initialization is accomplished, the subroutine proceeds to assign the value 1 to the local variable T; it then assigns the value 7 to the local variable O_1; and finally the local variable O_2 assumes the current value of the local variable T, which is 1. The new values corresponding to the pair i, A_1 are then transmitted back to the calling program. Thus i and A_1 exchange their values that existed just before invocation of the subroutine.

A different type of calling mechanism might transmit the final value of O_2 back to the program variable A_i, where i is instantiated as the *now-changed* value i. This would not result in the intended exchange of 1,7 to 7,1 between the *same* pair of elements, which becomes clear if we note that the name A_i does not represent a single element but rather a set of elements corresponding to the vector structure A. Some languages allow a mechanism equivalent to our definition of call by value only for input formal parameters, either as a standard or as an option. The passing of output formal parameters may then be done by some other mechanism. For our purposes, that is, in terms of user-oriented design, we recommend that both categories of parameters essentially be passed by the same effective mechanism. In particular, ALGOL 60 has, by option, a call by value, but it is applied only to input formal parameters. In ALGOL 60, the usual mechanism of passing values is *call by name.* The language PASCAL also permits passing of parameters by a mechanism equivalent to call by value, if the formal parameter is declared. It also permits the passing of the results of calculation back to the calling program by the use of the mechanism *call by reference.*

Call by reference

Call by reference is also termed *call by address, call by location,* and *call by simple name.* In general, a call by reference has a formal parameter that corresponds to a single variable. What is really passed, however, is not the value of the actual parameter but rather the address (the reference to) of the actual parameter. In cases where the actual parameter is not a single variable but rather an expression, what is forwarded to the subprogram is the address where the current value of the expression is stored. Thus, with this mode of call, the subprogram can modify variables existing outside its scope, if these variables are associated with the formal parameters of the subprogram. If during the execution of the subprogram, the formal parameter's initial value becomes changed to some other value, the contents of the location whose address has been passed, that is, the address of the actual parameter, will be changed.

Those occurrences may result in unintended side effects, since the programmer may have regarded the specified formal parameter as simply an input vehicle that would not affect the calling program. For arrays such as $A_{i,j}$, the values of the subscripts i and j are evaluated at the time the subprogram is invoked. Thus the address passed to the subprogram is a location of a particular element of the structure $A_{i,j}$.

The language FORTRAN uses call by reference as its usual mechanism to pass parameters. For certain implementations of FORTRAN, however, use of the call-by-reference mechanism can have catastrophic results. For example, suppose a particular implementation of FORTRAN scans the input program and, in addition to constructing a table that lists all variables of the program, creates an auxiliary table to contain all the constants mentioned within the program. That is, the constant is treated as a name, and its value, in its internal representation, is contained in an address referenced by that name. In those circumstances, a not-bright programmer might define the subroutine as

```
SUBROUTINE f(X).X = 100. RETURN. END.
```

and the main program might contain the statement

```
CALL f(1)
```

The call-by-reference mechanism results in the formal parameter X referencing the address used to store the actual parameter 1. That is, the assignment statement inside the subroutine essentially says, "Take the value on the right side of the assignment statement, go to the address referenced by the actual argument of *f*, and store the value in that address." The effect is that the value of 100 will now be assigned as the contents of a location linked to the *name* of constant value 1. Thus, if at some later point in the program we have the statements

```
Z = 5
Z = Z + 1
PRINT Z
```

then the value printed out would be the number 105. Similarly, the statement

```
Q = 1 + 1
PRINT Q
```

would result in an output value of 200. Of course, some implementations of FORTRAN do not process constants this way or do not use the standard call-by-reference mechanism. Instead, they use a mode similar to the call by value.

To illustrate another side effect of the use of the call-by-reference mechanism, suppose we define

```
FUNCTION f(z). z = z + 1. RETURN z. END.
```

and in the program we have the following fragment

```
x = 3, y = 4
E1 = x + f(x) + y
E2 = f(x) + x + y
```

The program will compute the values

```
E1 = 3 + 4 + 4 = 11
E2 = 4 + 4 + 4 = 12.
```

It would appear that addition is not commutative when the expression contains a function where the actual parameter is passed to the formal parameter by the call-by-reference technique. When there is an occurrence of an expression such as

$$E = x + y + f(x,y) + x + y$$

where x and y are affected by the execution of function $f(x,y)$, then the value of the second instance of $(x + y)$ may be different from the first instance of $(x + y)$. An optimizing compiler may consider $(x + y)$ to be a common subexpression and cause the evaluation of $(x + y)$ only once during the execution of E. Different values of E would be found when the program was compiled by a nonoptimizing compiler or interpreted during the debugging phase.

Call by name

The *call by name* as a method of passing parameters became well known when it was made the default method of parameter passing for ALGOL 60 (although call by value is an option). Section 4.7.3.2 of the revised report of ALGOL 60 states that a call by name is such that a "formal parameter...is replaced, throughout the procedure body, by the corresponding actual parameter, after enclosing this latter in parentheses wherever syntactically possible....(4.7.3.3)...finally the procedure body, modified as above, is inserted in place of the procedure statement and executed."

Thus the actual parameter expression becomes the initial value of a corresponding formal parameter. That is, the actual code that represents the expression and that will be used to evaluate the expression becomes the initial value of the formal parameter. In effect, the device must operate so that it is computationally equivalent to the actual parameter expression (that is, its code) and as though it were written in place of the formal parameter in every instance in the body of the definition of the subprogram. Implementation techniques that avoid this multiple copying of code make the implementation more efficient and still achieve the same effect. (See standard works on compiler theory and design for more details.)

A useful application of call by name is when one wishes to evaluate the definite integral of some function numerically, for example,

$$\int_a^b f(x)\,dx$$

which can be defined as the subprogram

$$\text{FUNCTION } integral\text{ (a,b,x,f)} = \sum_i \mathrm{W_i f_i}$$

where the code for $f_i = f(x_i)$ must be evaluated for each point x_i such that $a \leq x_i \leq b$ and W is a set of constants. If the function $f(x)$ is *passed by name,* then the integration algorithm may be easily implemented. One could also design a function representation such that the actual expression that defines f explicitly appears in the list of actual parameters.

Call by name can also generate unexpected side effects. For example, reconsider the SUBROUTINE *exchange* definition in the previous section "Call by Value." The same invocation causes the input formal parameters $\mathrm{I_1}$ and $\mathrm{I_2}$ to be initialized to the values

```
I₁ = i, I₂ = Aᵢ
```

The output parameters are also set to

```
i = O₁, Aᵢ = O₂
```

Then, according to the body of the subprogram,

```
T = i, O₁ = Aᵢ, O₂ = T = i
```

Originally, the program had set i = 1, $\mathrm{A_i}$ = 7 for i = 1; thus, as the body of the subroutine executes,

```
O₁ = A₁ = 7
```

But now i = 7 by the assignment i = $\mathrm{O_1}$. Thus the second output assignment gives $\mathrm{A_7} = \mathrm{O_2} = 7$. Not only is the intended exchange not accomplished but some unreferenced element, that is, $\mathrm{A_7}$, has now had its (unknown) value changed.

Still using the same subroutine definition and the same initial value for i and A_i, as specified in the previous program, consider a different call, where the order of actual parameters is interchanged, as in'

```
CALL exchange (A_i,i,A_i,i)
then
I_1 = A_i, I_2 = i, A_i = O_1, i = O_2
T = A_i, O_1 = i, O_2 = T = A_i
T = 7, O_1 = 1, O_2 = 7
```

In this case the input pair of actual values (7, 1) has been exchanged so that the output to the set of actual parameters is now the pair (1, 7). This sort of side effect is particularly confusing in debugging situations, since the subroutine works in some circumstances but not in others.

The same effect can be illustrated in a simpler example for a language where the conventions for the local and the global scope of variables is such that under certain circumstances the formal variables play *both* input and output roles. Thus we can define

```
SUBROUTINE interchanger (X,Y). T = X, X = Y, Y = T. END.
```

If the program fragment is

```
i = 1, A_1 = 7.
CALL interchanger (i,A_i)
```

then invocation of *interchanger* causes execution of the following code:

```
T = i, i = A_i, A_i = T
T = 1, i = 7, A_7 = 1
```

and A_1 is not changed from its original value of 7. Such is not the intended effect. Similarly, with the same values for i and A_1, the call

```
CALL interchanger (A_i,i)
```

causes execution of

```
T = A_i, A_i = i, i = T
T = 7, A_1 = 1, i = 7
```

which produces the intended result and no side effects, but only for this particular order of function arguments!

Other Considerations

The invocation of a subprogram, if the actual parameters are themselves subprograms, can lead to useful results in some situations, as illustrated by the previous integration example where the subprogram *f* is, in effect, an expression passed by name. Careless use of this "trick," however, can lead to programs that are either incomprehensible or that result in serious unintended side effects. Aside from the choice of a particular passing mechanism, the way a specific language treats scope in differentiating between local and global variables can have a crucial effect on the actual results that are generated.

For certain applications, a particular function may be used over in many different programs. In scientific, mathematical, and engineering applications programs, it is common to take certain functions, for example, those that compute the sine and the logarithm, and make them "built-in" facilities of the language. *Built-in functions* are also called *system functions* or *special functions*. Regardless of the nomenclature, it may be necessary to distinguish those system names from user-defined functions that may accomplish the same goal but with a different (presumably higher) precision. There are several ways to accomplish that in terms of forcing a specific implementation by language design. One way might be the explicit convention that when a user defines a function with a name identical to a system function, then all calls of that *name* will automatically invoke the user-defined function. A simpler, and more flexible, method would be to distinguish the system function from the user-defined function by a slight change of name. For example, *sine* might be the system name to compute the trigonometric function sine, whereas *hpsine* might be the user-defined equivalent function to compute the sine to a higher precision. There are other methods that can be used to achieve the same purpose. In general, however, implementation is facilitated and ambiguity avoided if function names are reserved so they cannot be used as names of other objects.

Another facility for subprograms is to specify the use of generic functions or subroutines. A generic function would be defined in a way that would allow its application to different types of data objects, for example, integers in one case, floating-point numbers in another case, or arrays in another case. Whether specific declarations of type are necessary depends on many factors. The application environment that dictates the specific language design is highly important, as is the level of implementation difficulty created by specific design choices. From a user-oriented point of view, it is usually more desirable not to make explicit declarations except where they are necessary to resolve situations of inherent ambiguity. As noted previously, if one deals only with statements of the simple form

$$X = Y + Z$$

in most situations the context of the program clearly implies the type category associated with X, Y, and Z. Thus it is not necessary to force explicit declarations of type, even though the plus symbol (+), which here stands for the addition operation, might invoke sharply different processes depending on whether X, Y, and Z are scalars or at least some of these variables are an array structure. It is difficult to specify exact rules to handle all cases. The language designer must make specific decisions appropriate to the application area and the level of implementation difficulty that he or she wishes to confront. A consequence of this point of view is that such decisions may be sharply influenced by the availability of what now may be considered novel machine architectures. What is difficult to implement on the classical von Neuman architecture may be easy to implement on some "non–von Neuman" machine design.

This viewpoint also implies that the intricacy or sophistication of language designs for subprogram manipulation should depend on the programmer, in the sense that what might be appropriate for the professional programmer may not be desirable for the individual whose goal is the computation of problem specifications, not a professional "style" of programming. Thus the specific class of user should be considered a component of the application-language design.

For applications that describe processes occurring concurrently, especially when those processes occur in an interleaved fashion, a special type of procedure may be designed. One special type of procedure is the *coroutine.* Since coroutines involve special considerations that are somewhat apart from our goal of user-oriented design, we refer the reader to standard texts on programming languages. A particularly useful discussion of this point is given in Ghezzi and Jazayeri.[1]

Iteration versus Recursion

Subprograms can be constructed so that they are either iterative or recursive by definition. An *iteration* is a repeated performance of a process until some explicit condition, which becomes operative during program execution, is satisfied. For example, consider the program fragment

$$\mathrm{SUM}(A_i,n) = \sum_{i=1}^{n} A_i$$

The next chapter will discuss higher-level languages that support conventional mathematical two-dimensional notation. In such languages this program fragment would be directly executable. Where

[1]C. Ghezzi and M. Jazayeri, *Programming Language Concepts,* 2d ed., John Wiley, New York, 1987.

this is not so, it would be possible to replace that fragment with the following, more procedural (and iterative) program fragment:

```
SUM = 0.
I = 1.
LABEL3. IF I > N RETURN ELSE
SUM = SUM + Ai
I = I + 1.
GO TO LABEL3.
```

where the notation A_i can be replaced by the more conventional A(i).

A procedure which adds up a list of values A_i can be defined in a more abstract manner. A procedure is *recursive* if it is able to reference itself. That is, a recursive procedure can call itself when the terminating condition is not satisfied and the basic computational cycle is not carried through to completion, in the sense of obtaining an explicit numerical value, until the entire process is completed. This can be illustrated by a recursive definition of the summation function:

```
FUNCTION SUM(Ai,n) = 0 IF n = 0 ELSE
SUM(Ai,n) = An + SUM(Ai,n - 1).
```

Execution of SUM(A_i,3) would take place as follows:

```
SUM (Ai,3) = A3 = SUM(Ai, 2)
SUM(Ai,2) = A2 + SUM(Ai,1)
SUM(Ai,1) = A1 + SUM(Ai,0)
SUM(Ai,0) = 0
```

We find the final result by *unwinding* the function thus:

```
SUM(Ai,3) = A3 + A2 + A1.
```

Consider the following iterative definition to compute the square root of a scalar value.

```
FUNCTION SQRT(N). S = N/2.
LABEL1. X = S. S = 0.5(X + (N/X)).
IF|(N/S) - X| < e THEN RETURN S ELSE GOTO LABEL1.
END.
```

where this is a possible program representation of the algorithm:

$$S_{i+1} = 1/2\ (S_i + \frac{N}{S_i})$$

S_0 = first guess of the square root of N. The iteration is carried through until the difference between subsequent computations is less than some predetermined precision e.

A recursive version of the square-root function might be written as

```
FUNCTION SQRT(N,S). IF|((N/S) - S)| < e THEN RETURN S
ELSE SQRT(N, 0.5(S + (N/S)). END.
```

That is,

$$
\begin{aligned}
&\text{SQRT}(100,50) \rightarrow \text{SQRT}(100,0.5(50 + \frac{100}{50})) \\
&= \text{SQRT}(100,26) \rightarrow \text{SQRT}(100,0.5(26 + \frac{100}{26})) \\
&= \text{SQRT}(100,14.9) \rightarrow \text{SQRT}(100,0.5(14.9 + \frac{100}{14.9})) \\
&= \text{SQRT}(100,10.8) \rightarrow \text{SQRT}(100,0.5(10.8 + \frac{100}{10.8})) \\
&= \text{SQRT}(100,10.2) \rightarrow \ldots
\end{aligned}
$$

The computation will terminate when the argument of the IF phrase becomes less than a predetermined precision *e*. At this point, the last value determined for S is the required SQRT of N.

Another example would be N factorial for integer N ≥ 1. In a high-level language that accepts mathematical notation, this might be defined as

$$\text{FUNCTION FACTORIAL (N)} = \prod_{i=1}^{N} \text{i}$$

which is equivalent to the iterative definition

```
FUNCTION FACTORIAL (N). f = 1. f = i * f FOR i = 1 TO N.
RETURN f. END.
```

A recursive definition of the same function might be

```
FUNCTION FACTORIAL (N). FACTORIAL (1) = 1.
IF N > 1 THEN FACTORIAL (N) = N * FACTORIAL (N - 1).
END.
```

The final value for FACTORIAL (N) is returned only after the sequence of operations terminates on FACTORIAL (1); then the intermediate stages are unwound.

Consider the higher-level definition

$$\text{FUNCTION P (n,x,a)} = \sum_{i=0}^{n} a_i x^{n-i}$$

which represents the series

$$a_0x^n + a_1x^{n-1} + \ldots + a_{n-1}x + a_n$$

This can be defined iteratively as

```
FUNCTION P(n,x,a). T = a₀. FROM i = 0 TO n - 1
T = xT + aᵢ₊₁. RETURN T. END.
```

When the program is executing, the following sequence occurs

```
T = a₀x + a₁                              (i = 0)
T = a₀x² + a₁x + a₂                       (i = 1)
T = a₀x³ + a₁x² + a₂x + a₃                (i = 2)
...
...
T = a₀xⁿ + ... + aₙ                       (i = n - 1)
```

A recursive definition equivalent to the previous one would be

```
FUNCTION P(n,x,a). IF n = 0 THEN P(n,x,a) = a₀
ELSE P(n,x,a) = xP(n - 1,x,a) + aₙ. END.
```

For n = 3, the computation would be executed as

```
P(3,x,a) = x*P(2,x,a) + a₃
P(2,x,a) = x*P(1,x,a) + a₂
P(1,x,a) + x*P(0,x,a) + a₁
P(0,x,a) = a₀
```

Therefore,

```
P₀ = a₀
P₁ = xa₀ + a₁
P₂ = x²a₀ + xa₁ + a₂
P₃ = x³a₀ + x²a₁ + xa₂ + a₃
```

In a language that permits recursion, a subroutine, even if not defined recursively, may be called recursively by the program.

For example, consider the subroutine with name

```
INT(a,b,x,F)
```

which computes

$$\int_a^b F(x)\,dx$$

for integrals of one variable. We might want to use this subroutine to compute an integral of more than one variable of integration, for example,

$$Z = \int_a^b \int_c^d F(x,y)\,dy\,dx$$

which could then be affected by

```
Z = INT(a,b,x,H)
H(x) = INT(c,d,y,G)
G(y) = F(x,y)
```

A nonrecursive language would not be able to evaluate such a recursive call, unless it used special programming tricks that amounted to a higher-level implementation of recursion itself. On the other hand, a nonrecursive language would have no difficulty in evaluating expressions such as

```
A = SQRT(SQRT(x))
B = SINE(SINE(τ))
```

as long as its implementation protocol was to evaluate the inner expression when encountering nested expressions. Thus, in the previous example, the inner SQRT function would return an explicit value to the outer SQRT function.

In general, implementation of full recursion is much more difficult than generation of iterative implementations for high-level notation. Implementation techniques for recursion are well known, however, and can be found in standard books on compiler-implementation techniques. The concern of this volume is not implementation techniques but rather language design that has the quality of user ease. From that point of view, iteration is much more desirable than recursive constructs. Since it is less abstract, iteration tends to lead to less confusion for the nonprofessional programmer. For most applications *at the user level,* recursion can be avoided by using the more desirable technique of high-level representation, as indicated by the previous expression for the double integral in normal mathematical notation. Recursion occurs on the implementational level and thus is not a concern for the nonprofessional user. For numerical computations, that is, the so-called number-crunching programs, iteration usually produces programs that run much faster than programs produced by recursive invocations.

It should be made clear, however, that recursion in and by itself is neither user-friendly nor -unfriendly. The evaluation of whether it serves a useful purpose in language design must take into account the specific application goals of a particular language. Indeed, recursion might be a useful attribute to language design even where the goals are simplicity, concreteness of language representation, and readability.

Certainly there is no problem, in terms of either understandability or implementation feasibility, in the use of a repeated function application which is nonrecursive. For example, if $F(x)$ and $G(x,y)$ have been defined as functions in the sense discussed previously, then the assignment

```
A = F(G(F(b),F(c)))
```

would be linguistically acceptable. It is reasonably understandable, does not involve an arbitrary number of repetitions, and is relatively easy to implement without side effects.

Also, recursion may be indirect, as when subprogram *P* calls subprogram *Q*, which, in turn, calls subprogram *P*. In the case of a subprogram that is defined recursively, it is possible that for certain arguments the subprogram may not terminate. For example, referring to the previous definition of FACTORIAL(N), the function will terminate as long as N is a positive integer. However, if N is a negative integer or has a fractional part, the subprogram will not terminate. It is beside the point that, mathematically, the subprogram is not a correct implementation of the *concept* factorial in those circumstances. Improper data or data that violate type declarations occur in programming practice in various ways. That, of course, is one argument for type declarations. But as indicated in Chap. 6, stronger counterarguments can be made with respect to the necessity of type declarations.

Chapter

8

The Language Design of a System for Scientific/Engineering/Mathematical Applications Programming

Basic Design Issues

Solution specifications to various scientific, engineering, and mathematical problems frequently can be represented by formulas where a required value is obtained as a function of one or more data-dependent variables. Unlike programs written in conventional programming languages, these solution specifications are characterized by two-dimensional representations, sometimes in a rather complex form. Symbols such as parentheses, brackets, and braces may be represented in different sizes to signal visually the scope of certain operators, even though in conventional mathematical notation the various-sized parenthetical symbols are functionally equivalent. Similarly, different-sized operator symbols are commonly used, for example, sigma $\sum$, integral $\int$, and pi as the product operator $\prod$, even though a small-sized operator symbol is semantically identical to a large-sized one.

The point is that it is easier to comprehend the scope of the intended operators and the span of the associated upper and lower limits of the expressions by varying the size of the symbols. Also, a two-dimensional textual display of solution procedures sometimes implies useful adjunct information. For example, two historically convenient representations of the derivative, with respect to time, have been

$$\dot{x}$$

or

$$\frac{dx}{dt}$$

The alternative forms have the same meaning. The second form is usually preferred, because it suggests that it can be treated like a fraction in certain circumstances, for example,

$$dx = \frac{dx}{dt}\,dt$$

It is explicit that the variable x is to be differentiated with respect to the variable t.

Another use of the conventional two-dimensional representation of mathematical forms can be illustrated by a representation of a continued fraction. For example, one may wish to represent a solution specification as the fraction:

$$\mathrm{R} = 1 + \cfrac{\mathrm{a}}{1 - \cfrac{\mathrm{a}}{2 + \cfrac{\mathrm{a}}{3 - \cfrac{\mathrm{a}}{2 + \cfrac{\mathrm{a}}{5 - \cfrac{\mathrm{a}}{2 + \cfrac{\mathrm{a}}{7 - \cfrac{\mathrm{a}}{2 + \cfrac{\mathrm{a}}{9}}}}}}}}}$$

In a conventional programming language, that would have to be represented in a linearized form such as

$$R = 1 + (a/(1 - (a/(2 + (a/(3 - (a/(2 + (a/(5 - (a/(2 + (a/(7 - (a/(2 + (a/9)))))))))))))))))$$

where the number of parentheses can be decreased if one relies on the rules of operator precedence for a specific programming language.

Historically, the representation of mathematical forms and the various notations associated with their representation have evolved in a relatively disciplined fashion. Two-dimensional representations have been favored, because pragmatic experience has shown that two-dimensional forms, particularly complex solution specifications represented in two-dimensional notation, are easier to understand than equivalent linearized text. Experience has also shown that a relatively small number of operator symbols have been sufficient to represent much of the literature dealing with computational solutions. Where new operator symbols are necessary, they can be created by easy-to-understand and straightforward definitions. Similarly, the syntax of mathematical representations can, in large part, be encompassed by a limited set of canonical forms, for example,

$$\frac{E}{F}, EF, E \pm F, \sqrt{E}, \int_l^u E\,dx, \sin E, \sin^{-1}E, (E), \{E\}, [E], \sum_{i=1}^{n} E_i, \prod_{i=1}^{n} E_i$$

and so on, where E and F are expressions and where the forms can be applied recursively. In addition, the solution specifications, as commonly used in mathematical text, encompass a relatively restricted set of syntactical forms and symbols, which in turn constitute a subset of English, more precisely referred to as technical English. Thus well-formed solution specifications for scientific/engineering/mathematical applications are characterized by limited variability in semantics and syntax and by a relatively small set of notational forms.

The computer processing to translate those representations can be handled by moderate-sized computational processes or translators. Figure 8.1 is a solution specification that is also an executable program, acceptable as input to a software system called the AUTOMATED PROGRAMMER.[1]

The obvious characteristic illustrated in Fig. 8.1 is the acceptance of such conventional notations as subscript expressions; superscript expressions as exponents; fractions to various levels of nesting; implied multiplication; logarithms to an arbitrary base; inverse trigonometric functions; numerator-over-denominator division; various forms for iteration; and symbols such as illustrated in Fig. 8.2, which include the operators for summation, product, definite integration, and square root. These operators and the square bracket and brace symbols may be input in various sizes and nested to arbitrary depth. Figure 8.3 shows these symbols taken to various sizes.

Not all mathematical text can be represented by a limited set of lexical symbols, notations, and syntactic forms. However, a substantial part of commonly used mathematical text can be so represented. This domain can be extended if easy mechanisms for the introduction of new tokens, notations, and forms are incorporated into a user system.

---

[1]AUTOMATED PROGRAMMER is a registered trademark of KGK Automated Systems, Inc.

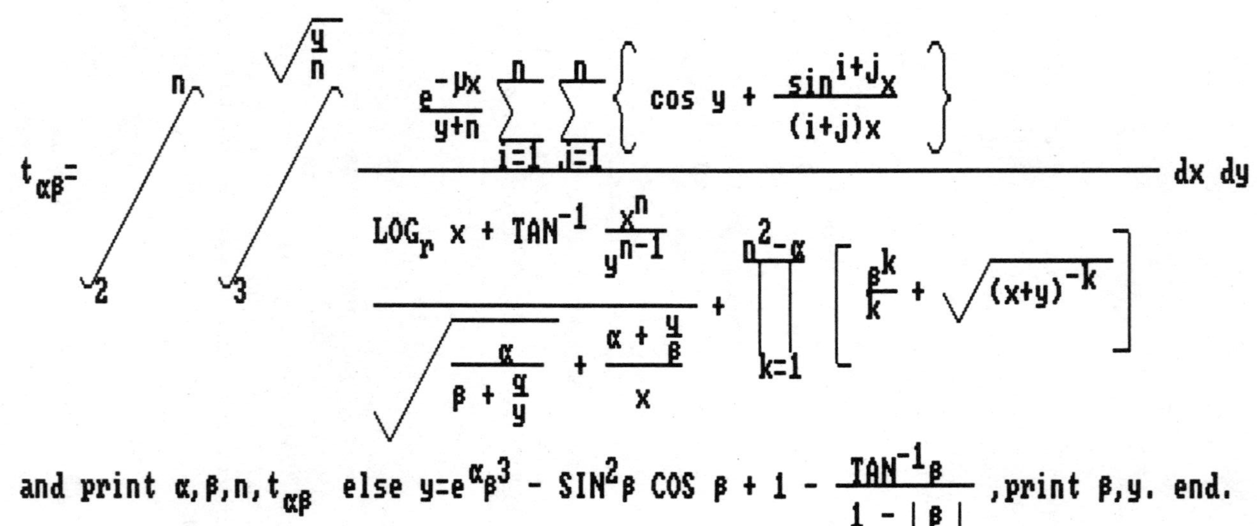

Figure 8.1 Actual program input as entered into the AUTOMATED PROGRAMMER. (*AUTOMATED PROGRAMMER is a registered trademark of KGK Automated Systems, Inc.*)

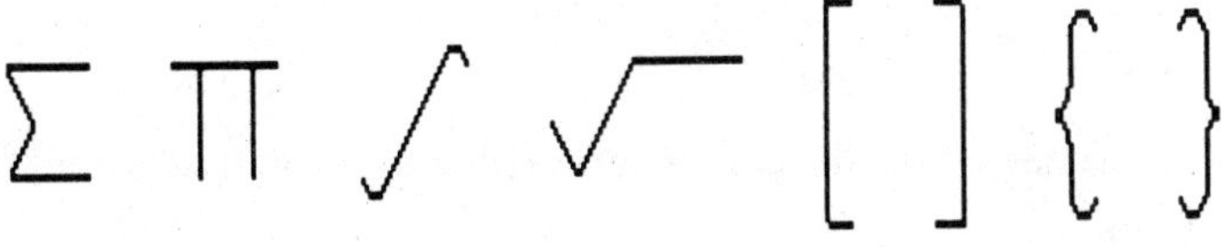

Figure 8.2

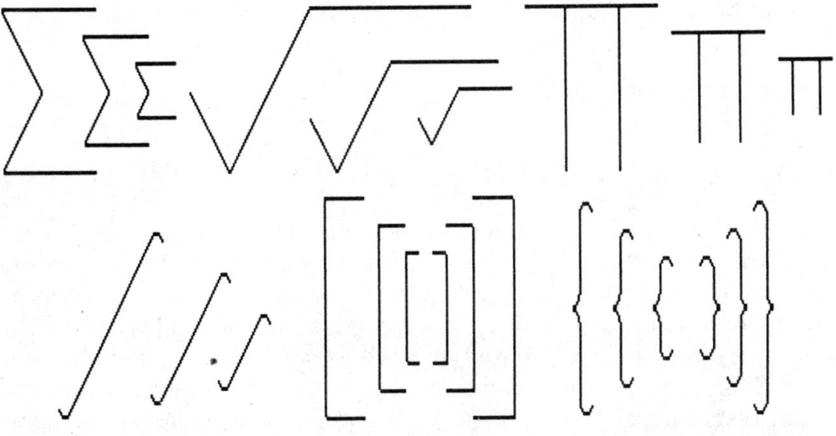

Figure 8.3

It is conventional to have a human being translate the cited examples into a linearized form, using some appropriate subroutine to do numerical (or symbolic) integration and other subroutines or functions to accomplish other operations. If one analyzes how a programmer translates the representation in Fig. 8.1 into a particular computer language, one can conclude that *the translation process, in this particular instance, consists of a series of purely mechanical steps and therefore can be automated.* The forms cited previously for double integration can be regarded as simply a graphical representation, and the various operators for integration, summation, parenthesization, square root, product, and the linear trigonometric forms can be recognized as simple distinct graphical substructures embedded in the overall representation. Once that is done, the process of translating from the graphical substructures to the equivalent conventional programming language constructs can be represented by the usual type of syntactical rewriting rules. For example, the form EF can be represented by the syntactical rule

EF → E * F

and the form $\frac{E}{F}$ represented by the rule

$$\frac{E}{F} \rightarrow E/F$$

A graphical substructure such as the integral symbol can be represented by the rule

$$\int_{l}^{u} f(x)dx \rightarrow \text{CALL SUBROUTINE INTEGRATION } (l, u, f(x), x)$$

or some other form more appropriate for evoking a subroutine.

Automated Programming

Thus a large class of solution specifications represented as conventional mathematical formulas can be translated automatically into a conventional programming language by using a translation paradigm equivalent to a set of conventional syntactic rewriting rules. The graphical substructures can be input as function-key *macro symbols,* thus avoiding complex pattern-recognition analysis, or more sophisticated, but viable, pattern-recognition analysis can be undertaken. It is not our purpose here to expand on various details of implementation, but rather to make the point that the process of translating conventional two-dimensional mathematical representations is, in principle, feasible. We can illustrate this with an example of a simpler instance of an integral embedded in a program that permits such forms. The program fragment containing the integral is shown in Fig. 8.4.

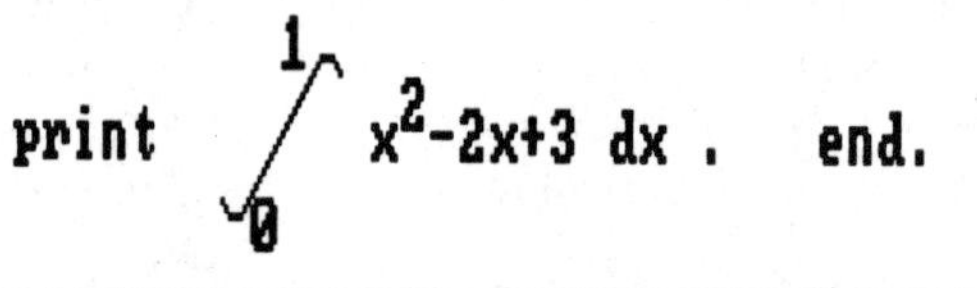

Figure 8.4

A *machine-generated* program, in the language C, which is computationally equivalent to Fig. 8.4 is shown in Fig. 8.5. Note that this program is not written in elegant style and is not optimal in terms of execution efficiency. That is because it was generated by a prototype "automated programmer," that is, a computer system that takes programs written in conventional (two-dimensional) mathematical notation and automatically translates them into a program written in a conventional language. Such machine-generated programs are not meant to be read by a human; they are to be input to an optimizing compiler to remove the code inefficiencies.

```
#include "stdio.h"
#include "math.h"
#include "clib.h"
 /* scalers: */
 float V0042; /* x */
 /* arrays: */
 /* system scalers: */
 float V0040 = 3.1415926535897930; /* c */
 float V0041 = 2.71828200; /* e */
 /* formats: */
 /* images: */
 /* functions: */
 /* statement functions: */
 double F0043(V0042) /* F0043 */
 double V0042;
 {
 return ( (double) (((pow(V0042,2.0000) - (2.0000*V0042)) + 3.0000)));
 }
 /* procedures: */
 int main(argc,argv)
 int argc;
 char *argv[];

 /* program acmint3 */
 {
 procargs(argc,argv);
 printf("%g ", integrate(0.0000,1.0000,F0043) );
 printf("\n");

 if (argc > 1) {
 if (IMAGEPOS ! = 0)
 printimage(twodoutput,LASTIMAGE,IMAGE);
 fprintf(twodoutput," -888 0 0\n");
 }
/* end of program */ }
```

Figure 8.5 Program produced by a prototype C-code-generation version of the AUTOMATED PROGRAMMER system.

The major point about this example is that the original program representation of Fig. 8.4, using conventional mathematical representation, would be understandable to anyone with minimal mathematical literacy, even one who did not originate that particular program or who is unfamiliar with the special idiosyncrasies of the particular automated programming system used to generate the C code. Such an assertion of obvious comprehensibility (*self-documentation*) could not be applied to the equivalent C program even if it were rewritten in a style that could be termed elegant and "documented" by more extensive comments. Furthermore, it would seem plausible that as the underlying problem formulation increases in terms of both visual and logical complexity, the attributes of comprehensibility between the two-dimensional representation and that of the equivalent linear-program representation will differ at a rate that may be closer to exponential than linear. Put concretely, for a *simple* mathematical problem, the difference in comprehensibility between a program representation permitting normal mathematical forms and a representation in a conventional programming language may be insignificant. But suppose program 1 has a complexity measure of a, and program 2 has a complexity measure of b, where the complexity metric is some plausible function of both visual and logical complexity and a is the same order of magnitude as b. Suppose the ratio of comprehensibility between program 1 in the "2-D representation" to the same program in the C language is close to 1, since a, the complexity of program 1, is small. The ratio of comprehensibility of program 2 compared to its C language representation can be expected not to differ substantially from program 1. But suppose another set of equivalent programs was such that the complexity ratio $b/a = 10$. Then what would the ratio of *comprehensibilities* (2-D representation)/(C representation) of program 2 compared to program 1 be? 10? 100? Or some even larger factor? In principle, the answer to that could be determined by controlled experiments to measure program comprehensibility (and programming performance). But the field of experimental studies of program comprehension and programming performance is still in a beginning stage, and no broad inferences can be drawn from the limited evidence available.

Not all problem-solution specifications, however, can be directly automated without some initial modification. This may require making explicit the limits to values that are neither explicit in the original specification nor implied by the text. Also, directions for input and output are usually necessary. An example of a solution specification that is not completely in a form appropriate for direct automation would be an algorithm for solving sets of linear algebraic equations of the form shown in Fig. 8.6. But this problem-solution specification can be rewritten with relatively minor syntactical and notational transformations and straightforward interpretation as the program (acceptable to an automated programmer system) shown in Fig. 8.7.

An automated programming system would generate the equivalent program coded in some conventional programming language or coded directly to machine language. It is more advantageous to generate the equivalent program in a conventional language such as FORTRAN, since there are vast libraries of programs, subroutines, and functions

For sets of linear algebraic equations of the form $\sum_{k=1}^{n} A_{ik}x_k = C_i$ where $i = 1, 2, \ldots, n$ and A_{ik}, C_i are given for $n \leqslant 20$, compute:

$$(1)\alpha_{ij} = A_{ij} - \sum_{k=1}^{j-1} \alpha_{ik}\alpha_{kj} \ (i \geqslant j);$$

$$(2)\alpha_{ij} = \frac{A_{ij} - \sum_{k=1}^{i-1} \alpha_{ik}\alpha_{kj}}{\alpha_{ii}} \ (i < j);$$

$$(3)g_i = \frac{C_i - \sum_{k=1}^{i-1} \alpha_{ik}g_k}{\alpha_{ii}}.$$

Then compute $x_i = g_i - \sum_{k=i+1}^{n} \alpha_{ik}x_k$ where $i = n, n-1, \ldots, 1$. For verification, compute the C's for $n = 3$ using the results for the x_i's.

Figure 8.6 An algorithm for linear algebraic equations.

Title CROUTt. Maximum n=20. Read"n=",n. Print "j=",j,"i=",i and read "A(i,j)=", $A_{i,j}$ for j=1 to n and i=1 to n. Print "i=",i and read "C(i)=",C_i for i=1 to n.

For i=1 to n and j=1 to n if i≥j then $\alpha_{ij} = A_{ij} - \sum_{k=1}^{j-1} \alpha_{ik}\alpha_{kj}$ else

$\alpha_{ij} = \dfrac{A_{ij} - \sum_{k=1}^{i-1} \alpha_{ik}\alpha_{kj}}{\alpha_{ii}}$. For i=1 to n $g_i = \dfrac{C_i - \sum_{k=1}^{i-1} \alpha_{ik}g_k}{\alpha_{ii}}$

For i=n,n-1,...,1 compute $x_i = g_i - \sum_{k=i+1}^{n} \alpha_{ik}x_k$. Print i ⟨2⟩,$x_i$ for i=1,2,...,n.

Print "C1=",$\sum_{j=1}^{n} A_{1,j}x_j$, "C2=",$\sum_{j=1}^{n} A_{2,j}x_j$,"C3=",$\sum_{j=1}^{n} A_{3,j}x_j$. end.

Figure 8.7 A two-dimensional program corresponding to Fig. 8.6.

that have already been written in FORTRAN and that can be incorporated (i.e., *linked*) with the FORTRAN code automatically generated by the automated programming system. Figure 8.7 is a graphics printout of program text as entered into the AUTOMATED PROGRAMMER. When this two-dimensional text is entered, and the command given to translate, this system will *automatically* produce the FORTRAN program shown in Fig. 8.8. Normally, this FORTRAN program will be *automatically* processed into object code and linked to external subprograms by the system using a conventional compiler and linker. The product of the program of Fig. 8.7 will be an executable module. The human effort (programming effort) has been confined to reformulating the form of the algorithm of Fig. 8.6 into the program—with almost identical mathematical text—of Fig. 8.7. The remaining effort has been completely automated! As we will indicate subsequently, entering the text of Fig. 8.7 can be done with less effort than usually needed for the input of mathematical text, i.e., by typing hard copy or by input via a mathematics word processor.

The machine-generated FORTRAN program differs in style from one that might be generated by a person using the specification of Fig. 8.6. In the corresponding two-dimensional program illustrated in Fig. 8.7, names may be of arbitrary length and may contain Greek or other characters not acceptable to FORTRAN. Therefore the specification/program names are replaced by "tokens" in the machine-generated FORTRAN program. The tokens are of the form *Vn* where *n* is an integer corresponding to the names of variables in the two-dimensional program. This has a positive effect on translation efficiency as well. Also, the linguistic constructs for a two-dimensional programming language may be made to be more general than FORTRAN in the use of iteration and selection. To accommodate this more general approach, GOTO statements may be generated even though they might be avoided in some specific instance of *simple* iteration or selection.

In any case, these machine-generated FORTRAN programs are not intended to be read or modified by people. The reading or modification should be done at the higher level of the two-dimensional program/specification. The advantage gained in generating the specific target language as FORTRAN (rather than executable machine code) is, as noted above, that the generated program can be linked easily with diverse FORTRAN libraries and other *human-generated* FORTRAN programs, embedded in a much larger program, or ported to other than the original host machine for subsequent compilation.

The same considerations apply to other possible target languages, for example, C or Ada.

```
      PROGRAM FIG$8$7
C ==>              This program has been generated by
C ==>
C ==>               The AUTOMATED PROGRAMMER System
C ==>
C ==> A trademarked product of KGK Automated Systems, Inc.
C ==>
      IMPLICIT REAL*8(T)
      COMMON /APALXTBE/ IMAGEL,V0058,V0061,V0063,V0064,V0066,V0074,V0075
     x,V0076,V0077,V0078,V0079,V0080,V0081,V0082,V0083,V0084,V0085,V0062
     x,V0065,V0069,V0071,V0073
      REAL*8 V0058,V0061,V0062(0:20,0:20),V0063,V0064,V0065(0:20),V0066,
     xV0069(0:20,0:20),V0071(0:20),V0073(0:20),V0074,V0075,V0076,V0077,V
     x0078,V0079,V0080,V0081,V0082,V0083,V0084,V0085
      CALL AP$INIT(-1)
      IF (IMAGEL .EQ. 0) THEN
      IMAGEL = 1
      CALL AP$RINIT(V0062,945)
      ENDIF
      WRITE (0,'(1X,/,1A,\)')'n='
      READ (INT(5),*)V0061
      TL2019 = V0061
      TI2019 = 0.1000D1
      DO 12019 V0064 = TI2019,TL2019,SIGN(1.0D0,TL2019-TI2019)
      TL2017 = V0061
      TI2017 = 0.1000D1
      DO 12017 V0063 = TI2017,TL2017,SIGN(1.0D0,TL2017-TI2017)
      WRITE (6,12012)V0063,V0064
12012 FORMAT (1X,2Hj=,G15.8,1X,2Hi=,G15.8,1X)
```

Figure 8.8 FORTRAN output automatically generated by the AUTOMATED PROGRAMMER from the input of Fig. 8.7.

```
      WRITE (0,'(1X,/,1A,\)')'A(i,j)='
      READ (INT(5),*)V0062(NINT(V0064),NINT(V0063))
12017 CONTINUE
12019 CONTINUE
      TL2027 = V0061
      TI2027 = 0.1000D1
      DO 12027 V0066 = TI2027,TL2027,SIGN(1.0D0,TL2027-TI2027)
      WRITE (6,12022)V0066
12022 FORMAT (1X,2Hi=,G15.8,1X)
      WRITE (0,'(1X,/,1A,\)')'C(i)='
      READ (INT(5),*)V0065(NINT(V0066))
12027 CONTINUE
      TL2030 = V0061
      TI2030 = 0.1000D1
      DO 12030 V0075 = TI2030,TL2030,SIGN(1.0D0,TL2030-TI2030)
      TL2032 = V0061
      TI2032 = 0.1000D1
      DO 12032 V0076 = TI2032,TL2032,SIGN(1.0D0,TL2032-TI2032)
      IF ((V0075 .GE. V0076)) THEN
      T2042 = 0.0
      DO 12042 V0077 = ANINT(0.1000D1),(V0076-0.1000D1)
      T2042 = T2042+(V0069(NINT(V0075),NINT(V0077))*V0069(NINT(V0077),NI
     xNT(V0076)))
12042 CONTINUE
      V0069(NINT(V0075),NINT(V0076)) = (V0062(NINT(V0075),NINT(V0076))-T
     x2042)
      ELSE
      T2054 = 0.0
      DO 12054 V0078 = ANINT(0.1000D1),(V0075-0.1000D1)
```

Figure 8.8 *(Continued)*

```
      T2054 = T2054+(V0069(NINT(V0075),NINT(V0078))*V0069(NINT(V0078),NI
     xNT(V0076)))
12054 CONTINUE
      V0069(NINT(V0075),NINT(V0076)) = ((V0062(NINT(V0075),NINT(V0076))-
     xT2054)/V0069(NINT(V0075),NINT(V0075)))
      ENDIF
12032 CONTINUE
12030 CONTINUE
      TL2063 = V0061
      TI2063 = 0.1000D1
      DO 12063 V0079 = TI2063,TL2063,SIGN(1.0D0,TL2063-TI2063)
      T2072 = 0.0
      DO 12072 V0080 = ANINT(0.1000D1),(V0079-0.1000D1)
      T2072 = T2072+(V0069(NINT(V0079),NINT(V0080))*V0071(NINT(V0080)))
12072 CONTINUE
      V0071(NINT(V0079)) = ((V0065(NINT(V0079))-T2072)/V0069(NINT(V0079)
     x,NINT(V0079)))
12063 CONTINUE
      DO 12082 V0081 = V0061,0.1000D1,((V0061-0.1000D1)-V0061)
      T2090 = 0.0
      DO 12090 V0082 = ANINT((V0081+0.1000D1)),V0061
      T2090 = T2090+(V0069(NINT(V0081),NINT(V0082))*V0073(NINT(V0082)))
12090 CONTINUE
      V0073(NINT(V0081)) = (V0071(NINT(V0081))-T2090)
12082 CONTINUE
      DO 12099 V0074 = 0.1000D1,V0061,(0.2000D1-0.1000D1)
      WRITE (6,12095)V0074,V0073(NINT(V0074))
12095 FORMAT (1X,F2.0,G15.8,1X)
12099 CONTINUE
```

Figure 8.8 *(Continued)*

```
      T2107 = 0.0
      DO 12107 V0083 = ANINT(0.1000D1),V0061
      T2107 = T2107+(V0062(NINT(0.1000D1),NINT(V0083))*V0073(NINT(V0083)
     x))
12107 CONTINUE
      T2114 = 0.0
      DO 12114 V0084 = ANINT(0.1000D1),V0061
      T2114 = T2114+(V0062(NINT(0.2000D1),NINT(V0084))*V0073(NINT(V0084)
     x))
12114 CONTINUE
      T2121 = 0.0
      DO 12121 V0085 = ANINT(0.1000D1),V0061
      T2121 = T2121+(V0062(NINT(0.3000D1),NINT(V0085))*V0073(NINT(V0085)
     x))
12121 CONTINUE
      WRITE (6,12122)T2107,T2114,T2121
12122 FORMAT (1X,3HC1=,G15.8,1X,3HC2=,G15.8,1X,3HC3=,G15.8,1X)
      CALL AP$ERR(0)
99    STOP
      END
      BLOCK DATA APBLXTBE
      COMMON /APALXTBE/ IMAGEL,V0058,V0061,V0063,V0064,V0066,V0074,V0075
     x,V0076,V0077,V0078,V0079,V0080,V0081,V0082,V0083,V0084,V0085,V0062
     x,V0065,V0069,V0071,V0073
      REAL*8 V0058,V0061,V0062(0:20,0:20),V0063,V0064,V0065(0:20),V0066,
     xV0069(0:20,0:20),V0071(0:20),V0073(0:20),V0074,V0075,V0076,V0077,V
     x0078,V0079,V0080,V0081,V0082,V0083,V0084,V0085
      DATA V0058/0.0000000010000000D0/,V0061/0.2000D2/
      END
```

Figure 8.8 *(Continued)*

The equivalent program coded in C, as produced by the automated programming system, is shown in Fig. 8.9. This machine-generated C program[2] was produced by a prototype C-language generator specifically designed to produce nonstructured code for purely experimental study purposes. In due course, this prototype generator will be replaced by a more sophisticated generator that will produce C code more susceptible to optimization by a standard C-language compiler.

```
#include "stdio.h"
#include "math.h"
#include "clib.h"
  /* scalers: */
  float V0051; /* n */
  float V0053; /* j */
  float V0054; /* i */
  float V0056; /* i */
  float V0060; /* i */
  float V0061; /* i */
  float V0062; /* j */
  float V0063; /* k */
  float V0064; /* k */
  float V0065; /* i */
  float V0066; /* k */
  float V0067; /* i */
  float V0068; /* k */
  float V0069; /* j */
  float V0070; /* j */
  float V0071; /* j */
  /* arrays: */
  float V0052[0021][0021]; /* A */
  float V0055[0021]; /* C */
  float V0057[0021][0021]; /* a */
  float V0058[0021]; /* g */
  float V0059[0021]; /* x */
  /* system scalers: */
  float V0048=3.1415926535897930e0000;   /*   */
  float V0049=2.7182818284590450e0000;   /* e */
  float V0050=1.0000e0099; /* INFINITY */
  /* formats: */
  /* images: */
  /* functions: */
```

Figure 8.9 C language output automatically generated by the AUTOMATED PROGRAMMER from the input of Fig. 8.7.

---

[2]This program was produced by use of a special prototype C-code-generation version of the AUTOMATED PROGRAMMER system, a registered trademark of KGK Automated Systems, Inc.

```
/* statement functions: */
/* procedures: */
int main(argc,argv)
int argc;
char *argv[];

/* program CROUTt */
{
procargs(argc,argv);
V0051 = getdata(stdin,"n=");
V0054 = 1.0000; /* code for from triple 2034 */
while ((V0051-V0054)*1.0000 >=0)
{ /* for body 2034 */
V0053 = 1.0000; /* code for from triple 2027 */
while ((V0051-V0053)*1.0000 >=0)
{ /* for body 2027 */
printf(
"j=");
printf("%g ",V0053
);
printf(
"i=");
printf("%g ",V0054
);
printf("\n");
V0052[round(V0054)][round(V0053)] = getdata(stdin,"A(i,j)=");
V0053 += 1.0000;
} /* for body 2027 */
V0054 += 1.0000;
} /* for body 2034 */
V0056 = 1.0000; /* code for from triple 2047 */
while ((V0051-V0056)*1.0000 >=0)
{ /* for body 2047 */
printf(
"i=");
printf("%g ",V0056
);
printf("\n");
V0055[round(V0056)] = getdata(stdin,"C(i)=");
V0056 += 1.000;
} /* for body 2047 */
V0061 = 1.0000; /* code for from triple 2055 */
while ((V0051-V0061)*1.0000 >=0)
{ /* for body 2055 */
V0062 = 1.0000; /* code for from triple 2062 */
while ((V0061-V0062)*1.0000 >=0)
{ /* for body 2062 */
if ((V0061 >= V0062)) { /* code for if triple 2098 */
```

Figure 8.9 *(Continued)*

```
V0063 = 1.0000; /* code for sum triple 2076 */
*++EXTRA = 0;
while (V0063 <= (V0062 - 1.0000))
{

(*EXTRA)+ =((V0057[round(V0061)][round(V0063)]*V0057[round(V0063)]
[round(V0062)]]);
V0063++;
}
V0057[round(V0061)][round(V0062)] =
(V0052[round(V0061)][round(V0062)] - (*EXTRA--)); /* code for assignmet
triple 2078 */
/* close then 2098 */ } else {
V0064 = 1.0000; /* code for sum triple 2092 */
*++EXTRA = 0;
while (V0064 <= (V0061 - 1.0000))
{

(*EXTRA)+ =((V0057[round(V0061)][round(V0064)]*V0057[round(V0064)]
[round(V0062)]]);
V0064++;
}
V0057[round(V0061)][round(V0062)] =
((V0052[round(V0061)][round(V0062)] - (*EXTRA--))/V0057[round(V0061)]
[round(V0061)]); /* code for assignmet triple 2096 */
/* close else 2098 */ }
V0062 += 1.0000;
} /* for body 2062 */
V0061 += 1.0000;
} /* for body 2055 */
V0065 = 1.0000; /* code for from triple 2106 */
while ((V0051 - V0065)*1.0000 >=0)
{ /* for body 2106 */
V0066 = 1.0000; /* code for sum triple 2119 */
*++EXTRA = 0;
while (V0066 <= (V0065 - 1.0000))
{
(*EXTRA)+ =((V0057[round(V0065)][round(V0066)]*V0058[round(V0066)]]);
V0066++;
}
V0058[round(V0065)] =
((V0055[round(V0065)] - (*EXTRA--))/V0057[round(V0065)][round(V0065)]);
/* code for assignmet triple 2123 */
V0065 += 1.0000;
} /* for body 2106 */
V0067 = V0051; /* code for from triple 2134 */
while ((0 == (V0067 < 1.0000)))
```

Figure 8.9 *(Continued)*

```
{ /* for body 2134 */
V0068 = (V0067+1.0000); /* code for sum triple 2144 */
*++EXTRA = 0;
while (V0068 <= V0051)
{
(*EXTRA)+=((V0057[round(V0067)][round(V0068)]*V0059[round(V0068)]));
V0068++;
}
V0059[round(V0067)] = (V0058[round(V0067)]-(*EXTRA--)); /* code for
assignmet triple 2146 */
V0067 += (-1.0000);
} /* for body 2134 */
V0060 = 1.0000; /* code for from triple 2157 */
while ((V0051-V0060)*(2.0000-1.0000) >=0)
{ /* for body 2157 */
printf("%2d ",(int) V0060
);
printf("%g ",V0059[round(V0060)]
);
printf("\n");
V0060 += (2.0000-1.0000);
} /* for body 2157 */
printf(
"Cl=");
V0069 = 1.0000; /* code for sum triple 2169 */
*++EXTRA = 0;
while (V0069 <= V0051)
{
(*EXTRA)+=((V0052[round(1.0000)][round(V0069)]*V0059[round(V0069)]));
V0069++;
}
printf("%g ",(*EXTRA--)
);
printf(
"C2=");
V0070 = 1.0000; /* code for sum triple 2180 */
*++EXTRA = 0;
while (V0070 <= V0051)
{
(*EXTRA)+=((V0052[round(2.0000)][round(V0070)]*V0059[round(V0070)]));
V0070++;
}
printf("%g ",(*EXTRA--)
);
printf(
"C3=");
V0071 = 1.0000; /* code for sum triple 2191 */
```

Figure 8.9 *(Continued)*

```
*++EXTRA = 0;
while (V0071 <= V0051)
{
(*EXTRA)+=((V0052[round(3.0000)][round(V0071)]*V0059[round(V0071)]));
V0071++;
}
printf("%g ",(*EXTRA--)
);
printf("\n");

if (argc > 1) {
if (IMAGEPOS != 0)
printimage(twodoutput,LASTIMAGE,IMAGE);
fprintf(twodoutput," -888 0 0\n");
}
/* end of program*/ }
```

Figure 8.9 *(Continued)*

The execution of the machine-generated C program of Fig. 8.9 produces the record of input data and output results shown in Fig. 8.10.

Thus the amount of translation necessary to go from problem-solution representation to two-dimensional-program representation is minimal compared to that necessary to go from problem-solution representation to a program written in a conventional programming language such as C, PASCAL, FORTRAN, or Ada. Thus, put in terms of the concepts treated in earlier chapters, we have illustrated how one can minimize the linguistic difference between problem-solution representation and executable program representation.

Another program that is acceptable as input to the AUTOMATED PROGRAMMER is given in Fig. 8.11. Its purpose is the same as the program illustrated in Fig. 8.7, but it uses a different algorithm for the solution of linear algebraic equations. The text between the left character { and the right character } is composed of comments and does not generate code. All other notations are to be interpreted as in conventional mathematical text. A much simpler program to calculate the mean and standard deviation of a set of input data is shown in Fig. 8.12. Here the text strings within quotes as arguments of the PRINT clause are printed as literals, as is conventional. The use of the word END to terminate a program is optional.

In the ideal sense, for a specific application domain, the goal of the language designer should be to produce a language system where the problem solution can be represented by syntactical and notational forms that are "natural" to that specific application domain and that are directly executable. The language designer who wishes to further

```
croutt
n=3
j=1.000000 i=1.000000
A(i,j)=1
j=2.000000 i=1.000000
A(i,j)=2
j=3.000000 i=1.000000
A(i,j)=3
j=1.000000 i=2.000000
A(i,j)=2
j=2.000000 i=2.000000
A(i,j)=3
j=3.000000 i=2.000000
A(i,j)=1
j=1.000000 i=3.000000
A(i,j)=2
j=2.000000 i=3.000000
A(i,j)=1
j=3.000000 i=3.000000
A(i,j)=2
i=1.000000
C(i)=1
i=2.000000
C(i)=1
i=3.00000
C(i)=1
  1 0.272727
  2 0.090909
  3 0.181818
C1=1.000000 C2= 1.000000 C3=1.000000
```

Figure 8.10 Input and output at execution of the program of Fig. 8.9.

the goal of automated programming must not only choose syntactic structures and notational forms already existing in a particular field, but must examine them for implementation feasibility, as well as determine if they are better comprehended, in a *cognitive* sense, than some equivalent, in a *logical* sense, alternative representation. The previous example of a continued fraction in two-dimensional representation compared to a linear representation illustrates this point. Logically, they are equivalent. But which is more comprehensible in a cognitive sense? The answer can be framed in the context of current practices of mathematical education or from the standpoint that all notations and syntax are a priori equivalent in a cognitive sense. We know of nobody of experience who would sustain the latter hypothesis.

```
title gaussian elimination.

maximum n=50. read n.
{ READ THE COEFFICIENT MATRIX ROW BY ROW }

    for i:=1 to n and j:=1 to n read W_ij.

{ READ RIGHT HAND SIDE }  for i:=1 to n read W_i,n+1.

{ INITIALIZE PIVOT VECTOR }  P_i:=i for i:=1,...,n.

for i:=1 to n D_i :=|W_i,1|,(for j:=2 to n if |W_ij|> D_i then D_i := |W_ij|),

if D_i:=0 then print "MATRIX IS NOT INVERTIBLE  " and stop.

for k:=1 to n-1 compute I:=k,
```

$$\text{colmax} := \left| \frac{W_{P_k,k}}{D_{P_k}} \right| \text{, (for } i:=k+1 \text{ to } n \text{ if } \left| \frac{W_{P_i,k}}{D_{P_i}} \right| > \text{colmax then}$$

$$\text{colmax} := \left| \frac{W_{P_i,k}}{D_{P_i}} \right| \text{, } I:=i\text{), (if colmax := 0 print "MATRIX NOT INVERTIBLE" and stop)}$$

```
{ INTERCHANGE P_i AND P_k WHERE i IS THE INDEX OF THE MAXIMUM COLMAX }
```

$$t:=P_I,\ P_I:=P_k,\ P_k:=t,\ (W_{P_i,j}:=W_{P_i,j} - \frac{W_{P_i,k}}{W_{P_k,k}} W_{P_k,j} \text{ for } i:=k+1 \text{ to } n \text{ and } j:=k+1 \text{ to } n+1).$$

```
if W_(P_n),n:=0 then print "MATRIX NOT INVERTIBLE " and stop.
{ SOLVE FOR UNKNOWNS BY FORWARD AND BACKWARD SUBSTITUTION }
```

$$x_k := \frac{W_{P_k,n+1} - \sum_{j:=k+1}^{n} W_{P_k,j} x_j}{W_{P_k,k}} \quad \text{for } k:=n \text{ to } 1.$$

```
{ OUTPUT THE RESULTS } for k:=1 to n print x_k.  end.
```

Figure 8.11 Another program for the solution of a set of linear algebraic equations.

```
title mean.
```

maximum n=20. read n. for i=1 to n read x_i. mean = $\dfrac{\sum_{i=1}^{n} x_i}{n}$,

std = $\sqrt{\dfrac{\sum_{i=1}^{n} (mean-x_i)^2}{n-1}}$ and print "mean = " mean,

"standard deviation = " std. end.

Figure 8.12 A simple program to compute the mean and standard deviation of input data.

All these considerations strongly imply that two-dimensional forms are critical for the design of computer languages intended for applications programming in engineering, scientific, and mathematical domains. Further, there should be a supporting vocabulary (reserved key words) and syntactic structures that mimic technical English. There should also be some underlying strategy to resolve ambiguity.

The previous examples in this chapter were chosen to illustrate that the linguistic differences between the problem representation and the representation of the executable program were either none or minimal. Thus the degree of feasible automation can be said to be directly related to the minimization of linguistic difference. Where this minimization is possible for a specific application domain, there is less need for detailed program comments or a separate requirements document to aid in future changes to the method of problem solution. Put a different way, the executable program becomes self-documenting because the programming structures, forms, and notations are already familiar to those professionals working in a specific area.

Linguistic Characteristics

If we wish to design a language suitable for automating the goal of scientific/engineering/mathematical applications programming, we might summarize the linguistic requirements of such a design as follows:

The lexical constraints governing the creation of an executable pro-

gram should be minimal. The underlying goal should be the capability for fast and accurate programming that mimics the documentation of the solution specification expressed in technical English.

We can illustrate this point by describing some of the lexical characteristics of the AUTOMATED PROGRAMMER. In this system variable names may be of arbitrary length *and names need not be declared.* Since implicit multiplication is also permitted (as in conventional mathematical notation), the system must resolve the possible lexical ambiguity in the statement $y = ab$. Is this to be interpreted as $y = a * b$ or as $y = ab$, where ab is a two-character name? The system scans the entire program looking for various semantic clues to make the proper lexical discrimination. Although not common, it is possible (intentionally or otherwise) to use a naming style that will create an inherent lexical ambiguity in analyzing a string of characters. For these cases, the system makes a default lexical analysis and then, on request, displays to the user the entire program where the system interpretation of juxtaposed names is clearly indicated by alternately highlighting each adjacent name. This is consistent with the philosophy of feeding back to the user the system interpretation of input so as to minimize semantic differences between *user intent* and *actual execution.*

Naturally, because of the available character set (see Fig. 9.4), names may include Greek characters as well as digits. Uppercase English characters are distinguished from lowercase characters, and periods (or decimal points) are allowed within names. This is to facilitate the reading of (distinct) long names such as *TheMinimumWaterVelocity* which could also be phrased as *the.minimum.water.velocity,* or perhaps as *The.Minimum.Water.Velocity.* The distinction between uppercase and lowercase serves to increase the availability of names constructed from English characters. Names may also be single Greek characters or mixed English-Greek character sequences. Similar names may also be distinguished by primes, that is, A, A′, A″ A‴.

However, upper- and lowercase are not distinguished for key words. Since the basic syntactic structure is a complex sentence, this facilitates a better literary style, such as permitting the capitalization of the first letter of a key word when it begins a sentence.

Noise words such as COMPUTE are optional. If used, they make for a more readable program document and also may help the system to resolve possible syntactical ambiguity by serving as a clause delimiter.

Solution specifications use different nomenclatures and different linguistic styles. Since the intent is to facilitate the translation (and in some cases, the copying) of the solution-specification document into the program document, various synonyms or synonymous phrases are also permitted. For example, *Print, Output, Write* are equivalent. Also, *skip a line* will produce the same effect as *skip 1 line*. Words may play dual roles. For example, the key word AND may simply serve as a connective between phrases or it may be interpreted as a logical operator within a boolean expression. The appropriate lexical identification is resolved by contextual analysis. The reason for this lexical flexibility is both to minimize the number of key words to be remembered and to allow use of common synonyms, that is, common to professional practice and prior familiarity with key words of conventional programming languages.

Punctuation rules are kept to a minimum. Blank spaces serve to delimit lexical tokens as well as to help in the resolution of syntactic ambiguity. The period (followed by a blank space) serves to signal the end of a sentence. Of course, the period character is also used as a decimal point. Any ambiguity between these two intentions is resolved in context. Parentheses, if used, serve to delimit the scope of a clause within a sentence. Colons and semicolons are not used, since experience with conventional languages indicates that they are prone to usage errors. Only the single symbol = is used, whether for assignment, equality, or constant definition. This avoids the arcane representations common in languages such as C and is consistent with conventional mathematical notation. The usual mathematical symbols for "not equal," "greater than or equal to," etc., are available as single characters. The character *d* is used as a differential operator in the context of an expression to be integrated. This does not interfere with its use as a variable name or as part of a variable name outside that context. The single character words *e* and π are reserved as system constants with double-precision values equal to the conventional mathematical representation. However, this does not interfere with their use as characters within a multicharacter variable name. There are some additional special characters which aid in simplifying the programming of complex output formats, especially those involving mathematical expressions or other two-dimensional graphic constructs, as well as some primitive graphic characters. The reverse-video characters which serve as placeholders have been discussed in Chap. 5. The remaining special characters appear in the keyboard layout of Fig. 9.4. The "primitive" characters \ | _ / { } ∩ ∪ may be used to manually construct mathematical symbols, or, more conveniently, a standard set of symbols of various sizes may be generated by using the function keys of the keyboard. This is discussed in more detail in Chap. 9.

Users desiring to indicate explicit multiplication may use an asterisk, center dot, or the conventional × symbol. The latter two symbols may also be used to distinguish between scaler (inner product) and cross product (outer product) when the operands are vectors. As is conventional, single or double quotes are used for literal strings in output formats. The beginning of a comment is a signaled by the { character and terminated by the matching } character. Comments may be positioned anywhere within the sentence or may precede or follow a sentence anywhere in the program.

The executable program should be represented in terms of syntactical structures, two-dimensional forms, and other notations conventional to the specific application domain.

The syntax for this language should be flexible, providing alternative forms and control structures. Such flexibility matches conventional usage of scientific documentation. Because the range of flexibility is limited for a large subset of scientific documentation, this is a feasible goal for computer automation.

One of the dividends of lexical and syntactic flexibility is the ability to generate programs that, while equivalent, are written in different programming styles. For example, the program in Fig. 8.13 is written in a textbook style (using a typeset representation). The program in Fig. 8.14 is written in a mixed FORTRAN-BASIC style.

Maximum $n=20$. Read n. Read A_i,B_i for $i=0$ to n.

$x = \sum_{i=0}^{n} \left\{ A_i \prod_{j=i}^{n} B_j A_j \right\}$. Print x. End.

Figure 8.13

Maximum $W=20$. Read W. $\delta=0$. For $x=0$ to W read u_x,v_x, Loop to formula 3 for $x=0$ to W. $\sigma=1$. For $y=x$ to W $\sigma=\sigma u_y v_y$. $\delta=\delta+u_x\sigma$. Formula 3. Print δ. End.

Figure 8.14

And finally, the program shown in Fig. 8.15 is written in assembly-language style using GOTOs.

Dimension x_{20},y_{20}.$\alpha=0$. Read σ. Statement 1. Read x_α,y_α.$\alpha=\alpha+1$. If $\alpha\leq\sigma$ goto statement 1. $S=\alpha=0$. Statement 2. $\beta=\alpha$. $P=1$. Statement 3. $P=Px_\beta y_\beta$. $\beta=\beta+1$. If $\beta\leq\sigma$ then goto statement 3. $S=S+Px_\alpha$ and $\alpha=\alpha+1$. If $\sigma\geq\alpha$ goto statement 2. Print S. End.

Figure 8.15

One conventional viewpoint might argue that syntactic flexibility is a drawback, since computationally equivalent programs, as illustrated in Figs. 8.13, 8.14, and 8.15 can have different representations. Indeed, this would be a drawback if it were customary to formulate problem-solution representations in a single style for a specific application domain. In reality, this is not the case. While scientific documentation can be considered to have a disciplined style of limited variability, in actual practice there is substantial diversity in representational and "literary" styles that cannot be ignored. Also, programmers are conditioned to different (conventional) programming styles. Since implementation of a uniform style of representation is unlikely, flexibility of programming style is desirable simply because it minimizes new programming effort. The arguments for strict uniformity of programming style are usually based on the belief that imposition of such uniformity will make proofs of program correctness possible for large, complex programs. But as yet, there is no convincing evidence that supports such a belief.

The basic linguistic structure should be a multiclause, multiline sentence where each "line" is a two-dimensional area. It should be multiclause in the sense indicated in Chaps. 3 and 4, where control structures may be regarded as modifying the basic core of the computational process. Usually this core is an assignment clause that represents the computational formula of classical numerical mathematics. Thus a FOR loop would modify some basic computational core represented by the underlying formula. In a similar fashion, other clauses such as WHILE and UNTIL can be regarded as modifying the essential computational core of the sentence. The basic sentence should be "multi-2D-line" since the historical concept of single lines dates back to the FORTRAN card image, an overly restrictive form that still haunts many more recent languages. We prefer to term the linguistic unit "sentence," since the intent is to model sentences of conventional mathematical text insofar as they represent a problem solution.

In the AUTOMATED PROGRAMMER a sentence may extend over an arbitrary number of 2-D lines and may contain various types of clauses. (A *2-D line* is one screen-width of the two-dimensional area occupied by a mathematical expression; see the discussion of the AUTOMATED PROGRAMMER editor in Chap. 9.) More than one sentence may start or terminate within the same line. Normally, the scope of control of a clause is the entire sentence, but, if desired, scope may be limited by parenthesizing that segment of the sentence which includes the specific clause. Clauses may be separated by spaces, commas, or words such as *compute* or *and,* the actual choice being a function of stylistic preference. Again, the idea is to permit a programming style which emulates that normally found in solution-specification documentation.

To implement such a style, it is necessary that the syntax be flexible in the sense that the order of clauses be unrestricted as long as the semantic intent is clear. This goal is further enhanced by the availability of various optional equivalent forms for the phrasing of a clause. These forms have been chosen so that they mimic the technical English explanatory style found in textbooks. Again, this tends to minimize the effort in translating from solution specification to executable program.

Conceptually, the simplest type of clause is the two-dimensional assignment statement. Essentially this uses the conventional notational representation of the formula where definite multiple integrals, definite summation and product operators, and square roots—these symbols constructed to various sizes—are accepted. Brackets and braces, drawn to various sizes, are available to enhance program document readability. Each of these forms may be nested to any arbitrary depth. Also, as illustrated in the previous figures, the usual textbook notations are used for exponentiation, subscripting, implied multiplication, numerator-over-denominator division, logarithms to a specific base, and inverse trigonometric functions. Since this system is oriented toward scientific, engineering, and mathematical applications, such a representation facilitates the *copying* of formulas from specifications.

The simplest way to cause repetitive execution of the contents of a sentence (or parenthesized sentence fragment) is to start or end a sentence (or parenthesized sentence fragment) with a FOR (or FROM) clause. Various acceptable syntax for this clause includes:

1. for v = E to G
2. FOR v = E by F to G
3. for v = E,F,G,...,H
4. For v = r(s)t
5. FOR v = E,F,G,H
6. For v = E by F while <*condition*>
7. for v = E by F until <*condition*>

where v is an index (iteration) variable; r, s, and t are linear expressions; E, F, G, and H are *two-dimensional expressions*; and <*condition*> is a logical or relational expression. In the first form, if E > G, then the index variable is decremented. In the third form, the difference between the last two expressions before the ellipses becomes the increment by which the index variable progresses to the next expression. In the fifth form, the list of expressions may be arbitrarily long. Spaces after a comma are optional and the key word FOR (or FROM) may be spelled with any combination of upper- or lowercase characters. For sequences of FOR clauses (nested loops), the "inner" loop is that clause textually nearest to the controlled program text. To enhance readability of sequences of FOR clauses, the second and later use of the key word FOR may be replaced by a space, a comma, or the word AND. For example,

```
For i=10 to 70, j=2 to 5 print i+j.
```

or equivalently,

```
Print i+j for j=2 to 5 and i=10 to 70.
```

Iteration of a sequence of clauses within a sentence may also be accomplished by inserting the clause WHILE <*condition*> or UNTIL <*condition*>. Repeated execution of a sequence of sentences may be accomplished by using the WHILE (UNTIL) clause (or a FOR clause) in conjunction with a LOOP TO clause. For example,

```
While x > A - B loop to statement 12.
```

In this case, the scope of the WHILE or UNTIL or FOR clauses is extended over the indicated sequence of sentences. This sequence culminates with the sentence STATEMENT 12. This may be interpreted as a labeled physical point in the text which does not associate with the next text sentence. Of course, a loop may also be set up in the usual way by using a GOTO, the idea being to accommodate various programming styles as well as documentation styles.

The justification for offering this flexibility of programming style is not only to minimize the translation from specification to program but also to recognize certain *psychological* aspects of the programming process. The design of the AUTOMATED PROGRAMMER assumes that constraint to a rigid, "unnatural" style—unnatural in the sense that it is in dissonance to the conventional linguistics associated with the application area—tends to make for an error-prone process. It recognizes that programmers come to their task with different backgrounds and that people have different conceptual styles. A programming language that is flexible and somewhat forgiving in its constraints is consistent with this sort of cognitive model. The following example further illustrates flexibility of alternative syntactic structures for iteration:

```
FOR n = 1,3,...,k, j = N(-3)k and i = j BY N to M
PRINT i,j,N.
FOR N = 1 (2) k AND j = N BY -3 to k AND i = j,
j + N,...,M PRINT i,j,N.
FROM N = 1 BY 2 TO k, FOR j = N, N - 3,...,k,
i = j(N)M PRINT i,j,N.
FOR N = 1,3,5,...,k AND j = N, N - 3,...,k AND FOR
i = j, j + N,...,M PRINT i,j,N.
FOR N = 1 (2) k, j = N ( - 3) k, i = j (N) M PRINT
i,j,N.
```

All of the forms in the example are computationally equivalent.

Consider the two sentences:

```
FOR i = 1 TO 10 j = i², print j.
FOR i = 1 TO 10, j = i², print j.
```

In the first sentence, the blank between 10 and j acts as a clause separator; that is, it separates the FOR clause from the assignment clause. There is no possible ambiguity here under our previous assumptions of the synonyms for the key word FOR. In the second sentence, the comma is a form that, *in context,* could serve as a synonym for FOR. Thus there is the possibility of interpreting the assignment phrase, $j = i^2$, as the initial value of a *second* (nested) loop in the index j. Since $j = i^2$ does not fit one of the previously cited forms for the argument of a FOR phrase, the possible ambiguity can be resolved automatically by default, or, and sometimes this is preferable, the user may be alerted to a possible error if the language permits a FOR phrase with a list structure (as in the AUTOMATED PROGRAMMER). This is illustrated by

```
FOR i = a + 2b, a - 2b, M(0.2)2M, C BY D - 1 TO E,
r,r + 1, F(G)H,z,...,w - a, L,M TO N, p - a PRINT
i,2i,3i.
```

This form does not permit an assignment phrase as an element of list, but a user might make such an error. The designer has to balance out the perception of the probability of user error with giving the "automated programmer" a great deal of intelligence in resolving ambiguity through context analysis. Of course, such a problem would not present itself if the user adopted a "literate" style of programming and produced the sentence

```
For i = 1 to 10 compute j = i² and print j.
```

The other major syntactical quality that must be considered in the design of a language is *selection* (conditional choice). In the AUTOMATED PROGRAMMER this is accomplished by the conventional programming construct, the IF...THEN...ELSE form where the ELSE clause is optional. What is unconventional is that the argument of IF may be a *two-dimensional* relational expression or logical expression using the logical connectives AND or OR. Subsequent IF forms may be nested within either the preceding THEN or ELSE clauses. Ambiguity is resolved by system-default choice or, preferably, by user-inserted parenthesization.

Notation that is unconventional or idiosyncratic in the specific application domain should be avoided in designing the language.

Explicit "programming" requirements should be minimized if the language system is to be successful. The need for training to use the system should not be a substantive effort. This may be illustrated by discussing the way that the AUTOMATED PROGRAMMER treats arrays, matrices, and vectors.

Normally, it is not necessary to declare the type, number of dimensions, or size of arrays, matrices, or vectors. By scanning the source program, the AUTOMATED PROGRAMMER can *infer* these attributes. In cases where this is not possible from a static analysis, as the system will inform the user, auxiliary declarations may be inserted in the program.

Arrays may be subscripted to an arbitrary number of dimensions and subscripts may be subscripted. Single-character variable subscripts need not be separated by commas. The system resolves this ambiguity and feeds back the information within the "dimension report" (see Fig. 8.16 and subsequent discussion) so that the user may verify the system interpretation. Again, the justification for this strategy is to attempt to relieve the programmer of the burden of creating all sorts of "boilerplate" but at the same time ensure that the source program has been correctly processed.

Matrix and vector arithmetic is supported *using standard textbook notation.* If the system infers that A and B are two-dimensional arrays, then the system will interpret AB, $A + B$, $A - B$ as the matrix product, matrix addition, and matrix subtraction, respectively. Multiplication may also be indicated explicitly by using an asterisk or center dot. The conjunction of a matrix and a vector will yield the appropriate matrix-vector or vector-matrix product. If one of the operands is a scaler, then the appropriate matrix-scaler arithmetic will be executed. Matrices may also be compared for equality or approximate equality. If two operands V and U are vectors, then placing a center dot between them, as in $V \cdot U$, will yield the vector inner product. Placing the special cross-product symbol between them, as in $V \times U$, will yield the vector cross product. (These symbols are illustrated in Fig. 9.4 at key positions 1 and 8, respectively.)

Entering

$A = B^t$

where t is a reverse-video character will result in the transpose of matrix B being assigned to matrix A. Entering

A^{-1}

will cause the calculation of the inverse of A *and automatic verification that A is neither singular nor so ill-conditioned as to lose acceptable numerical precision.* When desired, the user may enter *cond* A to cause explicit output of the condition number associated with the matrix A. Similarly, *det* A yields the determinant of A.

Entering

A^n

for a positive integer n, will give a result equivalent to the matrix multiplication of A by itself $n - 1$ times. Similarly, if n is a negative integer, the matrix product will be that of the inverse of A.

Entering

A°

yields the identity matrix whose order is the same as A.

Expressions of matrices, vectors, and scalars are also acceptable as long as they conform to conventional matrix arithmetic.

Normally, the indices of arrays start at 0. However, the user may specify that they start at 1. When matrix multiplication occurs between nonsquare matrix operands, the result must be sized appropriately, and the operation must be checked for mathematical consistency at *run time. This is all done automatically* to ensure that the final result is represented correctly when output.

When a READ MATRIX A is executed, where A has been determined to be an n-by-m array, then the system, at run time, will request the entry of m values for each of the n rows of A. All forms of input are free format, each data value separated by an arbitrary number of blanks or a comma, and erasable before pressing the enter key. The command READ MATRIX $A_{n,m}$ will cause the system, at run time, to request the entry of the first m values for each of the first n rows of A. PRINT A will cause the output of matrix A printed row by row. PRINT IMAGE 1 A will cause the elements of the matrix A to be printed in conformity with the placement of the reverse-video placeholders of IMAGE 1. (See the discussion in Chap. 5.)

The executable program should be as self-documenting as possible; it should be possible to insert nonexecutable comments anywhere in the program text. This would require the designation of "comment begin" and "comment end" symbols. For example, the character { could serve as the "begin" and } as the "end." But note that in a two-dimensional language where sentences have height as well as width, the begin-comment symbol can be placed anywhere vertically in the *column* which begins the two-dimensional comment. Likewise, the end-comment symbol can be placed anywhere vertically in the *column* which terminates the two-dimensional comment segment. Thus the comment itself can be *any* two-dimensional representation, either multiline text or graphics. Note also that even one character can serve both semantic functions.

The use of symbols with multiple meanings reduces the need for the user to memorize many unique tokens. An obvious example is the point mark, or period, which can serve as a decimal point (and possibly as a binary point) or as an end-of-sentence delimiter. In the examples cited previously, the point mark also has other semantic interpretations than can be resolved in the context of the characters before and after the point mark. Similarly, lexical complexity identification (such as arises when a point mark appears as a character in a variable name) is reduced if a sentence terminator is designated to be the juxtaposition "point mark" "blank." This "rule," since it is in accordance with good literary style, is consistent with a reasonable cognitive model of the user.

Techniques for editing program text should be highly user-oriented in the sense that they should be functionally obvious. In the previous examples of programs that contain two-dimensional mathematical forms, it is obvious that there should be at least two kinds of insertion: linear insertion and two-dimensional.

For linear insertion, since the left margin is usually (but not always) fixed for linear text, the easiest option for the user is to position the cursor at the point of insertion and press *one* "insert" key to accomplish a linear right-shift of one character space. Thus, when applied to a linear expression in the numerator position of a fraction, the numerator can be "opened up" without disturbing the rest of the two-dimensional representation. The limitation to a right-shift is usually not unduly restrictive, even when applied to a fragment of a two-dimensional expression. Of course, a linear left-shift could be implemented but at the expense of having to assign an additional key identifier. However, insertion that involves placing a two-dimensional form within a preexisting two-dimensional representation requires a "2D-right-shift" and a "2D-left-shift" in units of one vertical column of character space, the height of the column being bounded by the maximum height of the *implicit* rectangle that encloses the existing two-dimensional representation. This operation can be assigned either to two different keys or to one special key, with a case shift distinguishing left shift from right shift. Additional editing operations, such as block insertion, block deletion, and block copy, should be designed so that user protocol is *psychologically* obvious. This minimizes the user effort involved in learning a specific editing technique, as well as eliminates the necessity of detailed explanations such as found in conventional systems documentation. Major design goals are to avoid a complex time-ordered sequence; a complex simultaneous combination of keystrokes; and time-consuming call-ups of lists of options, or complex "menus." Menus that tend to be visually complex, contain long lists, contain items that themselves call other menus, or require reference to a user manual are not helpful to the user. (The editor used by the AUTOMATED PROGRAMMER to edit two-dimensional programs is discussed in Chap. 9.)

The language design should be such that conditioning the user to rigid syntactical forms is not necessary. Many so-called natural-language or natural-front-end systems use key words identical to words found in English. In itself, this is desirable, but for some systems the associated syntax tends to be rigid. Such systems do not, in any substantive way, "understand" commands or requests input by an untrained user. The user is *conditioned* in much the same way that one can teach a chicken to play a simple tune on a toy piano. The chicken is rewarded with grain after it pecks a correct key and given negative reinforcement after pecking a wrong key. When a user makes a request that does not conform to the very limited number of syntactic "templates" or semantic "frames," either the request is rejected or the system guides the user toward using the syntax and semantic framework acceptable to the system. (This system approach is discussed in more detail in Chap. 9.)

The difference between such an approach and what we have been discussing lies in the attributes of the specific application domain. As we pointed out in Chap. 1, true natural-language input poses problems of such complexity that a solution is not very probable within the current scope of linguistic knowledge. However, the domain of scientific, engineering, and mathematical applications programming can, in large part, be encompassed by a relatively small set of notational forms and a relatively small set of syntactical "phrases" that can be linked together into "sentences" that can be regarded as having a syntactic flexibility adequate for this specific (but wide) application domain. Put another way, some domains are incredibly difficult as far as language design and parsing are concerned, while other domains can yield to surprisingly simple strategies.

There should be intelligent, easy-to-comprehend feedback to the user of the system interpretation of input and an appropriate editing mechanism to resolve system misinterpretations. With respect to ambiguity resolution, there is no current theoretical model that is appropriate even for such a restricted domain as the recognition of formulas in conventional two-dimensional representation. To resolve this, the language designer should use contextual analysis where applicable and should attempt to construct a psychological model of the user in the context of the specific application domain. The language designer must determine what linguistic constructs are "normal" to the specific application domain and what constructs can be regarded as "pathological" so that prediction of possible interpretations of a program fragment can be implemented. For example, in a mathematical application program that contains the string

```
AcosB
```

was the intention of the user that AcosB be the name of a variable? Or that the string be interpreted as A * cos(B), where * denotes multiplication, *cos* is the name of the routine that returns the cosine of its argument, and *there is no other syntactic or semantic information that contradicts this interpretation?*

Either interpretation is *logically* admissible. The first interpretation, however, can be regarded as pathological to the specific application domain. The second is more probable only in the psychological, rather than the logical, sense. Decisions of language design, specifically strategies of ambiguity resolution, should not be regarded as fixed since they are functions of empirical experience. An important ingredient in ambiguity-resolution strategy is the willingness of the designer to amend, or even reject, a particular strategy if actual experience so dictates. In this sense, the *feedback loop is between the designer and the user.*

To further illustrate these points: When the program of Fig. 8.1 is entered into the AUTOMATED PROGRAMMER system to be translated, the system, after its initial scan of the program, will emit the warning message, "Possible misinterpretation of an assignment as a FOR clause." It will also give the two-dimensional line number, row number, and column number of the beginning of the phrase referenced. In this case, the system is calling attention to the character string $\beta = 2(2)n$ in the middle of the first line of the program of Fig. 8.1. Here the system has interpreted this string as the third (implicit) FOR clause with the iteration index β. (Reading from left to right, the first iteration clause is over n, the second iteration clause is over α.) For this specific example, this interpretation is consistent with the underlying algorithm and the programmer's intent. But since there is the possibility of ambiguity, that is, $\beta = 2(2)n$ *could be* an assignment in a different context, the system feeds back a warning of possible ambiguity. If the AUTOMATED PROGRAMMER should detect an actual error, i.e., unacceptable syntax or a fault in lexical naming, then it would not only emit an error message with a specific diagnosis but would immediately return to its editor and display the offending program and position the screen cursor at the incorrect point of the program so that editing corrections may be made immediately.

Another type of feedback would be caused by the processing of the program of Fig. 8.7. This program involves the manipulation of two-dimensional arrays. However, many of the subscripts are written as *ij* or *ik* or *kj* or *ii,* not as *i,j* or *i,k* or *k,j* or *i,i*. Both forms are conventional and acceptable, but the commas are generally not used explicitly if the *meaning* seems clear. The possible ambiguity here is that *ij* might be interpreted as the *product* of *i* and *j*. The AUTOMATED PROGRAMMER analyzes the entire program, evaluating the *global context* to decide which interpretation of the subscripts is more probable. Also, based on its analysis of the entire program, the AUTOMATED PROGRAMMER assigns the necessary storage even if a dimensionlike declaration is not present in the program; that is, it infers the amount of storage necessary. However, since the system interpretation is based on probable inference, and could conceivably not match the programmer's intent, the system feeds back a "dimension report" to the user. This is illustrated in Fig. 8.16. In the figure, the "warning" is caused by the lack of information in the program (of Fig. 8.7) that would allow the system to deduce a fixed array size for the named arrays. In fact, the actual array size is controlled by the *input* variable n. But maximum storage must be allocated based on the declaration that n has a maximum value of 20. The report lists the dimension of each array or vector variable and the maximum value of their respective

```
Automatic Dimensioning Report:

WARNING:  Unable to minimize subscript for any array.
The first physical index for all arrays is 0
The default first logical index for all matrices and vectors is 1

Array                         Largest Index for Each Dimension
Name                 Number       1      2
-----                ------     ----   ----
A                       2        20     20
C                       1        20
α                       2&       20#    20
g                       1        20#
x                       1        20#
Notes:
#     -- Unable to maximize subscripted expression in at least one occurence.
&     -- Unable to definitely determine the number of dimensions.
```

Figure 8.16 Dimension report generated by the AUTOMATED PROGRAMMER from the program of Fig. 8.7.

indices. The accompanying "notes" are sort of weak warnings feeding back the possibility of ambiguity or misinterpretation. In this case, the system's interpretation turns out to be correct; that is, it is consistent with the underlying algorithm. If it were not, the user, because of the warnings, could then rephrase the program to remove ambiguities by using more explicit constructs, i.e., constructs less prone to ambiguity or misinterpretation. This also supports the notion of permitting linguistic flexibility for a domain-specific language.

Others besides the original "programmer" should be able to verify, maintain, and extend a program. The type of program representation previously illustrated is intelligible to other professionals in the specific application domain who may have no specific experience with the programming language.

An appropriate language design should include a rich selection of output capabilities so that highly structured reports and graphical "picturelike" output are easily formulated. Examples of some output techniques applicable to scientific computation were illustrated in Chap. 5. Other domains may require additional techniques.

The requirements of a feasible system should encompass easy interfacing to already coded programs. For the domain of scientific/engineering/mathematical applications, there exists a vast collection of application packages and subroutine libraries. Most of these programs have been written in FORTRAN, a much smaller portion in BASIC, PASCAL, and C. More recently, the language Ada has been used for applications programming. An additional desirable property for the program examples illustrated previously is that they be capable of being embedded as subprograms into previously coded programs. The major advantage of this approach is that the user is not required to learn a new programming language, in the sense of conventional programming detail, or recode previous programs written in a conventional language. If the circumstances are such that there is no need to interface with existing libraries and programs written in a conventional language, then the choice of the "back-end" language can be anything that allows efficient execution. In this case, an automated programming system is similar to a compiler, except that the input is at a very much higher level.

More General Considerations

The language characteristics discussed previously are motivated by considerations having to do with evolution of linguistic expression in scientific and technical fields. The international nature of technical communication has been characterized by notational forms, vocabulary, and syntactical structures specific to scientific and technical communication. Thus, while technical communication is influenced by the framework of particular natural languages, it is limited to a specific knowledge domain. Historically, programming evolved as a discipline that sought to translate problem formulations and their solution specifications, expressed in conventional form, into equivalent representations that could be executed on a computer. Past experience in software development has made it abundantly clear that that translation process is expensive in terms of human effort. Proof of program correctness for even moderately complex programs is a goal seemingly beyond the current state of the art. The primary goal of the user is to produce reliable, easy-to-understand, executable programs in contradistinction to the practice of programming as an aesthetic experience. Most people working with computer computation have no interest in producing aesthetically pleasing or cleverly designed fragments of code. For such users, "programming style" is an uninteresting consideration.

If the goal is to automate the application programming process by the use of a suitable language design, it is necessary to adopt linguistic forms that are not only in the traditional (precomputer) applications domain but that are directly executable without the need for user coding. If the applications domain cannot be characterized by such forms, then automation is not feasible. In addition, variants of the traditional forms must be psychologically acceptable to the user; that is, they must be consistent with the user's normal mode of expression. If the language is suitably designed, various professionals in that applications domain, even though untutored in the computer language, should be able to grasp most of the content of the program.

In the language design previously illustrated, it was recognized that the formula is basic to scientific/engineering/mathematical applications programming and that the normal textbook representation of the formula is directly executable. A more general representation requires a richer vocabulary and more complex syntactical forms. Human-factors considerations require that these syntactical forms be flexible and that arcane or baroque representations be avoided. Intuitively, the intent of designing an automated programmer for scientific programming is to reduce the programming process to one of *copying* problem-solution methods from a textbook. This is possible in a literal sense only if the textbook solution is well formulated. If not, then a certain amount of "programming" must be done to transform the solution into a well-formulated form.

An executable representation that mirrors the textbook-style representation should reduce or, in some cases, eliminate much of the problems associated with program reliability. Obviously, there are areas in an applications domain that are not well formulated or cannot be directly expressed in an executable representation. The best that can be accomplished in those areas is to attempt to formulate a language design that minimizes the burden on the user for translation to well-formulated and executable forms. In this connection, a language facility that permits user definition and construction of new symbols that automatically invoke user-defined subroutines can be a powerful aid. As an example, say a user is given the facility to define and construct from the primitive characters \, /, and _ the symbol shown in Fig. 8.17*a* so that when this symbol appears in the text as a prefix to an appropriately defined function F, as in Fig. 8.17*b*, a previously user-defined subroutine for partial differentiation will be automatically invoked. What is required are techniques for inputting graphical structures (see the examples in Chap. 5) and appropriate techniques for either recognizing a constructed graphic or, in a keyboard-oriented system, assigning it to a key. There should also be the capability to link *defined* subprograms by using a user-oriented protocol.

Figure 8.17*a*

Figure 8.17*b*

In terms of a psychological model of the user, cognitive simplicity is enhanced by the use of the above technique because higher-level abstractions, for example, partial differentiation applied to a function of several variables, is represented by a single token, instantiated as a simple graphical structure.

This point of view is a straightforward extension of the more obvious replacement of the FORTRAN-like program fragment

```
   S = 0
   DO 5 I = 1,10
 5 S = S + 1**2
```

with the clearly superior (that is, more easily comprehended) representation shown in Fig. 8.18. Thus, by example, we have demonstrated throughout this chapter that conventional (historically evolved) mathematical notation is cognitively more comprehensible than the notational structures used in current programming languages.

$$S = \sum_{I=1}^{10} I^2$$

Figure 8.18

Another concept, related in the sense that cognitive simplicity is supported, is the use of lexical tokens and constructs that may have more than one meaning. An obvious example is the use of the token = , which can be used as an assignment operator; for relational equality, as in IF a = b...; for definition, as in π = 3.1415...(either as a system constant or by declaration); or for equivalence, as in A = B where semantic equivalence, rather than assignment, is meant. Given *appropriate* language design, these different meanings are resolvable in context. The alternative would be to use different tokens, for example, := for assignment and = for relational equality. The latter option, while *logically simpler* (that is, it generates no possibility of ambiguity), can be rejected because it is too cognitively complex and error-prone. It is simply easier to remember a smaller set of characters where implementation of ambiguity resolution is feasible. It also minimizes the effort involved in learning the rules of a computer-language system.

Another problem is that of extensive documentation associated with the use of a conventional programming language approach. Usually there are exhaustive manuals and texts to explain how to program in a specific language. Our approach avoids a great deal of that. Since users are already familiar with the notation and syntactical forms of their application domain, a user manual need contain only a concise summary of lexical formats and syntactical rules. Detailed explanation need be given only for idiosyncratic (optional) notations. An example of an explanation of such a notation would be: "Print X{5.2}" means print the value of X so that its integer part is no longer than 5 digits and its fractional part is no longer than 2 digits, but "Print X" results in a value printed in some standard format (for example, normalized floating point). Conceivably, the language designer might also wish to make explicit certain lexical rules, for example, that key words are reserved and that characters can be input in either lowercase or uppercase without changing their meaning, but that uppercase and lowercase characters are distinguished when they are used to construct names of variables. The only advantage of such lexical differentiation is that it permits a more "literate" programming style, since key words such as "print" may have their first character capitalized when at the beginning of a sentence and be all lowercase elsewhere. Differentiating cases in variable names can avoid unduly long or complex names since, in effect, the number of acceptable characters is doubled for single-character names, whereas the possibilities for multicharacter names are tremendously expanded.

Not *all* rules need be made explicit, however. If the (psychological) probability is low that a user, already conditioned to professional practice in an applications domain, will make certain errors, then such rules may be omitted in the interest of short, succinct reference manuals. This type of strategy is feasible only if the system gives immediate feedback to the user as to its interpretation of possibly ambiguous program input and if it is quite robust in its capability of detecting *logical* error or cases of inherent ambiguity where it would be too dangerous for the system to elect a default option. By "dangerous," we mean a situation where, while a default option is plausible, the probability of the default conforming with the intention of the user is not *overwhelmingly* great. If empirical experience shows that particular language interpretation strategies are not effective, then they can be changed without major effect on the surface language structure. This can be done by giving the user more explicit rules or by appropriate machine warnings or error messages. If experience reveals that there has indeed been a serious error in linguistic design, it is incumbent on the designer to reformulate that design. *Users tend to acclimate themselves to the products of bad design simply because they perceive no alternative.*

An example of undue detail with respect to implementation strategy is the case where the designer must make decisions as to various options for optimization of execution code. This has an overall effect on user-oriented design, because elaborate optimization usually results in a longer response time between when a user inputs a program to be translated and compiled and when the compiled code starts to execute. In this respect, many published papers have outlined elaborate schemes to optimize code generated from translation of long (many characters) assignment statements. Yet empirical evidence has shown that in using a language such as FORTRAN, programmers generate only very short assignment statements. Thus, *for FORTRAN,* optimization that assumes lengthy assignment would be counterproductive, but this effect is language-dependent. In the user-oriented computer language, previously illustrated, we can expect "long" (many characters) assignments since the "sentences" of the cited language mirror realistically lengthy formulas with qualifying and controlling phrases. Thus the "back end" may generate FORTRAN code, where execution efficiency may be improved by final compilation using a highly optimizing compiler. Again, what the designer does critically depends on the actual structure of the user language and the reaction of the user to the advantages or disadvantages of a specific language. For FORTRAN, which is coded by people, short assignments prevail because the original card-oriented structure of FORTRAN makes long assignments difficult to debug and edit. Thus the programmer may take a lengthy formula and break it up into shorter and less efficient fragments. For the two-dimensional language that we have sketched for scientific/engineering/mathematical applications, lengthy (many characters) sentences correspond to the source, that is, the problem-solution representation. Debugging therefore becomes more like proofreading, and editing becomes visually obvious. Also, the *machine*-automated programmer has no reluctance to generate long FORTRAN assignments.

As indicated in Chap. 6, declarations of type and storage reservation should be minimized where the assignment of type and allocation of storage can be inferred from scanning the program. That is, considerations of user ease far outweigh the possibilities of error detection by the use of unnecessarily detailed declarations. Further, detailed type distinctions can sometimes be avoided by the distinction between type abstractions and type representations. An example of a type abstraction would be "real-number." But "real-number" may have *several* representations, that is, integer representation, fixed-decimal-point representation, and normalized or unnormalized floating-point representation. Internal numerical computation may be in whatever representation is feasible or efficient for a specific architecture, regardless of any input type declaration. For example, subscripts of arrays normally are represented as integers. But calculation on such subscript expressions need not be done by integer arithmetic. What is of importance is that the result of such computation, that is, the output, should be in integer representation. What is crucial is not to declare certain variables to be integers just because they will play a role as subscripts, but to ensure that expressions that function as subscript representation yield results that have no fractional parts. More concretely, if x appears as a subscript for the variable Z_x, and if x is an expression computed to be $n.\epsilon$, $\epsilon << 1$, then it is clear that the value of ϵ can, in many cases, be regarded as arising from the accumulation of rounding error. Thus the value of x can be set to n. This is not *logically* compelling, but it is a highly plausible strategy if other than "infinite-precision" arithmetic has to be used to compute the final value of x.

Historically, powerful output-format capabilities have been neglected by conventional languages. For the programmer, the creation of complex output structures has been, up to now, a demanding, error-prone task. In the current programming environment, this chore has been eased by the availability of so-called fourth-generation packages for report generation and various packages for integration of text, charts, and graphical output. We illustrated in Chap. 5 a powerful approach, the IMAGE, that can be incorporated as an output format for a language designed for scientific/engineering/mathematical applications programming. This image can be treated as an iterated graphical structure with different embedded values for each iteration and, in principle, integrated with output linear text. The major asset of IMAGE is that it is intuitively obvious to the user. Here *debugging is literally proofreading*. The output is *visually* identical to the program format, IMAGE. The embedded computed values are automatically scaled to the representation (signed or unsigned integer, signed or unsigned fixed-point, signed or unsigned floating-point to arbitrary normalization, and flexibility in exponent placement and connection to its mantissa), which is determined by the placeholders of the program format, IMAGE.

In scientific/engineering/mathematical applications programming, there is a widespread reluctance of users to learn and integrate a new programming language. Our approach suits that point of view. The user need not learn a new language in any substantive sense.

The Anthropomorphism Problem

It must be clear that we are not advocating "natural-language" design for an area as disciplined as scientific/mathematical/engineering applications programming. But because the input notations and structures appear "natural," i.e., obvious to the professional user who has been conditioned by previous technical training, naive users may identify with the system, in a way analogous to psychological transference, and attribute to the "automated programmer" an "intelligence" and linguistic flexibility far beyond that for which it was designed. This type of anthropomorphism or reification can be countered by disclaimers of "naturalness;" by emphasis on explicit, albeit flexible, linguistic rules; and, most important, by immediate feedback to the user of the system interpretation of a program, including warnings (possible misinterpretations) and rejection of unacceptable or inherently ambiguous structures. While the psychological aspects of reification and transference that occur with so-called natural-language front-end systems should, in general, be seriously considered, our experience with systems designed for scientific applications programming is that this is a problem that is controllable in the real-world environment. In any event, the final conclusion on this point can be determined only by empirical observation of actual user experience with systems such as discussed in this book.

Chapter

9

Additional User-Oriented Concepts

The Design of Human-Machine Interfaces

The point of view expressed in previous chapters, particularly Chap. 8, is consistent with the engineering model that the software user is part of the overall system: computer hardware plus software plus interface plus user. Thus design of an interface must take into account not only feasibility considerations determined by hardware and software limitations but also a psychological model of the user.

Given these considerations then, the major engineering goal of interface design is to produce an interface that is economically efficient, that is, an interface that allows the user to achieve input to the system with the least expenditure of effort. The user-oriented aspects of design are advanced if learning to use the interface involves minimal effort. In the ideal case, no design tradeoffs between expected novice and expert use are necessary. Situations where such tradeoffs *appear* to be necessary usually arise because the system designers do not clearly understand certain programming strategies to obviate such a distinction. Traditionally, system programmers have overestimated the difficulty of implementing system attributes that would make life easier for the user. Typically, detection of a syntactic error will result in an error message, such as ERROR 8097, and that is all. The user must then look up ERROR 8097 in the typically thick and not-too-well-organized reference manual to finally find some not-too-informative explanation. In most cases, there is no technical reason why a detailed, easy-to-comprehend message cannot be fed back to the user immediately. The reason usually offered for not doing this is that it would result in degradation of execution performance and increase system cost. Such excuses usually mask poor strategies of system implementation.

Some of these design criteria can be illustrated by a brief consider-

```
The AUTOMATED PROGRAMMER (TM) System V1.22
(C) Copyright KGK Automated Systems, Inc. 1988 Serial AP-13621

DIRECTORY PATH__________ C:/AP/PROGS
INPUT FILE NAME__________                      (Leave blank for NEW file)
OUTPUT FILE NAME_________
LIST FILE(S)_____________ ????????.2D
DELETE FILE(S)___________
RUN OUTPUT_______________ SCREEN      PRINTER
LANGUAGE_________________ FORTRAN     C          ADA

Edit  Translate  Run  Print  Image  iNterpretation  Files  Delete
Subprogram  Link  Help  Quit
```

Figure 9.1 AUTOMATED PROGRAMMER access menu.

ation of the interface design for the automated programming system discussed in Chap. 8. Our goal might be to assess whether it is possible to accomplish a first-instance contact between user and system via *one* displayed screen menu. Consider the user who has entered, via the keyboard, an operating system command such as cd\ ap ("call the automated programmer"). The immediate response would be the screen menu display of Fig. 9.1.

All system operations of the AUTOMATED PROGRAMMER are controlled through this front-end access menu, which is partitioned into a main portion and a command panel. The main portion allows the user to amend the default directory path (*first line*), to list an input file name if he or she intends to edit an existing program (*second line*), and to list an output file name (*third line*) in order to name a new program or to give an old program a new name. A fourth line may be used to name specific files in memory that are to be listed, a fifth line to name files to be deleted from memory, a sixth line to switch output to printer rather than the default screen, and a seventh line to switch to some output target language other than the default language of FORTRAN. Selection of the switch option is achieved by moving the cursor within the respective line.

The bottom command panel lists the choices:

Edit—call the two-dimensional screen editor to create or edit a two-dimensional source program

Translate—recognize and parse the two-dimensional source program named in the input filename slot; translate to a target language; compile, link, and create an executable module; and run this module

Run—execute a previously created module named in the input file slot

Print—print the two-dimensional source program named in the input file slot

Image—output results within a formatted "picture" (see Chap. 5 for an explanation of this concept as a two-dimensional format structure and for examples)

iNterpretation—display the system interpretation of the source program to resolve possible ambiguity between implicit multiplication and multicharacter variables

Files—activate the list-files slot

Delete—activate the delete-files slot

Subprogram—similar to Translate except that the named input file is not linked or executed, in the expectation that this separate object module will be linked to other modules or libraries

Link—call a screen link-editor which automatically links listed object modules and program libraries and provides other functions helpful to the creation of programs to be assembled from separate modules

Quit—exit to the operating system

Switching between the main panel and the command panel is accomplished by using the [Esc] key. Movement within a panel is via the cursor keys. As the user moves the cursor from one command to the other, each command is highlighted and an explanation of its purpose, similar to the above descriptions, is displayed at the bottom of the access menu. When a command is highlighted, pressing the enter (return) key initiates execution of the selected command. Alternatively, from the command panel, the user can select a command and initiate its execution by just typing the letter of the command which is capitalized, such as T for Translate or N for iNterpretation. (From the main panel, the user can select a command by pressing the [Alt] key *and* typing that letter of the command which is capitalized.)

All operations available within the system always return to the access menu upon completion. All protocols within other aspects of the system are consistent to that used in the access menu.

The first command option of the access menu is *Edit*. When activated, this provides input to a full-screen, two-dimensional editor. When the system is in the normal edit mode, a "banner" at the top of the screen lists the appropriate directory path, input filename, output filename, the sequence number of the current "2-D line" (*see below*) within which the cursor is positioned, the sequence number of the top 2-D line of the current screen, the sequence number of the bottom 2-D line of the current screen, and the number of 2-D lines in the entire source program. This is illustrated in Fig. 9.2 for the program whose input filename is GAUSS. Pressing the escape [Esc] key on the keyboard switches the banner into a list of editing instructions to facilitate the creation and editing of two-dimensional mathematical expressions. As each instruction is tentatively selected, via the cursor, a short explanation appears as to its function. This is illustrated in Fig. 9.3 for the program MEAN, where the instruction "Save" has been selected.

Historically, input (typing) of mathematical expressions has posed a problem. Mathematical word processors have adopted two main approaches. The first is similar to the conventional programming approach in that the user must translate the mathematical expression, in conventional textbook representation (normally a two-dimensional form), to a linear string of characters *and associated codes* that eventually will result in a document where the mathematical expression is given in a typographic style similar to its original form. The other major approach is to adopt a WYSIWYG ("what you see is what you get")

```
Directory: C:\AP\PROGS  Input File: GAUSS  Output File: TEST
Current 2D: 4   Top 2D: 1  Bottom 2D: 9   Last 2D: 17
================================================================
TITLE gaussian elimination.

maximum n=50. read n.

{ READ THE COEFFICIENT MATRIX ROW BY ROW }

   for i=1 to n and j=1 to n read W_ij.     █

{ READ RIGHT HAND SIDE }  for i=1 to n read W_i,n+1.

{ INITIALIZE PIVOT VECTOR }  P_i=i for i=1,...,n.

for i=1 to n D_i =|W_i,1 |,(for j=2 to n if |W_ij |> D_i then D_i = |W_ij |),

if D_i=0 then print "MATRIX IS NOT INVERTIBLE  " and stop.

for k=1 to n-1 compute I=k,
```

Figure 9.2 First screen of a two-dimensional program with normal editor banner.

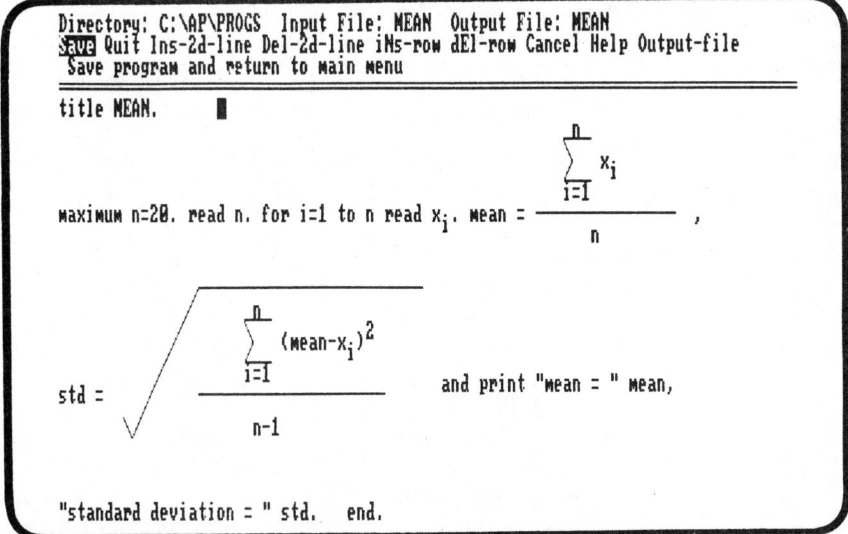

Figure 9.3 A two-dimensional program with editing commands banner.

approach in constructing the mathematical document on a screen editor. However, in most instances, the input process also involves the insertion of special control codes to create mathematical symbols or to properly position characters.

The approach used by the AUTOMATED PROGRAMMER is far simpler and is a WYDIWYSIWYG, i.e., *"what you do is what you see is what you get,"* approach. Entering mathematical expressions into the screen editor tends to be more of an intuitive process and is accomplished by using a standard IBM PC keyboard or compatible input device. However, the usual character set has been expanded to four cases, which include the standard uppercase and lowercase characters, Greek characters, special math characters, and some special format control characters. The third and fourth cases (Ctrl and Alt) are not complete, leaving room for future incorporation of additional characters. Also, the function keys may be used for fast generation of the common symbols for summation, product, integral, square root, brackets, and braces *to various sizes.* The input process is easy since each character, and its associated case position, is displayed on a keyboard template supplied with the system. This template, in reduced form, is illustrated in Fig. 9.4.

The up-down-right-left cursor keys are used to reach the desired typing position within the screen editor. While the right-left keys operate as in linear text mode, the up-down cursor keys move the cursor vertically only one-half character space at a time. This permits the po-

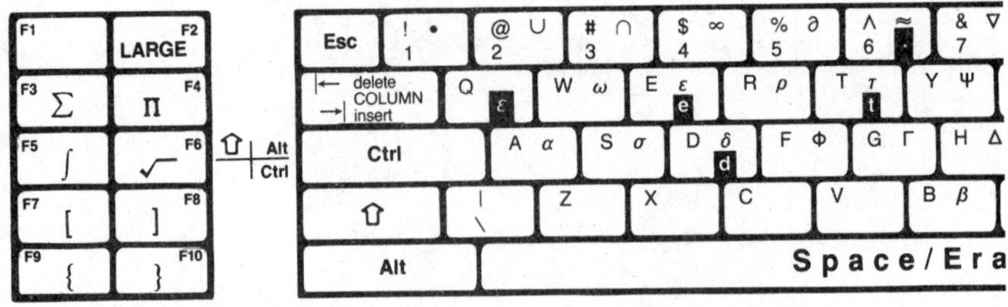

Figure 9.4 Keyboard template of the AUTOMATED PROGRAMMER.

sitioning of subscript or superscript expressions one-half line below or above the respective subscripted or superscripted variable.

Fortunately, a great deal of mathematical notation can be encompassed by the use of a limited character set for the most common operators. The symbols for summation operator, product operator, integral operator, square-root operator, left/right brackets, and left/right braces may be drawn using a small set of primitive characters or they may be automatically constructed by tapping the appropriate function key. As may be noted from Fig. 9.4, function key F2 is marked "LARGE." Function key F3 is labeled Σ, the symbol for summation. Similarly, the other function keys are labeled with the mathematical symbols for product, integral, and square root, as well as for square brackets and braces. Thus a single stroke of key F3 will produce a standard-size summation symbol. However, pressing F2 once before pressing F3 will produce a larger-size symbol. Pressing F2 twice before pressing another function key will produce an even larger symbol, and so on. Therefore all the symbols marked on the function keys may be automatically drawn to arbitrary size. This enhances the self-documenting characteristic of the program, since it makes it easier to distinguish nests of expressions. These automatically generated symbols may be extended, contracted, or otherwise modified manually.

A mathematical expression is usually two-dimensional in the sense that it has width and height. This two-dimensional character arises from the use of subscripts and superscripts, the numerator-over-denominator form of division, the use of various-size operators, and different types and sizes of parentheses, often in a nested form. While these forms are not *logically* necessary (all representations may be replaced by a linear string of codes), this notation has been accepted historically as facilitating the understanding of mathematical representation. The constraint enforced by the AUTOMATED PROGRAMMER is that the maximum width and height of any *portion* of a mathematical expression is the width and height of the editor screen. This constraint has been adopted

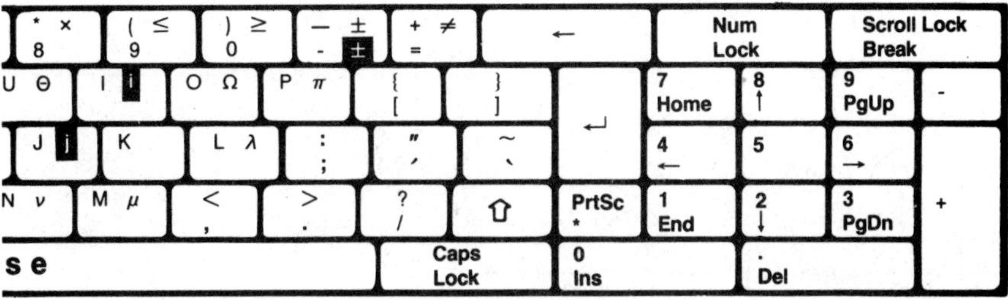

Figure 9.4 *(Continued)*

primarily for human-factors reasons. There is no technical impediment to allowing an expression to exceed screen limits by using vertical or horizontal scrolling. This has been avoided since it would make use of the editor less "intuitive."

The actual width and height of the entered portion of a mathematical expression determines the physical size of its 2-D line and the number of 2-D lines representable on one screen. The mathematical expression may be continued over an arbitrary number of 2-D lines, using vertical scrolling of the screen when desirable.

The few rules for placing characters within an expression and forming the limits of operators are reasonably liberal, easily remembered, and quite tolerant of a sloppy typing style. For example, the expressions for the upper and lower limits of a summation operator should not exceed the horizontal width of the respective upper and lower arms of the summation symbol. The reason for this specific rule is to remove possible ambiguity between the sum limits and the summand expression while still retaining flexibility in the two-dimensional placement of limit or summand expressions. If either the upper-limit or lower-limit expression is longer than the respective upper or lower arm of the sum symbol that was produced by function-key automatic generation of the summation symbol, *then the respective arms can easily be extended manually.* The final sum symbol need not be symmetric. In general, as long as the final representation is recognizable to the human reader, the system, using accurate and efficient *pattern-recognition* procedures, will make a correct classification.

As noted above, one of the commands in the command panel of the access menu of the AUTOMATED PROGRAMMER is *Link,* which calls the link editor. This is also a full-screen editor,[1] illustrated in Fig. 9.5. The screen is divided into three sections of fixed viewing size. The upper-left section allows the user to amend whatever default val-

[1]Copyright 1986 by KGK Automated Systems, Inc.

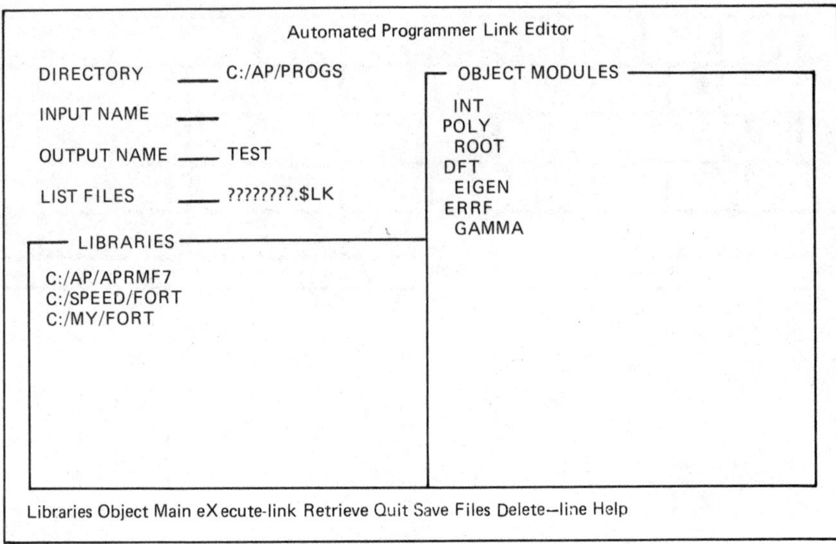

Figure 9.5

ues first appear on the lines DIRECTORY, INPUT NAME, OUTPUT NAME, and LIST FILES which specify the working directory, input and output filenames, and listing of information regarding previous linked files. The lower-left section is a window where users may list all the libraries they are using. The filenames of the library supplied by the AUTOMATED PROGRAMMER (\AP\APRMF7) and the library belonging to the installed FORTRAN compiler will appear automatically. The filenames of other libraries which contain subprograms to be incorporated in the final program are also entered into this window. If the listings exceed the horizontal or vertical limits of the window, the text will be scrolled in the appropriate direction automatically. The right portion of the screen is the window where users may list the names of all the object modules they wish to incorporate into the final complete program. As in the libraries window, if the listings exceed the window's horizontal or vertical limits, the text will be scrolled in the appropriate direction automatically.

As in the access menu, the bottom of the screen contains a command panel. This may be accessed by using the [Esc] key. The protocol for activation of commands is the same as used in the access menu and in the two-dimensional editor. (*Protocol consistency is very important in the design of user-oriented systems.*) Activating the *Libraries* command places the cursor inside the library window for editing. Similarly, the *Object* command places the cursor within the "object modules" window. *Main* puts the cursor within the upper-left portion of the screen. Activation of the command *eXecute-link* causes the link editor to parse all the various entries, verify for consistency, save this information, run the linker program to produce an executable file, and then return to the access menu for further instructions. (The remaining commands are useful if one wishes to do editing involving previous files, but for our purposes here it is not necessary to go into any further detail.) As in the access menu, each command is highlighted when selected and an explanation of the command appears at the bottom line of the screen.

Again, the design purpose here is to perform a complex programming function by using a *single* screen menu, using *simple* protocols that are *consistent* with the protocol used in other parts of the system and that *automate the process as much as possible.*

We have sketched out the above to indicate that what may appear at first glance to be a difficult interface design problem can be accomplished for a highly technical domain in a way that makes operating-system and system-processing details invisible to the user.

Natural-Language Input

Several commercially available systems claim to comprehend input, using natural language, for the purpose of information retrieval or the automatic generation of complex reports. A retrieval request might be

> How many salespersons in the appliance division made sales in excess of $100,000 total for 1985?

A request for a report might be

> List total sales per month for the period 1975 through 1985 and also produce a plot.

Most of the currently available commercial systems use an approach grounded in the syntactic analysis of the input string. Other, still-experimental research systems use an approach grounded in extracting conceptual information, relating this to a knowledge base, and then discarding the syntactical structure of the input. For those systems that attempt to parse the input by using syntactical structures, the processing program constitutes a complex software package. As pointed out in Chap. 1, true natural language has characteristics that make its comprehension by machine, in the full sense, to be in principle not completely possible (or at least extraordinarily difficult). This is because linguists have never demonstrated a completely adequate syntax for natural-language communication between people nor are there dictionaries that are complete in their list of lexical tokens (words). Also, natural-language communication is heavily context-dependent and constantly prone to ambiguous interpretation. Thus, regardless of the programming complexity of these systems, they "work" because of various techniques (tricks?) that may not be apparent to the user.

All available systems can cope only with a finite (usually relatively small) set of syntactic structures and/or conceptual representations. Put another way, the system "understands" an input string only if the string matches one of the syntactic or conceptual "templates" *anticipated* by the program. A cleverly designed system can parse "mildly" complex input by using and/or rearranging composite structures or by recursively matching primitive templates. So if you say what the system *expects* you to say, a correct parse is made. For example, if you input "Total sales equal $979,120," then *if* there is a template "L = R," the system can parse the input as "L = total sales," "R = 979,120," and "L ← R."

Obviously, this approach is limited in principle and is not sufficient for general use. However, it may be made feasible by certain ad hoc augmentation rules. For example, suppose the input was "I wonder if you could tell me what the total sales were for 1985?" Suppose there was no adequate single template available for this question, but there was a template of the form *"What were X in Y?"* The system could match *X* with "total sales" and *Y* with "1985" if there is the rule

> If there are key words (words that are in italic in the sample template) present, then disregard unrecognizable words in finding the best template match, or else *assign a new variable name to any unrecognizable (not decomposable) string* if that allows a match to either side of a primitive template.

This simple rule can be remarkably effective in certain domains of discourse. Of course, the variables *X* and *Y* can be tagged with sets of admissible semantic attributes. For example, if *X* is "total sales," then *Y* is accepted as "1985" (one of a subset of admissible numbers for the class "years"); or *Y* may be accepted as "Boston" (one of a subset of admissible names for the class ("cities"). The input "June" in the template "hole" for *Y* could be resolved, by default, as the month June of the current year or result in a request for more specific information.

For these systems to function effectively, it is important that they feed back to the user their interpretation of the user input. Feedback can be represented in "natural" language form but closely matched to the internal system syntax. Or feedback can be represented in some intermediate form resembling statements in a higher-level programming language.

More commonly, the system will not be successful at parsing a user query at the first instance of input. An effective system will engage the user in a dialogue structure designed to elicit more information from the user, in a sequence that fits into precoded syntactic and conceptual structures of the system. In a certain sense, the "dialogue" is like a nested set of visual menus, except that the communication medium is verbal, that is, output sequences of question-sentences from the machine and input answers from the user (usually one-word replies).

Typically, these systems have a dictionary ("lexicon"), annotated with synonym relations and facilities for users to create their own vocabulary lists. A good deal of lexical analysis is done to relate user-defined names to the coded tokens, fields, and records in the database of the system and to relate "command words," such as "percentage net profits" to the assignment

```
PNP = 100*( (TOTAL.REVENUES - TOTAL.EXPENSES)/
                                     TOTAL.REVENUES)
```

Actually, building a lexicon is a highly detailed, manual process that is heavily influenced by the structure of the system's database, the overall system strategy toward linguistic analysis, and the idiosyncrasies of the specific application domain. Lexical ambiguity is usually handled by requesting more information from the user or giving the user a short menu of options from which to choose.

In the sense that these systems "work," they do so because the user is subtly conditioned to communicate with the system using a vocabulary, syntactic structure, and semantic concepts that the system expects. A user who does not do so will not get a request fulfilled; will be badgered by detailed requests for more information, decisions as to various options, or certification of system interpretive feedback; or will even be discouraged from opting for expensive processing. The best that can be said for most of these systems is that they represent an easy way for a user to learn, informally, a computer language whose key words are already familiar. Of course, this is not really natural-language comprehension by machine, but it may very well be better than requiring users to learn a conventional programming language. The major potential of these systems will be realized when accurate and cost-effective speech-input devices are available as front ends, a possibility that, for noncontinuous speech, appears to be on the horizon, if not imminent.

The major drawback of such systems is the anthropomorphic effect (discussed in Chap. 8), where certain susceptible individuals relate to machines as though the machines were human. Part of this phenomenon is the possibility that accommodation to the limitations of machine input will have wider ramifications. For example, current speech-recognition capability by machines requires that words be spoken in clear monotones with pauses between adjacent words. Will widespread use of this technology affect the way people speak to each other?

Our overall attitude to natural-language input can be summarized by stating that "natural-language" input can be realized in restricted application domains by viewing the problem as one of designing a new programming (formal) language that is linguistically more flexible and general than its predecessors. Feedback of system interpretation and easy editing techniques play important roles in system efficacy. The syntax, lexical aspects, and semantic attributes of the "natural" programming language must be constructed so that ambiguity is resolvable and expectation of error minimized. This is primarily a *psychological* design problem, rather than a question of linguistic synthesis, even though linguistic considerations enter into the design process. It must be stressed that the validation of such a design ultimately lies in experimental verification.

Design Considerations for "Natural-Language" Front Ends

As we have previously emphasized, the use of true natural-language input is beyond current capabilities for interfacing with a computer. We have also suggested that selection of a linguistic subset is feasible only if it models linguistic use in a specific application environment. If the front-end design is to be successful, then the linguistic flexibility it will accept should in some substantive sense reflect the flexibility found in the actual application environment.

The use of synonyms simply mirrors the observation that humans use different words for the same action or categorization. Thus the acceptance of synonyms in a front-end system substantially increases the probability that the input statement will be correctly parsed by the computer. The major point here is that synonyms (lexical or structured forms) must reflect actual usage in the application domain.

In Chap. 8 we indicated that both lexical ambiguity and syntactic ambiguity can be resolved, *to a limited extent,* by strategies of context analysis and/or by opting for default options based on an empirical cognitive model of the user. Where either strategy is not sufficient, the user input must be rejected. In both cases, feedback to the user of specific system interpretation and/or detailed information as to the nature and location of the "error" is highly desirable for an effective front-end design. In essence, this is equivalent to asking users, explicitly, to detail their intentions. Context analysis is more desirable, however, since a system that interminably asks a user questions as to intent or for additional information quickly becomes wearisome. A system is well designed if it can successfully resolve most ambiguities automatically. Feedback then functions as a user-acceptable fail-safe mechanism.

In Chap. 8 we indicated that for the area of scientific/mathematical/

engineering applications programming, the appropriate fundamental linguistic structure should be a "sentence" consisting of a possibly large number of clauses modifying an assignment computation or sequence of assignment computations. We choose this design because it simplifies semantic interpretation. An example of this is the anaphoric implicit reference in the following sequence of segmented English statements:

```
     Begin
Q1.  Who is president of the Banana Computer Company?
A1.  James Q. Jones
Q2.  What is his address?
A2.  43 Slippery Way, Scarsdale, NY.
     End.
```

In question 2, it is assumed that "his" refers to the "who" of question 1. If Q1 and Q2 had been combined into one sentence, "Who is the president of the Banana Computer Company and what is his address?" there would be no ambiguity. What we are suggesting is that a "sentence" structure, as outlined in Chap. 8, is less prone to ambiguous "reference binding" than simple sequential statements typical of FORTRAN-like languages or the block structure imposed on simple sequential statements typical of ALGOL-like languages. This concept is further supported if index variables are local to the sentence in which they are embedded and if clause scope can be delimited by parentheses (for example, a parenthesized FOR clause has scope delimited by enclosing parentheses, else the clause scope is the entire sentence). For the specific domain of scientific applications programming, it may be useful to disregard our previous caveat against global variables. Scientific computation is characterized by the use of variable names with widely recognized meanings, that is, π, e, gamma, eigenvalue, etc. Thus specifying that variables (except indices and formal parameters) be global may simplify referencing and avoid duplications in assignment within subprograms. Of course, our underlying assumption is that the "programmer" is intimately familiar with the technical terminology of the application domain.

Where the application domain is linguistically sparse, the design of a front end can use a sequential-template approach set in menu screens that are presented to the user. First a choice of key words is presented to the user. Selection of a particular key word causes (1) a second menu to pop up, giving a choice of additional key words appropriate to the first slot in the template that matches the first key word, or (2) a prompt to the user to input a value or a name in the space to the right of the selected key word. If the user inputs a name, it must be in the system lexicon. The procedure is then repeated until a complete command is constructed. This approach is feasible only for applications that can tolerate simple, rigid grammars and where the user population will accept what is a tedious and boring protocol. The advantage of the approach is that implementation is easy, execution is fast, and input errors are minimal. The major disadvantage is that even minor changes in the form of input may require substantive implementation revisions.

An attempt to generalize natural-language input would lead to constructing all-inclusive grammars for the English language and a vast body of linked semantic attributes to distinguish which syntactic constructions are appropriate for a particular domain. In practice, such an approach to generality has failed, since it cannot distinguish among sentences that have nontrivially different syntactic structure but that in the *context of a specific application domain* can be interpreted to have identical meanings. (In some other context, the same sentences may yield different meanings.) The programs in Fig. 8.13, Fig. 8.14, and Fig. 8.15 illustrate how, for the cited application, three syntactically different structures map into equivalent computations. This is not to say that the individual object codes into which they are translated are the same. Generally, they are not. Yet they are computationally equivalent in the sense that the same input will generate the same output for all cases.

Programming Style, Program Verification, and Software Engineering

Much of the current academic view toward programming style has been centered about the concepts of "structured" programming. Briefly, adherents of structured programming style hold that every program should be written so that it can be represented as a sequence of processes P_i, P_{i+1} $P_{i+2}, \ldots, P_n$. Each particular process P_j can only use combinations of three control structures:

1. P_{i1} (concatenation): A sequence of computations S_i (or a set of parallel sequences) with one entrance and only one possible exit for each computation.
2. P_{i2} (selection): IF <CONDITION> THEN S_1 ELSE S_2. <CONDITION> tests if something is true or false, for example, $X>1$. Whether or not S_1 or S_2 is executed, P_{i2} exits to the same point of the program.
3. P_{i3} (repetition): WHILE <CONDITION> LOOP S_1. S_1 is repeatedly executed as long as <CONDITION> is true. If <CONDITION> is initially false, then S_1 will not be executed at all. P_{i3} has one entrance and exits to the next P_i when <CONDITION> becomes false.

Each S_i may be of type P_{i1}, P_{i2}, or P_{i3}. P_{i2} need not have an explicit ELSE statement. The WHILE may also be replaced by its negation, UNTIL.

The principal idea here is that *all* programs should be written in this style and that control structures such as GOTO should not be used, since they confuse the structure of a program. This attitude views a program hierarchically. Overall, the program is a goal. In implementing that goal, the program can be broken up into subgoals, and each subgoal into sub-subgoals, and so on. When a subgoal is executed, control returns to the point just after the subgoal was "turned on." Thus the control flow is basically sequential if the subgoals can be regarded as nodes (points) in the flow graph. Of course, each node can itself have a detailed structure on a deeper subgoal level. A GOTO of any sort destroys this hierarchical structure, and the graph of program flow can no longer be represented as a sequential flow from one node to another. A GOTO allows a jump from one goal level to a qualitatively different goal level. The "ideological" purpose of structured programming is to be able to prove that programs are "correct"—that is, they conform to their formal specifications—or to be able to construct probably correct programs in a stepwise manner. An adjunct claim is that programming in the structured programming style is efficient as a software-engineering technique. That is, it produces better programs faster at lesser cost and makes programs easier to maintain and revise.

Examples abound of programs that make excessive use of GOTOs and that are difficult to understand. One example was given in Chap. 8 where we compared three computationally equivalent programs. Figure 8.13 is a program that was written using conventional *mathematical* notation, which is a highly structured form. Figure 8.15 is a program that was written using GOTOs. Obviously, the program using conventional mathematical notation is easier to understand and easier to prove correct. It also appears to be more efficient for someone who is familiar with conventional mathematical notation. However, it is also possible to demonstrate that certain programs written in a structured style become more efficient and easier to comprehend by use of a few GOTOs.[2]

Programming is an *empirical* discipline. Despite the efforts of many clever theoreticians, an effective theoretical framework to demonstrate "correctness" in any but the simplest of programs does not exist. There is also a fundamental problem even with the concept of correctness. Even if one proves that a program is consistent with its specifi-

---

[2]The best treatment of this subject may be found in D. E. Knuth, "Structured Programming with GOTO Statements," *Computing Surveys*, 6, no. 4, 261–301, 1974.

cation and therefore "correct," it does not mean that the program does what it was *intended* to do. As any skilled practitioner of the art of programming knows, what people *say* they want is often not what they really *intend*. A scientist may give an applications programmer the following specification: "Run my data through an analysis of variance procedure and report the levels of significance." However, the underlying statistical properties of his data may vitiate the assumptions on which the analysis-of-variance test of significance is based. Thus the reported results, while technically correct, may be of no value. What the scientist really means is: "Use a standard statistical test of significance *that conforms to the nature of my data,* so that the results are meaningful." This is an entirely different matter and a much more difficult request to satisfy and validate. Even a *correct* program may not do what it was intended to do. The argument made in Chap. 8 is that, among other things, use of conventional mathematical notation for *appropriate applications* tends to narrow the gap between formal specification and intention only in the sense that it makes the specification and its explication as a program easier to understand. Of course, it does not *prove* that the program conforms to user intention; it only increases the probability that this *may* be so by removing unnecessarily opaque programming representations.

Notwithstanding the previous declaration that it is essentially an empirical art, programming starts with the concept of a specification, which in its formulation involves abstraction, that is, the discarding of presumably unnecessary details. It is at this level that user intention may be obscured by an inappropriate program representation. But even where representation is appropriate, there does not now exist any intellectual framework that can, in a systematic manner, relate the model underlying any specification to the real world (that is, the world of intentions) to which the model supposedly corresponds. Our point is that claims for the efficacy of a particular programming style, particularly the claims for structured programming, cannot be justified theoretically. Even in the small number of cases where "correctness" can be demonstrated, all that really has been shown is relative consistency between the specification representation and the program representation. With the current state of knowledge, the best that can be done is to seek empirical validation in matters of programming style.

There have been a small number of laboratory studies, most using a small population of subjects, that attempted to test the effects of programming style on software practice. Most of the studies used FORTRAN, PL/1, or some simple language developed specifically for the experiment. Typically, program sizes were very small. Even with these quite-restricted experimental designs, the results obtained were generally equivocal in supporting the claims of positive benefits from use of a structured programming style. There have been even fewer field studies, that, ex post facto, collected data relating to the viability of a structured programming style. Oddly enough, most of the published studies have been on commercial COBOL usage. Again, overall results were inconclusive or contradictory. In summary, there has been a paucity of empirical studies of programming style that can be said to meet minimum criteria of acceptability as controlled scientific experiments. What has been done gives no clear-cut understanding of the value of any particular programming style. This is not to say that programming style has no effect. It is just that the present state of computer science has not been able to demonstrate any objective effect. Likewise, there have been few studies on the effects of the selection of a particular programming language on programmer productivity. We happen to believe that language—its lexical form, syntactic structure, and notation and the link of its semantics to the psychology of the user—is crucial to productivity. Unfortunately, experimental evidence to support any conclusions on this topic is sparse, and the entire field of experimental studies of programmer performance is still in a nascent stage.

Object-Oriented Software

The object-oriented viewpoint of computer-language design focuses on the concepts of

Process and data abstraction. The statement of a solution is worked out at various conceptual levels of generalization.

Information hiding. Access to data and procedures within demarcated segments of a program is restricted by some protocol.

Modularity. A program is constructed as a set of modules subject to well-defined structure, communication, and activation protocols.

As software, an object can be considered to be a specific program entity that contains a data structure *and* a set of computational processes (methods) that operate on (transform) the private data structure of the object. The local state of the object is preserved. The control of an object is affected by passing a "message" to it. In general, the messages specify what transformations are desired but do not specify the details of such transformations, i.e., the actual details of the implementation that would give the desired result. Thus message sending supports the concept of *abstraction,* since the sending program does not assume a specific implementation or data representation associated with the object. Thus it is possible to change the internal implementations within the object without changing the outside program.

Objects can be considered to be concrete instances of a more general category termed a *class,* and a class may be included within a *superclass*. The class may be considered to represent a data type with associated behavior. Objects may *inherit* the data structure and operations that characterize their class. Thus an object characterized as belonging to a specific class need only be specified by those attributes which are unique to it within its class. The specific modes of inheritance may differ among different approaches to object-oriented software. The goal of the inheritance mechanism is to avoid the need to explicitly specify redundant information. It also simplifies the modification of a program since new information, applying to a set of objects, need only be entered at one point.

An additional aspect of the object-oriented viewpoint is the desirability of having different classes of objects react to the same message protocols. The goal here is to make objects reusable, modifiable, and interchangeable.

The actual implementation of these concepts from one object-oriented programming language (e.g., Smalltalk) to another (e.g., C++) varies widely, and currently there is no widespread agreement on necessary and fundamental principles among the many object-oriented languages described in the literature. Areas of activity for practitioners of the object-oriented viewpoint have been simulation, graphics applications, systems programming, and artificial-intelligence applications.

Despite the seeming attractiveness of the object-oriented viewpoint of design, there does not currently exist any substantial body of experimental evidence to bolster the claims for the advisability of using an object-oriented language for the creation of software. Implementations of such languages appear to be more complex than conventional procedural languages and appear to pay a penalty in run-time efficiency. However, from our point of view, i.e., the design of very high level user-oriented languages for the goal of automating application programming, these drawbacks, even if substantiated, are of relatively little importance. What *is* important is that the object-oriented paradigm does not correspond to a domain-specific computational environment. Thus it is not surprising to hear the claim that learning to program in the object-oriented mode is more difficult than the conventional approach. Certainly, none of the existing language implementations appear to have the qualities that would allow them to be characterized as user-oriented. However, this field has not yet reached a mature state, and it would be entirely premature to foreclose the possibility of developments that would work in favor of more automation of the programming process and more enhancements in the direction of user-oriented characteristics.

Direct-Manipulation Technique

By *direct manipulation,* we mean the manipulation or processing of icons displayed on a screen by pointing or drawing on screens sensitive to finger touch; use of a light pen or an acoustic pen; manipulation of a trackball, a control stick, or a "mouse"; or finger pressing or stroking of an auxiliary sensing pad. Icons may be either data structures, such as arrays, or graphical symbols (pictures) representing data structures or functions. The point of direct manipulation is that it is a *nonverbal* way of communicating to a computer. Direct manipulation replaces verbal commands for the processing of abstract entities by physical operation on concrete (visible) objects that are representations of the abstract entity. The direct manipulation results in immediately visible effects displayed on the screen.

Direct manipulation avoids the use of verbal commands such as "delete filename." Instead, the action could be effected by, or example, displaying a menu of icons on the bottom of a split screen. One icon might be a small cartoon that could be easily visualized as representing erasure (with or without the word *erase*). Touching that icon, on a touch-sensitive screen, and then touching a specific name in a table of names displayed on the upper part of the screen would cause the deletion of the file from the displayed list. Similarly, if dealing with displays of graphical information, one could "circle" interesting groups of data and then cause further processing by touching an appropriate function icon symbol.

Lexical tokens are the objects that are displayed on the screen and that are to be manipulated. There is no explicit syntax in the conventional sense, but there is an implicit syntax in that actions are constrained to certain patterns. Mistakes (errors) in positioning objects are immediately visible and thus require no output of error messages.

The major limitation to the use of concrete representation is that the size of the screen display limits the number of icons and the labels associated with those icons. For example, it is not difficult, on current screens, to display 30 filenames, with annotations, in a two-column table. If, however, each file was represented by an icon in the form of a drawing of a cabinet, with embedded name and other annotations, the screen would be too cluttered for easy direct manipulation.

The advantages claimed for the direct-manipulation approach stem from the obvious concrete expression of nonverbal communication and the immediate display of the effects of that communication. Spreadsheet programs are examples of some aspects of the direct manipulation approach. Some computer-aided design packages also use techniques of direct manipulation.

The major drawback in the use of direct manipulation *as a language* is the lack of generality. Direct-manipulation techniques may not work very well if the set of actions (drawing, pointing, and so on) and the set of function icons (or function keys) are quite small. Most important, the actions and the representations of the icons must be obvious to the user in the context of the application domain. Otherwise, a set of verbal commands, given the same range of processing possibilities, may turn out to be more efficient and more general in expressing the intentions of the user.

Direct manipulation may also use windows. A *window* is a part of a document that is displayed on part of a screen. Thus one screen can display several windows simultaneously, each window corresponding to a different document or different parts of the same document. This permits the concurrent viewing of two or more applications. Usually, in window software offered commercially, the user need only manipulate a mouse device to point at various labeled rectangular areas around the perimeter of the window and actuate the corresponding commands. Use of this technique removes the need for the user to memorize a long list of combinations of function key–case key pushes to effect a particular action. Depending on the particular software design, windows can lie contiguously or edge to edge, or they may be of arbitrary sizes and overlap. The basic idea underlying this design approach is to simulate documents scattered on a desk, with the user processing several documents simultaneously. "Papers" can be rearranged by using the mouse device to point to a particular window (document) and clicking the mouse button to cause that particular document to be displayed foremost. One method of moving a window from one part of the screen to another is to press the mouse button while the mouse is moved on the display table. The window moves in correlation with the movement of the mouse. Usually the user has to start the move by "pointing" the mouse at some particular area on the labeled border of the window. Inside the window, the document can be scrolled vertically or horizontally. Some software packages have window markers that indicate whether the portion of the document visible is near the top or the bottom of the document. This is done by displaying a "bubble" that moves up and down a vertical column. The relative position of the bubble within the column indicates the position of the screen in relation to the entire document. To scroll the document, the user points the mouse to areas of the control border or to icons and then clicks the mouse.

An icon can be thought of as a representation of an object, where the object is *both* particular data and the rules to operate on that data.

The picture that is the concrete manifestation of the icon may be opened into a window that displays the data of the object by pointing a mouse to it and clicking the mouse button or by some equivalent pointing/switching action.

Use of windows and icons requires high-resolution displays and complex implementation techniques. The methods of pointing and effecting actions vary. Some "mice" have only one button, some two buttons, others three. The tradeoff is that a one-button mouse requires more labeled control areas on the screen, thereby limiting the viewing area. Disadvantages of a mouse are that it may need to be recalibrated often, a special reflecting board may be necessary for tracking, and, for simple roller-ball versions, the desk area needs to be kept uncluttered.

Pop-up menus also fall into the category of direct manipulation. One way of handling many menus is to constantly display major categories of information as names in a menu bar at the bottom row of the screen. Pressing the appropriate function key or using a pointing device causes the subsidiary menu to "pop up." Subsidiary menus can, in turn, be used to call subcategories. Action can also be initiated by typing in the number corresponding to that listed for the desired submenu. Unfortunately, many commercial menus are inadequately designed and do not convey easily comprehended information to the user. Adequate design means that users can make choices almost by intuition and that "incorrect" choices will result in *informative* error messages and explanations to guide users to input that which expresses their intentions. Some menu systems are so badly designed that the user may be mystified as to the correct procedure to exit the menu after making a selection, because different protocols are used to exit different menus or different processes. Good design requires consistency in the command structure available to users across the scope of all possible actions. Thus any protocol for exiting any menu or process should be the same. Similarly, all menus should have the same structure and similar protocols for effecting other actions. If pressing function-key 1 produces an edit action in one menu, then the same key should be used for a similar edit action in another menu.

Language Design and Artificial-Intelligence Techniques

A language can be made more user-oriented with techniques that are usually considered to be in the subject area of artificial intelligence. One of the prime distinctions between a conventional programming system and an artificial intelligence (AI) system in that the AI system uses heuristic rules. A heuristic rule, contrary to an algorithmic process, cannot be analyzed to prove that it will be successful under certain conditions. A heuristic rule is like a rule of thumb. *Its justification lies in its success rate.* A good heuristic is one that works most of the time.

Another important characteristic of AI programs is the use of an "inference engine," that is, a set of procedures that conform to the axioms and inference rules of elementary logic. Given a certain set of conditions, an AI program will come to a logically valid conclusion. In Chap. 8, we illustrated a computer system, the AUTOMATED PROGRAMMER, designed to translate programs expressed in conventional mathematical notation and technical English into executable code. In this system, it is not necessary for the user to explicitly "dimension" arrays, that is, to declare the exact amount of storage necessary for a subscripted variable. The system is able to do this by the use of both heuristic rules and *simple* inference procedures that scan all sentences of the program and infer how much storage is necessary for each subscripted variable. These procedures are not guaranteed to be *always* correct in allocating storage, however. Whether they are of value depends on the observed success rate of the heuristics used, which, in turn, depends on the system detecting *and reporting to the user* situations where the system infers that there may be ambiguity in its analysis of storage requirements. The system can be judged to be successful if (1) most of the time, its report of the amount of storage allocation and the flagging of possible ambiguous allocations turns out to be correct and requires no corrective action from the user, (2) the number of times its heuristics and inference procedures fail is relatively small, and (3) the amount of undetected error *specifically* due to the use of heuristics is negligible. Even when the heuristics and inference procedures fail, the situation is usually detected during some phase of the program. Thus the use of these techniques is justified only if the language designer is willing to tolerate the small, but nonzero, possibility that the executable program will fail in return for greater ease in user programming. Even in those instances where program failure can be demonstrated, the particular program pattern that escaped analysis by the heuristic and inference procedure can be put on a list of special cases. Each case can be tested for future programs and corrected, or an appropriate (warning) notification passed to the user. In a practical sense, the possible rate of program failure can asymptotically approach zero at the expense of increased system size and processing time. However, the increase in system size and processing time may not be linear. Fortunately, in this instance, it appears that the number of cases of program construction that require special treatment is small enough that analysis is feasible.

Other techniques of AI, such as expert system-construction methodology, may also be used to deal with semantic ambiguity and context-dependent syntactic analysis. Language designers would do well to acquaint themselves with elementary concepts and techniques of AI, since many are applicable to the resolution of problems arising in user-oriented language design.

As should now be clear to the reader, our approach to user-oriented language design is domain-specific. That is, design is keyed to the language and notations of specific professional fields. Chapter 8 (and the figures in the latter part of Chap. 5) illustrated a concrete design addressed to scientific, engineering, and mathematical applications programming. This is in contradiction to the approach of designing languages of great universality applicable in all conceivable contexts. Historical experience indicates that such a universal approach engenders logical complexity, difficulty in comprehension, and difficulties in the ease of application programming. The user-oriented, domain-specific approach aims for "do-it-yourself" programming and tries to automate as much of the programming process as is feasible, using context-dependent analysis, a psychological model of the user, and feedback to resolve possible ambiguity. (We add, parenthetically, that "domain-specific" does not imply "narrow applications." The programming system discussed in Chap. 8 applies to a broad range of applications even though limited to one specific large domain.) On the other hand, the historical, largely universalist approach results in the inability of the noncomputer professional to do easily his or her own application programming, thus requiring either the employment of professional programmers or consultation with programmer "gurus."

An alternative approach to what we have presented aims to assist *professional* programmers rather than to replace them and attempts to do so in a non-domain-specific framework. This appears to be the viewpoint of the MIT project "The Programmer's Apprentice," as formulated by C. Rich and R. C. Waters.[3] Its long-term goal is to discover how *expert* programmers perform the act of creating programs. It is intrinsically based on an artificial-intelligence viewpoint and also has the declared goal of automating the programming process. However, true automation appears to be a long-term ideological goal of this project. Its immediate emphasis centers on developing intelligent assistance for programming tasks.

The Programmer's Apprentice uses the metaphorical term, *cliché,* to characterize stereotypical programming constructs. Thus by "inspecting" a program specification, one can recognize clichés and make use of implementations from a library of clichés. The formal representa-

---

[3]C. Rich and R. C. Waters, "The Programmer's Apprentice," *Computer,* pp. 11–25, November 1988.

tion for programs and programming clichés is affected by a "plan calculus." A *plan* can be represented as a hierarchical graph using boxes to denote operations and tests with connecting arrows denoting control and data flow. Each operator and test in a plan is associated with a set of conditions specified in a (formal) logical language. If the operations and tests are primitives of some programming language, then the plan is a concrete program. But the plan may also be used to represent partially designed programs. A cliché library may contain different "overlays" corresponding to different ways of implementing the same specification (where an *overlay* is a mapping from specification instances to implementation instances).

The degree of automation provided depends on special-purpose techniques and reasoning using a formal logic, essentially propositional. It also uses special-purpose decision procedures for algebraic properties of operators, such as commutivity, transitivity, set algebra, etc. The concept of *frames* is used to support inheritance and instantiation. Hybrid reasoning is used, involving the structure of the diagrams and functions as expressed in the logical annotations. The names of plans play the role of predicate symbols, and names of overlays are function symbols.

An operational prototype of one part of the Programmer's Apprentice is a knowledge-based editor called KBEmacs, which uses a library of implementation clichés that provide high-level editing commands for changing the algorithmic structure of a program. KBEmacs also generates documentation to explain the program in terms of the clichés used. It can also extract the underlying plan of a program text which can then be used in combination with plans for other clichés to synthesize new programs.

The interface language of the Programmer's Apprentice uses a large vocabulary of clichés expressed in terms targeted at expert programmers. However, as of late 1988, this aspect was not fully designed. Also being built is a Design Apprentice, which would include a declarative input language, detection of programmer errors, and automatic selection of reasonable implementation choices. The knowledge embedded in the Design Apprentice would be clichés for typical applications, designs, and hardware. The intention is to build a capability so that the programmer can interact with the Apprentice at the level of detailed program design. The (intended) scenario would begin with the programmer supplying a specification describing both hardware aspects and software aspects of the projected program. Terminology would be consistent with the philosophy of cliché usage. The Design Apprentice would detect *and explain* programmer errors that represent incompleteness or inconsistency. After errors were resolved, the Apprentice would generate executable code.

Another part of the Programmer's Apprentice is a Requirements Apprentice to support requirements acquisition and analysis. The Requirements Apprentice focuses on the transition from informal to formal descriptions. To do this, software-requirements clichés must be codified. This library of clichés must be extensive to cope with the range of real-world possibilities. Eventually the Requirements Apprentice and the Design Apprentice will be connected.

The Programmer's Apprentice represents an interesting research endeavor. Whether or not it is ultimately successful in a practical sense remains to be seen. Since its basic intent is not domain-specific, its success seems to depend, in a crucial sense, on whether or not its library of clichés can be made large enough and flexible enough to encompass the wide-ranging variety of real-world problems. Other subsidiary questions are whether its hybrid-reasoning system is sufficiently general and whether its interface can encompass a user-oriented approach.

Fifth- and Sixth-Generation Concepts

The basic concepts of fifth-generation computing were outlined by the Japanese in the early 1980s. Their goal was to produce, for the 1990s, knowledge-information-processing systems having problem-solving functions of such a high level that the systems would be comparable in intelligence to humans. The integrated system would understand problem descriptions and requirement specifications, synthesize processing procedures, be able to understand speech in natural language, recognize images, and perform other intelligence-interface functions. There would be an extensive knowledge base to support these functions and an inference mechanism for intelligent programming.

A typical application system was envisaged as configured into three subsystems—namely, interactive, processing, and management. The interactive subsystem would accept input, perhaps in natural-language or visual form, and convert it into an intermediate form using context-dependent analysis. The processing subsystem would accept this as-yet-incomplete description of the problem and use its knowledge-base description of the problem domain to generate an answer. The answer would be further processed by the interactive subsystem to produce an output comprehensible to humans. The management subsystem would control access to the various knowledge bases and coordinate various inference techniques.

The hardware-system structure was envisaged as consisting of units of greatly varying sizes appropriate to various applications, all sharing a common programming language. These machines would have three functional components—namely, inference machines, knowledge-base-management machines, and intelligent interface machines. All fifth-generation machines were to be linked to a global network capable of high-speed data transfer.

It is interesting to note that one of the five basic goals for application system research and development mentioned in the 1981 International Conference on Fifth-Generation Computer Systems (Tokyo, October 19–22) was an "applied problem-solving system." A major research and development theme of such a system was to develop a formula-understanding system for mathematical expressions. In this sense, we can regard the AUTOMATED PROGRAMMER system, described in Chap. 8, as consistent with the characterization of being, at least partially, a fifth-generation application system. The original Japanese conception seemed to see such a system as also incorporating symbolic manipulation capability and a knowledge base of formulas, attributes consistent with possible extensions of the automatic programming system that we have discussed.

The Japanese plans for an intelligent human-machine interface are particularly interesting, because they further the goals of user-oriented computer applications. Their plans fall into three main categories: (1) natural-language understanding, (2) speech recognition, and (3) image processing. They envisage these systems to consist of a front-end processor of input/output linked to a knowledge base and an inference engine. Their concept of natural-language processing appears to be dominated by a syntactic-analysis approach oriented to specific application domains, which they hope will permit the use of less than 2000 grammar rules, 5000 to 10,000 words for a question-answering system, and more than 50,000 words for text processing. Their initial implementation of a syntactic parser will use a modified version of Prolog, which is a logic programming language structured after the first-order-predicate calculus.

Speech recognition is seen as particularly useful for question-answering systems. The Japanese see the system as having ability to recognize continuous speech (no pauses between words) for a vocabulary of 50,000 words, for multiple speakers (with moderate training), at a word-recognition rate of 95 percent, and at processing speeds equal to three times real time.

Image processing is viewed in the framework of providing an environment in which pictures can be processed as a knowledge source and stored in an image database. Pictures are considered to be two-dimensional signal data. A typical subtask would be to recognize a handwritten drawing in a computer-aided-design system. Another subtask would be to develop language suitable for image manipulation and retrieval.

The major accomplishments of the first three years of the Japanese project were reported at the November 1984 international conference of the Japanese Institute for New Generation Research (ICOT). These accomplishments seem centered in the design of advanced workstations for research in artificial intelligence. Prototype machines were a "Personal Sequential Inference" machine and a relational database machine using as a language core versions of a logic programming language. Their commitment is to logic programming as their principal software methodology and hardware development emphasizing parallel processing capabilities. The initial prototype machines use microprogrammed architectures so the viability of different instruction sets can be explored.

Despite the declarations of the original Japanese fifth-generation proposal of 1981, actual commitment has been narrowly focused on machine architecture for knowledge-based systems and not on the original emphasis on broad studies of artificial intelligence and development of human-machine interaction. Because of this, an additional proposal was launched in 1985 for the purpose of a broader investigation of the human-related aspects of computing. The intent is an interaction of the fields of physiology, psychology, linguistics, and logic. Technological orientations are in the subject areas of pattern recognition, cognition, problem solving, natural-language and image processing, and speech recognition. Application orientations are toward expert systems, machine translation, intelligent computer-aided design, computer-aided-manufacturing systems, and intelligent robots. This proposal has been named the *Sixth*-Generation Computing System and was formally submitted to the Japanese Ministry of Science and Technology in March 1985.

As of mid-1990, it is clear that the original grand design of the fifth- and sixth-generation goals have not yet crystallized into marketable products. However, it would be premature to conclude that these goals are not attainable. What did become clear in mid-1990 was that the Japanese were shifting their immediate attention to the design and eventual production of machines (*and concomitant software*) for massively parallel processing. This would involve producing a single machine capable of orchestrating tens of thousands of independent processors running simultaneously. It is hoped that such machines will critically increase the capabilities of computer recognition of visual scenes, speech, and cursive handwriting, among many other activities which are currently better performed by humans than by machines.

Bibliography*

Texts on Programming Languages

Barron, D. W., *An Introduction to the Study of Programming Languages,* Cambridge University Press, Cambridge, 1977.

Barron, D. W., *Recursive Techniques in Programming,* Elsevier, New York, 1968.

Berg, H. K., W. E. Boebert, W. R. Franta, and T. G. Moher, *Formal Methods of Program Verification and Specification,* Prentice-Hall, Englewood Cliffs, N.J., 1982.

Clark, K. L., and F. G. McCabe, *Micro-Prolog: Programming in Logic,* Prentice-Hall, Englewood Cliffs, N.J., 1984.

Clark, K. L., and S. A. Tarnlund, eds., *Logic Programming,* Academic Press, London, 1982.

Clocksin, W. F., and C. S. Mellish, *Programming in Prolog,* 2d ed., Springer-Verlag, Berlin, 1984.

Elson, M., *Concepts of Programming Languages,* Science Research Associates, 1973.

Feuer, A., and N. Gehani, eds., *Comparing and Assessing Programming Languages,* Prentice-Hall, Englewood Cliffs, N.J., 1984.

*Ghezzi, C., and M. Jazayeri, *Programming Language Concepts,* 2d ed., John Wiley, New York, 1987. (This text is a sophisticated, but concise, treatment of conventional concepts of programming language structure.)

Glaser, H., C. Hankin, and D. Till, *Principles of Functional Programming,* Prentice-Hall, Englewood Cliffs, N.J., 1984.

Goldberg, A., and D. Robson, *Smalltalk-80: The Language and Its Implementation,* Addison-Wesley, Reading, Mass., 1983.

Gordon, M. J. C., *The Denotational Description of Programming Languages,* Springer-Verlag, New York, 1979.

Helmes, H. L., *Computer Language Reference Guide,* 2d ed., Howard Sams Co., Indianapolis, 1984.

Higman, B., *A Comparative Study of Programming Languages,* Elsevier, New York, 1967.

Horowitz, E., *Fundamentals of Programming Languages,* 2d ed., Computer Science Press, Rockville, Md., 1984.

Horowitz, E., ed., *Programming Languages: A Grand Tour,* Computer Science Press, Rockville, Md., 1983.

IEEE, *Transactions on Computers,* vol. c-25, no. 12, December 1976.

*Ledgard, H., and M. Marcotty, *The Programming Language Landscape,* Science Research Associates, Chicago, 1981. (This book is particularly suitable as an undergraduate textbook.)

MacLennan, B. J., *Principles of Programming Languages: Design, Evaluation, and Implementation,* Holt, Rinehart and Winston, New York, 1983.

*Items preceded by an asterisk are worthy of special note.

Marcotty, M., and H. Ledgard, *The World of Programming Languages,* Springer-Verlag, New York, 1987.
Martin, J., *Fourth Generation Languages,* vol. I, *Principles,* Prentice-Hall, Englewood Cliffs, N.J., 1985.
Martin, J., with J. Leben, *Fourth Generation Languages,* vol. II, *Representative 4GLs,* Prentice-Hall, Englewood Cliffs, N.J., 1986.
*Nicholls, J. E., *The Structure and Design of Programming Languages,* Addison-Wesley, Reading, Mass., 1975. (Although this text is somewhat dated, it contains well-written treatments of certain areas not available elsewhere.)
Organick, E. I., et al., *Programming Language Structures,* Academic Press, New York, 1978.
Peterson, G. E., *Object-Oriented Computing,* vols. 1 and 2, IEEE Computer Society Press, Los Angeles, 1987.
Peterson, W. W., *Introduction to Programming Languages,* Prentice-Hall, Englewood Cliffs, N.J., 1974.
Pratt, T. W., *Programming Languages: Design and Implementation,* 2d ed., Prentice-Hall, Englewood Cliffs, N.J., 1984.
Ralston, A., *Introduction to Programming and Computer Science,* McGraw-Hill, New York, 1971.
Reynolds, J. C., *The Craft of Programming,* Prentice-Hall, Englewood Cliffs, N.J., 1981.
Rosen, S., ed., *Programming Systems and Languages,* McGraw-Hill, New York, 1967.
Salman, W. P., O. Tisserand, and B. Toulaut, *Forth,* Springer-Verlag, New York, 1984.
*Sammet, J. E., *Programming Languages: History and Fundamentals,* Prentice-Hall, Englewood Cliffs, N.J., 1969. (This is a classic volume that contains a veritable treasure of little-known information about the many programming languages designed prior to the late 1960s. It is required reading for anyone seriously interested in the evolution of programming-language design.)
Schneider, H. G., *Problem Oriented Programming Languages,* John Wiley, New York, 1984.
Schwartz, J. T., *On Programming,* New York University Computer Science Department, New York, 1975.
Schwartz, J. T., R. B. K. Dewar, E. Dubinsky, and E. Schonberg, *Programming with Sets: An Introduction to SETL,* Springer-Verlag, New York, 1986.
Tennant, R. D., *Principles of Programming Languages,* Prentice-Hall, Englewood Cliffs, N.J., 1981.
Truit, T. D., and S. B. Mindlin, *An Introduction to Nonprocedural Languages: Using NPL,* McGraw-Hill, New York, 1983.
Tucker, A. B., Jr., *Programming Languages,* McGraw-Hill, New York, 1977.
Wasserman, A. I., ed., *Tutorial, Programming Language Design,* IEEE Computer Society Press, Los Alamitos, Calif., 1980.
Wasserman, A. I., ed., Special Issue on Programming Language Design, *ACM SIGPLAN Notices 10,* no. 7, July 1975.
Wegner, P., *Programming Languages, Information Structures, and Machine Organization,* McGraw-Hill, New York, 1968.
Wirth, N., *Programming in Modula-2,* 2d ed., Springer-Verlag, Berlin, 1983.

Texts from a Human-Factors Viewpoint

**ACM Computing Surveys,* Special issue on the psychology of human-computer interaction, vol. 13, no. 1, March 1981. (This is an interesting survey of some aspects of human-machine communication.)
*ACM SIGCHI Proceedings, *Human Factors in Computing Systems.* (These volumes are useful for their information on the current state of understanding of human-machine communication.)
Badre, A., and B. Shneiderman, eds., *Directions in Human/Computer Interaction,* Ablex, Norwood, N.J., 1982.
Brown, C. M., *Human-Computer Interface Design Guideline,* Ablex, Norwood, N.J., 1986.

Card, S. K., T. P. Moran, and A. Newell, *The Psychology of Human-Computer Interaction,* Lawrence Erlbaum, Hillsdale, N.J., 1983.

*Curtis, B., ed., *Human Factors in Software Development,* 2d ed., IEEE Computer Society Press, Los Alamitos, Calif., 1986. (This is a broad collection of what is of current interest to those doing research or development in the area of human-machine communication.)

Galitz, W. O., *Handbook of Screen Format Design,* 2d ed., QED Information Sciences, Wellesley Hills, Mass., 1985.

Kantrowitz, B. H., and R. D. Sorkin, *Human Factors: Understanding People-System Relationships,* John Wiley, New York, 1983.

Martin, J., *Design of Man-Computer Dialogues,* Prentice-Hall, Englewood Cliffs, N.J., 1973.

Norman, D. A., and S. W. Draper, eds., *User Centered System Design,* Lawrence Erlbaum, Hillsdale, N.J., 1986.

Rubinstein, R., and H. Hersh, *The Human Factor,* Digital Press, Boston, 1984.

*Shneiderman, B., *Designing the User Interface,* Addison-Wesley, Reading, Mass., 1987. (This is a valuable survey of current research in user-interface design.)

Shneiderman, B., *Software Psychology,* Little, Brown & Co., Boston, 1980.

*Soloway, E., and S. Iyanger, eds., *Empirical Studies of Programmers,* Ablex, Norwood, N.J., 1986. (This is the proceedings of the first conference devoted to empirical studies of programmers, a field that has great potential for providing a scientific basis for software engineering.)

Thomas, J. C., and M. L. Schneider, eds., *Human Factors in Computer Systems,* Ablex, Norwood, N.J., 1984.

Vassiliou, Y., ed., *Human Factors and Interactive Computer Systems,* Ablex, Norwood, N.J., 1984.

*Weinberg, G. M., *The Psychology of Computer Programming,* Van Nostrand Reinhold, New York, 1971. (A classic work, this was the first serious treatise of the psychological aspects of programming.)

Texts on Fifth-Generation Concepts

Feigenbaum, E. A., and R. McCorduck, *The Fifth Generation,* Addison-Wesley, Reading, Mass., 1983.

Moto-oka, T., ed., *Fifth Generation Computer Systems,* North Holland, Amsterdam, 1982.

Muller, R. L., and J. J. Pottmyer, eds., *The Fifth Generation Challenge,* Proceedings of the 1984 Annual Conference of The Association for Computing Machinery.

Relevant Articles on Language-Design Considerations

Backus, J., "Can Programming Be Liberated from the Von Neuman Style? A Functional Style and Its Algebra of Programs," *Comm. ACM* 21, no. 8, 613ff., August 1978.

Berk, T., ed., Proceedings, ACM Symposium on Graphics Languages, *ACM SIGPLAN Notices* 11, no. 6, June 1976.

Bierman, A. W., and B. W. Ballard, "Toward Natural Language Computation," *Am. J. Computational Linguistics* 6, no. 2, 1980.

Bierman, A. W., B. W. Ballard, and A. H. Sigmon, "An Experimental Study of Natural Language Programming," *Int. J. Man-Machine Studies* 18, 71–87, 1983.

Bierman, A. W., R. D. Rodman, D. C. Rubin, and J. F. Heidlage, "Natural Language with Discrete Speech as a Mode for Human-to-Machine Communication," *Comm. ACM* 28, no. 6, 628ff, 1985.

Brooks, R., "Toward a Theoretical Model of the Comprehension of Computer Programs," *Int. J. Man-Machine Studies* 17, 1983.

Carbonell, J. G., R. E. Cullingford, and A. V. Gershman, "Steps toward Knowledge-

Based Machine Translation," *IEEE Trans. Pattern Analysis and Machine Intelligence* 3, no. 4, July 1981.

Curtis, B., "A Review of Human Factors Research on Programming Languages and Specifications," *ACM Proceedings, Human Factors in Computer Systems,* 212–18, 1982.

Curtis, B., I. Forman, R. Brooks, E. Soloway, and K. Ehrlich, "Psychological Perspectives for Software Science," *Information Processing and Management* 20, nos. 1 and 2, 81–96, 1984.

DeMillo, R. A., S. C. Eisenstat, and R. J. Lipton, "Can Structured Programs Be Efficient?" *ACM SIGPLAN Notices* 11, no. 10, 10ff., October 1976.

*DeMillo, R. A., R. J. Lipton, and A. J. Perlis, "Social Processes and Proofs of Theorems and Programs," *Comm. ACM 22,* no. 5, 271ff., May 1979. (This is an interesting, well-reasoned work on the inherent difficulties in proving the correctness of real-world programs.)

Draper, S. W., and D. A. Norman, "Software Engineering for User Interfaces," *IEEE Trans. Software Engineering* 11, no. 3, March 1985.

*Fink, P. K., A. H. Sigmon, and A. W. Bierman, "Computer Control via Limited Natural Language," *IEEE Trans. Systems, Man, Cybernetics* 15, no. 1, 54ff., 1985. (This is a well-written paper that illustrates some of the difficulties, as well as the potential, of natural-language input to a computer.)

Gannon, J. D., and J. J. Horning, "Language Design for Programming Reliability," *IEEE Trans. Software Engineering* 1, no. 2, 179ff., June 1975.

Good, M. I., J. A. Whiteside, D. R. Wixon, and S. J. Jones, "Building a User-Derived Interface," *Comm. ACM* 27, no. 10, 1032–43, October 1984.

Gould, J. D., J. Conti, and T. Hovanyecz, "Composing Letters with a Simulated Listening Typewriter," *Comm. ACM 26,* no. 4, 295ff., 1983.

Grafton, R. B., and T. Ichikawa, eds., Visual Programming Issue, *IEEE Computer* 18, no. 8, 1985.

Halpern, M., "Foundations of the Case for Natural Language Programming," *Proceedings, Fall Joint Computer Conference (AFIPS),* 639ff., 1966.

Hobbs, J. R., "What the Nature of Natural Language Tells Us about How to Make Natural-Language-Like Programming Languages More Natural," *ACM SIGPLAN Notices* 12, no. 8, 85–93, August 1977.

IEEE Computer Society Workshop on Visual Languages, *Proceedings,* IEEE Computer Society Press, Los Alamitos, Calif., 1984.

*Jarke, M., J. A. Turner, F. A. Stohr, Y. Vassiliou, N. H. White, and K. Michielsen, "A Field Evaluation of Natural Language for Data Retrieval," *IEEE Trans. Software Engineering* 11, no. 1, 97ff., 1985. (This is a well-written paper that illustrates some of the difficulties in experimental design and appropriate statistical treatment for studies on natural-language input.)

Karna, K. N., ed., Intelligent Human-Machine Interface Issue, *IEEE Computer* 17, no. 9, September 1984.

*Klerer, M., "Experimental Study of a Two-Dimensional Language vs. Fortran for First-Course Programmers," *Int. J. Man-Machine Studies* 20, 445–67, 1984. (This paper accumulates experimental data that is interpreted to show the advantages of two-dimensional notation for a programming language and the extraordinarily large variance in performance by programmers.)

*Klerer, M., F. Grossman, and R. Klerer, "The Automated Programmer System: Language Design Issues for Scientific-Mathematical-Engineering Applications Programming," in *The Role of Language in Problem Solving* 2, J. C. Boudreaux et al., eds. Elsevier, North Holland, New York, 245ff., 1987. (This paper treats in some detail specific design issues concerned with the linguistic structures associated with an automated programming system, the AUTOMATED PROGRAMMER.)

Knuth, D. E., "Literate Programming" *The Computer Journal* 27, no. 4, 97ff., 1984.

*Knuth, D. E., "Structured Programming with Goto Statements," *Computing Surveys* 6, no. 4, 261ff., 1974. (This is a very well written paper that puts the use of GOTO constructs into appropriate perspective.)

Knuth, D. E., "An Empirical Study of Fortran Programs," *Software-Practice and Experience* 1, 105–33, 1971.

Laughery, K. R., Jr., "Human Factors in Software Engineering: A Review of the Literature," *Journal of Systems and Software* 5, 3–14, 1985.

Ledgard, H., "Misconceptions in Human Factors," *Abacus* 3, no. 2, 1986.

Ledgard, H., J. A. Whiteside, and W. Seymour, "The Natural Language of Interactive Systems," *Comm. ACM* 23, no. 10, 556ff., October 1980.

Meyrowitz, N., ed., OOPSLA'86 Conference Proceedings, *ACM SIGPLAN Notices* 21, no. 11, November 1986.

Naur, P., "Programming Languages, Natural Languages, and Mathematics," *Comm. ACM* 18, no. 12, 676–84, December 1975.

Perlman, G., "Natural Artificial Languages: Low Level Processes," *Int. J. Man-Machine Studies* 20, 373–419, 1984.

Pooch, V. W., ed., Interactive Graphics Issue, *IEEE Computer* 9, no. 8, August 1976.

Proceedings, International Conference on Reliable Software, *ACM SIGPLAN Notices* 10, no. 6, 1975.

Proceedings, Symposium on Artificial Intelligence and Programming Languages, *ACM SIGPLAN Notices* 12, no. 8, August 1977.

Reisner, P., "Human Factors Studies of Database Query Languages: A Survey and Assessment," *Computing Surveys* 13, no. 1, 13ff., March 1981.

Reisner, P., "Formal Grammar and Human Factors Design of an Interactive Graphics System," *IEEE Trans. Software Engineering* 7, 229–40, 1981.

Reisner, P., "Use of Psychological Experimentation as an Aid to Development of a Query Language," *IEEE Trans. Software Engineering* 3, no. 3, May 1977.

Rich, C., and R. C. Waters, "The Programmer's Apprentice," *IEEE Computer,* 11–25, November 1988.

Rich, E., "Natural-Language Interfaces," *IEEE Computer,* 39ff., September 1984.

Simmons, R. F., "Man-Machine Interfaces: Can They Guess What You Want?" *IEEE Expert,* Spring 1986.

Soloway, E., J. Bonar, and K. Ehrlich, "Cognitive Strategic and Looping Constructs: An Empirical Study," *Comm. ACM* 26, no. 11, 853–60, November 1983.

Stefik, M., and D. G. Bobrow, "Object-Oriented Programming: Themes and Variations," *AI Magazine* 6, no. 4, Winter 1986.

Tucker, A. B., Jr., "A Perspective on Machine Translation: Theory and Practice," *Comm. ACM* 27, no. 4, April 1984.

Waltz, D. L., "Natural Language Interfaces," *ACM SIGART Newsletter* No. 61, February 1977.

Wasserman, A. I., and S. Gutz, "The Future of Programming," *Comm. ACM* 25, no. 3, 196ff., March 1982.

Wasserman, K., "Physical Object Representation and Generalization: A Survey of Programs for Semantic-Based Natural Language Processing," *AI Magazine* 5, no. 4, 28ff., 1985.

*Wegner, P., "Capital-Intensive Software Technology," *IEEE Software* 1, no. 3, 7ff., July 1984. (This is a well-written paper that explores, among other issues, some of the problems associated with Ada programming.)

Wegner, P., and B. Shriver, eds., Object-Oriented Programming Workshop, *ACM SIGPLAN Notices* 21, no. 10, October 1986.

Wile, D. S., "Program Developments: Formal Explanation of Implementations," *Comm. ACM* 26, no. 11, 902–10, November 1983.

Wilensky, R., Y. Arens, and D. Chin, "Talking to UNIX in English," *Comm. ACM* 27, no. 6, 574–93. June 1984.

Woods, W. A., "Transition Network Grammars for Natural Language Analysis," *Comm. ACM* 13, no. 10, 591–606, 1970.

Yau, S. S., ed., Japanese Computer Technology and Culture Issue, *IEEE Computer* 17, no. 3, March 1984.

Index

ABOUT THE AUTHOR

Melvin Klerer is professor of computer science at Polytechnic University in Brooklyn, New York. Dr. Klerer has also been a professor at New York University; a visiting scientist at the Weizmann Institute of Science; and head of the computer science program at Hudson Laboratories of Columbia University. He has published numerous reports and studies in his field, presented papers before national scientific conferences, and led seminars for leading research institutes and universities. Dr. Klerer is the author of four previously published books, including the highly successful *Digital Computer User's Handbook*. He is also a codeveloper of a user-oriented automatic programming system for the IBM PC, the AUTOMATED PROGRAMMER System.